WHAT A
Church Boy
WANTS

Darnell Durrah

Trilogy Christian Publishers
A Wholly Owned Subsidary of Trinity Broadcasting Network
2442 Michelle Drive
Tustin, CA 92780

For information, address Trilogy Christian Publishing
Rights Department, 2442 Michelle Drive, Tustin, Ca 92780.
Trilogy Christian Publishing/ TBN and colophon are trademarks of Trinity Broadcasting Network.

For information about special discounts for bulk purchases, please contact Trilogy Christian Publishing.

Manufactured in the United States of America

10 9 8 7 6 5 4 3 2 1

Library of Congress Cataloging-in-Publication Data is available.

ISBN 978-1-64773-528-9 (Print Book)
ISBN 978-1-64773-529-6 (ebook)

To Jesus Christ, the one who *inspires* me. Your precious Spirit provided the wisdom, discipline, and skill needed to achieve such a task. To the one who *encourages* me, my sweet Lois. You are my number one cheerleader and greatest supporter. After twenty-two years, we're still standing strong. To God be the glory! To my mother, my children, and my loving family, both near and far, your amazing love and support *motivates* me every single day. To Bishop Kirkland and Minister Gloria Smith, your *influence* has caused me to achieve in ways that have changed my life and family forever. I praise God for your leadership. Finally, to every pastor, minister, and church leader, and to all who are of the household of faith worldwide; I dedicate this book to you.

Prologue

From the start, she knew it was a stupid idea. But Lisa needed the money, and she needed it fast. She was preparing to enter into what she originally thought was her last semester of classes at the University of North Carolina-Greensboro. That is, until she found out that she had been placed on academic suspension, a penalty that restricted her from receiving financial aid. There was no way she was going to tell her mother about it—not that it would have mattered, anyway. In Lisa's mind, all her mother cared about was getting home from work each day so that she could spend some quality time with her best friend, alcohol. Besides, she lived three hours away in Columbia, South Carolina, so what she didn't know wouldn't hurt her. Lisa decided to spare herself the unwanted criticism and ridicule, as she'd had enough of that from her mom to last her a lifetime. She'd just have to figure this out for herself.

Lisa knew that no normal job would pay enough to cover both her tuition and housing costs. What she didn't know was that the illegal activity she had become involved in didn't happen because of some coincidental twist of events; instead, she had been set up by a financial aid employee named Jarvis, who was a key player in an ongoing scheme targeting students like Lisa who were close to finishing school but who were in trouble with their financial aid. Jarvis, a graduate of UNCG, had landed a job working for the university right after his graduation from the school five years prior. However, instead of being diligent and working his way up through the ranks, he had been lured into a meticulous, illegal scheme. As a result, he received thousands of dollars each semester from a local drug dealer named Roquan in exchange for revealing the identities and financial hardships of struggling students, particularly those who were past the point of no return—those who would do just about anything to get the money needed to finish what they'd started.

Jarvis usually chose student leaders of various clubs and organizations on campus that were likely to host events or parties of some sort. Little did these prideful trailblazers know that it was all a part of the scheme for them not to receive the initial probation message instructing them to contact Jarvis in the financial aid office and warning them of the future suspension of their financial aid if no corrective action was taken. Having never received the first message, the students would inevitably wrongly assume that they had somehow managed to slip through the cracks. It wasn't until they received the e-mail regarding suspension with only two or three weeks left in the semester that panic, dread, and fear would all but consume them. The messages were strategically sent out to one person at a time, on the Thursday or Friday of the event that was to be hosted by the student leader, and by the time the student received the e-mail, the financial aid office, which closed at one on Friday afternoons, would already be shut down for the weekend.

Needless to say, after the e-mail was sent, Jarvis's job was easy. He would simply show up at the event legitimately posing as school staff who was there to chaperone and to make sure that things flowed smoothly. In reality, he was there solely to find his victims. He did so one by one, event by event, party by party. He would usually find them already tipsy in the name of temporarily mellowing out before facing the music to figure out what in the world they were going to do about the news they'd received. Although most students wouldn't recognize him as a financial aid employee, he certainly knew his targets very well, having prepared his responses in advance.

He would introduce himself to his victims as Jarvis from financial aid, saying that he was simply at the event serving as a chaperone. Once he mentioned the words *financial aid*, the student would attempt to seize the moment to talk to him about the letter and possible solutions to their newfound problem. Since the students were outside of a business environment, they normally felt like they could talk to him as a peer as opposed to a school official. This relaxed environment fit perfectly into his scheme, and after a few minutes of conversation, he could assess pretty accurately how eager each victim was to get the money needed to finish school. After his assessment, he would normally refer them to one of a few different places around town where they could find work.

Of course, each contact person, usually a manager, was in cooperation with Roquan, the drug dealer, since he was the owner of each establishment recommended to the students. Inevitably, each semester, Roquan would have a couple of students willing to do just about anything. The desperate victims would carry out a host of tasks, such as making large drops, usually across state lines, lending their cars for use in transporting drugs and posing as decoys. Some would even perform sexual favors in exchange for cash to help pay tuition.

After working as a waitress for a couple of months, Lisa had been introduced to Roquan. He had actually seen her in action a couple of times, so when he asked Steve, the manager, about her, he learned what a hard worker she was and how many hours per week she was willing to work. Noticing how beautiful she was, Roquan further inquired of Steve as to why he hadn't introduced them sooner, implying that he was perhaps attempting to keep her to himself. Steve's response was that he didn't know quite how to take Lisa. He explained that Lisa's striking beauty was compromised by her ability to double as a bouncer. He told Roquan how, on her third day on the job, she single-handedly kicked a drunken and unruly man out of the restaurant, but not before disabling him and flipping him over her back. He also told Roquan how she put another guy in some type of wristlock, making him squeal and writhe in pain after he touched her inappropriately. Roquan agreed with Steve that she was definitely not his type, yet he was intrigued by her and wanted to meet her.

For a while, Lisa's moneymaking scheme had worked. Her strategy was to be the campus drug pusher, but to do so stealthily. She would get the money from the students seeking to get high, then pretend to go off campus to get the goods, which usually consisted of weed, pills, and occasional acid tabs. Then she would show up a little while later with the drugs, which she usually kept hidden in a couple of unobtrusive places on campus. Her trouble began when she decided to stay in the game a little longer than she needed to. She had already walked for graduation, but she had one more class to take before she could actually earn her degree. She told her mother that she would be staying on campus to take that final class, but in reality, she had taken her hustle to the streets, and she found it hard to let the quick money go.

By association, she already had a few off-campus customers who quickly became instrumental in helping her acquire more. Lisa had made it through the majority of the summer and had easily acquired the remaining six thousand dollars needed to pay off her school debt. But she figured that she might as well make a few extra thousand so she would not have to depend on her mother for anything while she continued her search for a legitimate job back home in Columbia. Although she had recently begun working on her relationship with her mother, the more she considered her current situation, the angrier she became—and she was filled with bitterness and contempt toward her mom.

Between waitressing and dealing, Lisa had made close to $30,000, and she could have pulled it all off without incident had she only taken her money and walked away. She had a deep longing, however, to prove to her mother that she could do it on her own. So she set out to make as much as she possibly could in that one summer. In her anger, she had even determined to purchase a car and to give her mother's back to her after she returned home from school.

As she pulled up in the abandoned park, she had an eerie feeling about the unknown customer she was supposed to meet. She had purchased a small handgun from one of Roquan's connections the previous weekend, as she was a little apprehensive about the streets. The guy she was meeting was supposed to be cool, a lowlife no doubt, but otherwise, just a weed-smoking dude who was not known to be a troublemaker. Still, she always left her car in drive as she waited on her customers.

When the unknown Randall, a man known on the streets as Fats, approached her, she could tell that he was already high on something. Once she recognized him from the description she'd been given, she let down the window as he came toward the car. Then what should have been a quick, smooth exchange went very wrong when Fats lunged at Lisa and attempted to grab the package and run. Thinking quickly, Lisa raised her foot off the brake and caused him to lose his footing, but he fell farther into the car. When he refused to release the package, she warned, "Let it go, man!" through gritted teeth.

"Nah, baby, you ain't gettin' this back!" Fats growled. "A pretty girl like you shoulda known better than to be out here on these streets, anyway."

Lisa's head was spinning. This was all happening so fast. In the midst of dragging Fats's body and trying to wrestle the package out of his huge hand, she kept seeing images of her mother's face, which only angered her all the more. Because of her mother's lack of control, she had been lured into a trap that now had her in a potential world of trouble. Here she was, not knowing whether she was going to make it to the next day, and all she could think of was the one person she blamed for all of it—her mother, Betty Monroe. In Lisa's mind, it was her mom's fault that she lacked the resources she needed. If she couldn't have provided the money, at least she could have given some type of guidance, some motherly advice or instruction to help her to figure out what to do during the difficult times. Better yet, she could have been there for her daughter at some point, at any point, to instill in her the values, strength, and self-confidence needed to resist the foolishness in which she now found herself entangled. But Lisa's mom had not been there for her, and as a result, Lisa couldn't share her experiences—the joys and sorrows of her life—with the one person from whom she sought approval more than anyone else on the planet.

Recognizing that she was no match for the big man who was now trying to regain his footing, Lisa managed to slip her right hand away. She retrieved the small handgun tucked between the driver's seat and the center console and squeezed the trigger of the Saturday night special, placing one .22-caliber round into the big man's shoulder. However, that one squeeze of the trigger was loaded with so much anger and bitterness that it summoned yet another squeeze from somewhere deep within her soul. It didn't matter that her assailant was already incapacitated, howling in pain and trying to escape, leaving package and all. She shoved the gun against his jacket and squeezed the trigger again, this time placing the second bullet somewhere into the upper torso of her struggling target.

"How dare you!" she screamed. She wasn't sure if she was talking to Fats or to her mother. Again, she repeated forcefully in a much lower tone through gritted teeth, with eyes wide and a scowl on her face, "How dare you." Planting her hand across the large man's face, she pushed with all her might, successfully dislodging his wounded body from her car window.

In a frantic effort to get away, she sped to the top of the park's parking lot. Out of habit, Lisa stopped to check for oncoming traffic, though there was none. Sitting still, she found herself actually contemplating returning to her attacker, who had somehow become the victim. Regrouping from her moment of temporary insanity, she punched the accelerator and left the man for dead. Nothing was going to stop her from getting her degree, not even her alcoholic sorry excuse for a mother.

Chapter 1

Revival was fully underway at Miracle Center Church. In preparation, Pastor Johnson and the intercessory ministry had committed to praying for God to show up in amazing ways by saving souls, administering healing, performing miracles, and delivering people from demonic possession and oppression. It was the second night of the four-day revival, and the praise team had just finished leading worship. The normal order of service had been a call to worship, Scripture, prayer, praise and worship, and then the spoken Word. Pastor Johnson had spent much of the day asking God to blow their minds with even more than what they had witnessed on the previous night. It was time for him to deliver the Word, and now he wished that he hadn't asked God to fit such a tall order into his cookie-cutter worship agenda.

Through much prayer, Pastor Johnson and his leadership team had concluded that they were not to have a *guest* speaker this year. Though unusual, it was obviously the plan of God, and indeed He had moved mightily on the previous night. His amazing power had penetrated the souls of several people who were not likely to be seen attending a church service, let alone in the middle of the week during the summer, and especially at Miracle Center. This was not the traditional church that the casual churchgoer would attend to hear some good singing or to receive a gentle lesson on the Golden Rule. Rather, it was a church for people who were at their wit's end, those who had exhausted all their resources and concluded that they needed to see the power of God revealed in their situation, or else. Miracle Center had a reputation in the community, even though it

11

was often the butt of jokes as people would say to family and friends, "We're going to take you to Miracle Center to get those demons cast out if you don't stop cutting up." Still, despite the teasing, the entire community knew that if something was seriously wrong, this was certainly a place where they could find miracle-working power, and many miracles had taken place there over the years.

The congregation was made up primarily of two types of people: those who had been the subject of a miracle and had since dedicated themselves to helping the ministry and those who were simply fascinated by miracles and spent their time supporting the ministry in hopes of witnessing yet another miracle. The previous night of revival had produced several instances of what Miracle Center believed to be the greatest miracle, being born again. In addition, many others had been prayed for with regard to everything from broken relationships to healing from sickness, disease, and emotional scars. Pastor Johnson could tell that yet another miracle was about to unfold when a giant of a man showed up at the altar for prayer. He had certainly noticed the man during the service, merely because of his size and height. He didn't appear to be with anyone, and he didn't seem to utter one single "Amen" the entire service, although he did clap a time or two. After the sermon, Pastor Johnson was moving into the altar call. "This is your time," he said. "This is your night. Something good is going to happen in this place tonight. Do you believe it?"

"Amen!" the congregation shouted and clapped their hands.

"Everyone who can, please stand. We're about to ask the Spirit of God to work some miracles among us tonight." Before he finished speaking, he noticed the big guy was already making his way down to the altar. "Somebody praise the Lord in this place! Here comes a young man who has determined that he is not going to wait any longer to get his breakthrough. Let's praise God for him." The congregation erupted in applause, and the ushers scrambled to catch up with the gentleman, whose long legs seemed to be in full stride. "Look at him," Pastor Johnson said. "He's moving like he has faith to believe that God is able to do anything, like God is able to work a miracle. Is there anyone else here who believes that God is able to move on your behalf tonight?" Once again, the congregation began to praise God aloud and clap their hands. "Come on, keep praising Him just for a moment. God's about to do something in this man's life right now."

As the praise began to settle down, Pastor Johnson stood face-to-face, looking up at the man, who was now looking down at him. "Young man, we don't know each other, but—"

Before he could finish his sentence, the man extended his huge right hand and said, "I'm Marvin Erickson."

Attempting not to appear caught off guard, Pastor Johnson said, "I'm Aspen Johnson. It's nice to meet you. Marvin, sometimes God shows me things. I have the ability to see spiritual things like visions and dreams. Do you mind if I share with you what I saw as you were coming here to the altar?"

"Not at all, sir," Marvin replied as he stood there looking and sounding like a younger version of the character John Coffey from the movie *The Green Mile*.

"I saw a little boy wearing a glowing purple shirt, kind of like a jersey. He was running and playing in a field, with a smile and an expression of true contentment on his face. But the scene suddenly changed, and when I looked again, he was lying in a hospital bed, and the jersey he was wearing was a badly faded green-and-yellow color with faint white numbers on it. It had holes in it and was almost slimy to the touch. It was very disturbing to look at. Even more disturbing was the expression on the boy's face, which was extremely sad. The look is hard to describe, but it appeared as if he were about to pass away.

"Suddenly, you and another man, who was just a bit shorter but with the same build as you, walked into the hospital room. Immediately, everything changed. The two of you were wearing the glowing purple shirts, just like the boy had on in the field, and you were carrying a package—a gift for the little boy. He was so weak, however, that he was unable to open it. You gave it to the man with you, but he could only open it a portion of the way. The man returned it, and you ripped the top off it. Inside was a shirt just like the one that the two of you had on. It was just like the original jersey the boy had been wearing—a glowing purple jersey.

"When the boy saw it, he reached out to you with both arms. That was when you walked over and ripped the green-and-yellow jersey off the boy and put the purple one on him, while the other guy stood in the background, smiling, clapping his hands and praising God. The boy's health and vitality were restored, and he sprang up from the bed and leaped into your arms. Does this vision mean anything to you, Marvin?"

The huge man just stood there nodding for a moment. He was stunned, yet he tried to speak. "Yes...yes, sir, it does," he whimpered. He puffed his cheeks and blew out a big breath. Then he lifted his gigantic hands to his face, covered it, and began to sob.

Pastor Johnson, being the leader that he was, knew that he needed to give the man time to collect himself. He also needed the man to respond so that, hopefully, he could find out what the vision was fully about, although he had some idea. Under his breath, he spoke the words, "Come on, Holy Spirit, we need Your help right now." Instantly, as if he knew exactly what was needed, the organist began to play and sing "You Are Great," by Juanita Bynum. It was perfect for what both Pastor Johnson and Marvin needed, which was time to compose themselves.

"I'm sorry for being so emotional, Reverend Johnson," Marvin offered. "I just never..." He was unable to continue. He buried his face in his hands again, and his massive frame began to quake uncontrollably. Again, the musicians and praise team began singing, "You are great, You do miracles so great, there is no one else like You, there is no one else like You." They sang the chorus over and over, and the congregation joined in while the ushers tried to soothe Marvin, giving him tissues and gently rubbing his back.

As Marvin settled himself, Pastor Johnson signaled to the minister of music to fade. "Sometimes," Pastor Johnson said to the congregation, "when we witness God's presence and His miraculous power, it's hard not to become emotional. It doesn't matter who you are, or what your title is, or how many miracles you've witnessed in the past. When you come in contact with the miracle-working power of God, it *will* have an effect on you. Now I'm going to give Marvin a mic for just a moment, so get ready to witness the testimony of yet another miracle. Can you shout, 'It's already done'?"

"It's already done!" the congregation shouted. Big Marvin reached down and grabbed the mic from the adjutant, who was there to assist the pastor, and turned to face the congregation. He cleared his throat and said, "Again, my name is Marvin Erickson, and I am originally from the Bronx, New York. I have an eight-year-old nephew named Kevin who is like a son to me. He lives here in Columbia with my sister, and he has been battling cancer for about three months. The doctors told her just the other day that they discovered that Kevin now has some other rare form of brain cancer and that, barring a miracle, he has only a few days to live, maybe a couple of weeks at best. Somehow, Kevin overheard his mom talking about it, and believe it or not, it didn't scare him. But he told his mom that his only request was to see me again, because using his words, 'I know Uncle Marv can figure out something. He'll get us through this, Ma.'"

"I have never felt so much pressure, man," he continued, shaking his head and tearing up again. He took another deep breath and blew it out, puffing his cheeks again. "So I knew...I knew I had to do something. I had no idea what to do, so I asked God that, if He was real, to do something to help me so that I could help Kev to live and to enjoy a normal, healthy life. You can probably tell that I don't know much about God and faith. I ain't no atheist or nothin' like that. I just never really been big on church. You know what I'm saying? So the thought came up in my mind to talk to my friend named Tyson Degraffenridge. We call him Big Ty." The congregation began to applaud. "Oh, y'all know him like that, huh?" he asked.

"Yes, we know Tyson well here," Pastor Johnson replied.

"Cool," Marvin said. "We play side by side on the offensive line for the Minnesota Vikings." Again, the congregation applauded. "Oh, y'all are Viking fans too?" he asked, smiling.

Pastor Johnson seized the moment to utilize humor to keep the atmosphere light, thus preparing Marvin to continue to push through his testimony, no matter how difficult.

"Uh, let's just say we're Tyson fans," he offered. The congregation laughed and applauded.

"Okay, that's cool," responded Marvin. "Well, Big Ty is always talking about God to anybody who will listen. So one day, I began to ask him questions about what God had done for him. I admit that I was just giving him a hard time by asking him all the questions, but he told me about how God had healed him from some type of deformity at a church service when he was a young boy. I got to be honest, it was a very interesting story, especially seeing how strong this man is and how amazing an athlete he is, but since there was a group of guys from the team hanging around, listening to this story, my pride wouldn't let me express my true interest. But I never forgot it. When I got the call from my sister about Kevin, though, all that pride went out the window. I stayed up most of the night, and believe it or not, I prayed and asked God to help me to know what to do for my nephew.

"I always hear people like Big Ty talking about how they heard God say this and that, but man, let me tell you, I ain't heard nothing. I was left alone with just my thoughts—that's it. No loud voice, no soft voice, just thoughts. *What if he doesn't make it? He's just a kid. What did he do to deserve this? Should we get a second opinion? Why does Kev believe in me so much, anyway? God, are You real? Can You show me some kind of sign to let me know that You are even listening to me?* All these thoughts were going through my mind, and I became so frustrated because I felt like God wasn't giving me any answers. I wondered why He wouldn't speak to me like He speaks to other people. Finally, I said, 'Okay, God, I know I'm not the best dude, but Ty always says that You'll look past that. If that's true, can You just look past me and help my nephew, Kevin? Come on, God, he's a kid. I know I'm kinda out there, and I don't go to church and all like Ty, and if that offends You, I'm sorry. And I will put forth a true effort to do better. But Kev? That kid ain't done nothing!'

"I was a basket case, kind of like I am right now, but much worse. So I ended up crying myself to sleep. When I woke up the next morning, all I could think about was Ty's story about how he got some type of healing or something when he was a little boy. I didn't think about it at that time, but maybe that was God's way of answering me. You know what I'm saying? Maybe allowing Ty's story to be so strong on my mind was His way of giving me some kind of answer or something. I don't know. Maybe you can tell me?" he said quickly, glancing over at Pastor Johnson. He continued, "But I do know that it was so heavy on my mind that I called Ty at 4:25 in the morning. I told him what was going on and that I needed to know more about this church because I felt like I needed to come here. I explained to him that the feeling was so strong that I was willing to skip my workouts to come here and have y'all pray for my nephew—and trust me, I don't miss my workouts for nobody. But I just couldn't shake it. Ty's story was etched in my brain, and I just knew somehow that coming here was the right thing to do. I just had this feeling that if God healed Ty many years ago, maybe He would be kind enough to heal Kevin too. So my plan was to come here, ask for help for Kevin, go spend a few days with him, then get back before training camp starts next week.

"Ty told me that this was a miracle in the making. He said that you all were having a revival this week and that he and I needed to drop everything and get to South Carolina, since God had laid this on my heart so heavy. He insisted on coming with me for support, but I wouldn't let him. I told him that this one was personal, and if God was real, which I now believe He is, then He could prove Himself to me, without Ty's help.

"Before we hung up, Ty told me, 'You don't know what you're asking for, Marv. God is about to blow your mind!'" The church exploded in applause.

"Well, Marvin," responded Pastor Johnson, "I believe that Ty is right. Thank you for sharing that with us tonight. The vision now makes a lot more sense. You see, you and Big Ty represent life. When the boy was in the field, playing, he was full of life and he was wearing the colors of the home team. He must really be a huge Vikings fan," he said, looking at Marvin.

"Yes, sir, he is," said Marvin. "But I don't get it. You said that when you saw him again, he was wearing a faded-out green-and-yellow jersey with white numbers on it. That's the Green Bay Packers' jersey—the archrival of the Vikings. And let me tell you, Kevin can't stand them."

"So for him to actually be wearing that jersey," Pastor Johnson interrupted, "represented that he was under serious attack by the enemy—that would be the cancers attacking his body. Are we on the same page, Marvin?"

"Yes, sir, I'm with you, I'm with you," he answered. "But what I don't understand is that last part. You said that I, and I assume it was Big Ty, went to see Kevin and took him a package. Now, that package, the purple jersey, represented Kevin getting his health back, right?"

"You're absolutely right, Marvin," said Pastor Johnson.

"Well, I understand that Kevin was too weak to open the package, but why couldn't Big Ty open it? He's stronger than I am!" Marvin asked.

"Because Tyson's faith alone was not enough to convince you to abandon your workout routine and come to Columbia in hopes of seeing your nephew's health restored. It is not a coincidence that you said to Tyson that this was between you and God. It certainly is, son. You were the one who had to cry out to God for help. You were the one who had to trust Him enough to believe that Tyson's story being so heavy on your mind was God's way of speaking to you, and most of all, Marvin, you had to have faith enough to act on what you believed. And you're standing here right now as a result of your faith in action. Kevin is healed right now because you dared to believe God."

"So wait," Marvin interrupted, "you're saying that my nephew is healed?"

"Yes! I'm saying that the miracle-working power of God has already touched Kevin's life, which is what the vision was all about. That's why God showed it to us, gave us the interpretation of it, and if you need more proof, guess who I saw come in while your back was to the audience?"

In that moment, Big Ty stood up in the back of the sanctuary and made his way down the aisle. Marvin was once again overcome with emotion. The two men embraced and beat each other's backs with a strength that likely would have left the average man badly bruised. "You two men get down to that hospital and use your influence to talk to that staff about taking another look at Kevin's brain and his entire body. I declare it now that because of what the Lord has done, the cancer that was there before is no longer there! Little Kevin is totally free, in Jesus's mighty name!" The congregation rose to its feet and began to praise and worship God.

Chapter 2

It had been only five years since Pastor Johnson had come to Miracle Center Church. It was after the death of the previous pastor, Ronald Calavar. The membership had dropped off tremendously, just as the eighty-one-year-old pastor had informed the church leadership that it would. He shared with them how he felt he had failed them in his latter years by allowing disagreements and arguments within the church to fester instead of bringing the parties together to settle the matters. He also told them he recognized that, as the leader, it was his job to diffuse such foolishness so that the work of ministry could be fully effective. However, his health was failing, and he didn't have the strength he'd once had to settle such discord. Worse yet, while there were other ministers in the church, he had not taken the time to train and develop them; thus, oftentimes, they were the culprits of the disputes and confusion, or at least were involved somehow. Realizing that it was far too late to raise up a successor, he began to pray fervently that God would send them a pastor, a true shepherd whose concern would be for the people and not his own selfish agenda.

The last two times he was able to attend church, although he was unable to preach, he slowly approached the pulpit and addressed the congregation with the same message each time. "First of all, I want you all to understand that I am not speaking from man's wisdom right now," he would say slowly. "But I speak from the knowledge that the Holy Spirit has given to me through prayer and supplication. You need to know that I won't be with you much longer, but God has given me peace in regards to the future of this ministry. He has a certain man whom He has prepared for this work since before time began. It doesn't mean that the other ministers within this church aren't fine men and women of God. They simply are not the one that God has assigned to lead this ministry. This man is going to come in and feed you with knowledge and understanding. Though he will have a different style, the message will be the same. He's going to teach and preach with simplicity yet with great authority. He's going to come in with a fresh vision, and that vision will not only cause the church to live up to its name again, but it is also going to bring revival to the communities around the area. I need you to get ready, Miracle Center. If you have unsettled issues against your brother or sister within this ministry, please do not let it linger any longer. I implore each of you to search your heart. And if you discover that holding on to your issue with your neighbor is more important than the work of ministry, then please keep your seat. The rest of you, I ask you to come to the altar for prayer."

Not surprisingly, several people came to the altar for prayer, although many of them came not because they had an issue with anyone but because they weren't sure if it would be the last time they would get to pray with Pastor Calavar. Their attendance, however, made others who actually had issues with other people feel more comfortable coming to the altar. This happened on two consecutive Sundays. Then on Wednesday of the following week, Pastor Calavar slipped away during the night, having total peace about Miracle Center Church.

After a little while, the leadership team put together a search committee to begin looking for a new pastor. It took them less than thirty days from the time they began searching to find their new pastor, Aspen Lamont Johnson, the assistant pastor of Flintwood Baptist Church in North Charleston, South Carolina. He was forty-nine years old and married for the second time, after his first wife and two-year-old son were killed in a horrible car accident after only four years of marriage. This man knew what it was like to lose everything. After the death of his wife and son, he became very angry with God. While he didn't lose his faith, he lost virtually everything else, including his job, his home, his sobriety, and a measure of his sanity. Although he knew it wasn't wise, he just could not bring himself to receive help from members of his family and friends, from his job, or even from his pastor and church family. He was no longer mentally sound, as his mind kept telling him that if God wanted to help him, he would have spared the life of his wife and child. In his mind, God Himself was going to have to help him if he was ever going to get better.

That was exactly what happened for him, as it was during this time that he developed an entirely new relationship with God. He knew what it was like to be hopeless, to be in the depths of depression, to be addicted to crack cocaine and nicotine, and to be totally broken, yet he knew what it was like to be totally set free by the hand of the Almighty. Aspen Johnson was a walking miracle. One would be hard-pressed to find someone who could relate more than him to people who were broken, brokenhearted, and sometimes just plain broke. He had been through all of it, and yet here he was, the newly elected pastor of Miracle Center Church.

No one believed in miracles as much as he did. After God delivered him, Aspen was what some referred to as a ball of fire. Over the years, however, his style changed from that of a fire-breathing demon-chaser to a truth-teaching God-chaser. He eventually learned that if he gave people enough of the truth that is found in God's Word, they would be able to resist any demon and put it to flight as long as they were willing to commit to and apply the teaching. He knew that providing such for his parishioners required that a host of Christ-centered services be offered by the ministry, and thus he went to work establishing various ministries within the church, which included providing food to the less fortunate, counseling services, financial literacy, health and wellness classes, and biblical studies for ministers, deacons, and those in training.

Pastor Johnson had greatly exceeded his congregation's expectations. In just five years, the church membership had grown from a diminishing 60 to about 225 strong and counting. They had moved to two services and were being forced to consider three since they could seat only 150, and the second service was usually at full capacity. Pastor Johnson had a way of preaching and teaching the Word of God that was so easy to understand and yet so powerful. He seemed to stir a desire within people to hear more of what God had to say through His Word. He rarely preached longer than twenty to twenty-five minutes, and most of that time was used to correct misunderstandings about how the kingdom of God was really designed to operate.

Usually at the apex of his sermons, the presence of God would be so strong that people would sometimes begin to come to the altar even before any altar call was given. Sometimes, people would experience emotional healing, and occasionally, people would experience physical healing during the preaching of the Word. There were also times when people who had demonic spirits would begin to cry out while he was preaching, in an effort to distract him or to disrupt the service. Most times, he would ask the people to praise God, while the doorkeepers would come and escort the person to the back so that some of the ministers could assist. Other times, he would simply command the evil spirit to be silent as he kept preaching and teaching God's Word. Oftentimes, he would then cast the demons out of the person. He taught with authority about spiritual concepts, but he made them seem so practical. His teaching caused people to believe that it was realistic to expect God to help them overcome any obstacle whatsoever.

During the past five years, Aspen Johnson had come to expect nothing less than the miraculous from God. Certainly, he had seen miracles take place throughout the course of his life and ministry, but he stood in awe of how God was now using him of all people in this way. He recognized, however, that the grace God had given for such signs and wonders was not limited only to him. It was just the nature of the ministry that God had given him charge over, and on any given day, whether in or out of the physical building, God was likely to perform something mind-boggling in the lives of his parishioners. Yet as unusual as this was for him, he knew that he was definitely the one God had assigned to the people at Miracle Center Church.

It gave him a sense of peace to hear some of the elders talk about how God had moved in their church for a very long time. They told him story after story about how God had used the late pastor Calavar to teach them about the power of God. They shared with him how it seemed like, all of a sudden, God decided to begin backing up his sermons with various forms of real-life demonstrations, which was why they eventually changed the name from Metropolitan Nondenominational Church to Miracle Center Church.

As Aspen pondered some of the stories he'd heard over the years, he thought about how much he missed his friend Deacon Bolden. One embarrassing moment in particular came to mind, which happened as they were first getting to know each other. This particular story had a greater impact on Pastor Johnson than any of the numerous stories shared by others. Deacon Bolden, who was seventy-one, was serving as chairman of the church leadership team when he shared with Aspen that the church was located across town in 1962. It was actually closer to downtown Columbia, and two nightclubs were just a couple of blocks away from the church building in a rough part of town. The one closest to the church was for blacks, and the one two blocks down was for whites only.

One Friday night in August, when the church was in the midst of a revival, a group of five young black men was walking past the white club on their way to the black club. People were standing on the sidewalk in a line, waiting to get into the white club, when somehow the two groups began arguing. It quickly escalated into a fight, and eventually, a couple of shots rang out. One of the white men had accidentally shot a bystander, who had merely been standing in line, waiting to get into the white club, and the man was now lying on the sidewalk, literally bleeding to death.

When the crowd began to scatter, one of the black guys was hiding on the side of the nightclub, paralyzed with fear. Back then, a white Baptist minister who was loved and respected by virtually everyone in that area was known for being a street preacher. In fact, he had been nicknamed Street Preach. When he wasn't evangelizing the streets on a Sunday evening, he would visit various churches for afternoon worship. While everyone admired his boldness, he was known for breaking the color barrier of his day and demonstrating God's love to everyone.

Deacon Bolden told how, seemingly out of nowhere, Street Preach came walking down the sidewalk and immediately recognized the seriousness of the situation. He told the only two people still there that there was no time to wait for an ambulance, given the reputation of the neighborhood. He also said a couple of nurses were a few blocks away and directed the dying man's girlfriend to grab one leg and the club owner to grab the other. They struggled to carry the man up the sidewalk.

Witnessing all this was the guy who was still clinging to the building, who knew Street Preach very well. This young man wondered what Street Preach was talking about, because he had grown up not too far from this neighborhood and knew full well that there were certainly no doctors' offices anywhere around where any nurses worked other than the hospital. Struggling to carry the man's lifeless body, Street Preach began to cry out to God.

"All right, I need some help, God!" he yelled. "Don't you see us down here, trying to save this man's life? My flesh is trying to convince me that You are just gonna let him die. But I know You to be a merciful God. One day You showed up and had mercy on a sinner like me. So right now I ask You to show up and help this young man, too, in the name of Jesus! Have mercy upon him according to Your lovingkindness. I don't know what happened, or why this man was shot, but, God, I know that You are full of mercy! Save his life right now, I pray! Send us help right now, Jesus, while there's still time!"

As he pleaded for God's help, Street Preach, who had been walking backward, carrying the man's upper body, tripped over an uneven place in the sidewalk and fell flat on his butt. The man's body fell right between his legs, and both the girlfriend and the club owner fell down too.

Suddenly, the building-hugger sprang into action, hoping that no one who saw him realized where he'd come from. He didn't know, however, that he was not alone. Another building-hugger wearing a varsity sweater and penny loafers had been hunkered down behind the next building over. Also, the cowardly security guard, who had been checking people into the club earlier, suddenly showed up to lend a hand too. He later lied to the club owner, saying that he had stayed behind to secure the building and that as he was making his way out, he saw them fall and had rushed over to help. Actually,

WHAT A CHURCH BOY WANTS

he, too, had been hiding beside a building. Without giving the club owner time to question him, the security guard asked where they were taking the man. Street Preach spoke up and said that they were taking him to the church.

"What?" the girlfriend shouted. "To the church? I thought you said we were taking him to some nurse's station or something! And isn't that a black church?"

"Listen, lady, this is his only hope. We're taking him to the nurses in the church." These were the people who primarily served as aides to the pastor and other ministers. "This is where he's going to get the help he needs. You don't see any ambulance here, do ya? You don't even hear any sirens. They're not coming, lady, and your friend here is not getting any better! He needs a miracle, ma'am, and unlike us, God is not hung up on skin color."

"Yeah, I guess so," she responded.

"Now, come on, men. I don't know where you guys came from, but I do know that God will provide. Grab a limb and let's go!" Street Preach shouted. "Lady, now would be a good time for you to start believing in the Lord Jesus Christ," he said between breaths. "He didn't send these men out of nowhere for your friend here to end up dying on us. This is a miracle in the making!" he declared as they carried the man to the church. "Come on, guys, quick! Up the steps! Let's go!"

When the group arrived in the front of the church, the service was about to come to an end, as Pastor Calavar had asked the congregation to stand for the benediction. As he prepared to close out the services, the delegation burst through the front vestibule, and once again Street Preach lost his footing and fell straight down, causing the others to fall as well.

"He's bleeding!" someone shouted. "Oh, mercy, is he dead?" someone else asked. By then, Pastor Calavar had rushed to the back of the church and was asking Street Preach what was going on.

"He's been shot!" Street Preach yelled. "We need a miracle right now, brother!"

The two preachers instantaneously began calling on the name of the Lord together. Despite the situation's intensity, it was a very

humbling sight to see the two men on the floor with their arms out-
stretched over the dying man, crying and pleading for God's help.
The club owner, the girlfriend, and the security guy, not knowing
what else to do, also extended their hands over the man's body. The
other building-hugger, who had attended the church as a child, also
began crying and asking God for forgiveness.

The nurses brought towels and began to put pressure on the
wound as they, too, joined in to pray for the dying man. The congregation was gathering around and doing the same when suddenly the
man began to cough. At the same time, a red streak seemed to circle
around the inside of the church vestibule. Pastor Calavar heard the
cough, but he hesitated to open his eyes after seeing the red streak.
He wasn't sure what God was doing, but he knew that he wasn't just
seeing things. It happened again. Was this an angel or some miraculous sign from God? Again, he saw it, and this time his prayer turned
to praise as he just knew that God was moving somehow.

Street Preach was experiencing similar thoughts when he realized what was going on. Although it was not at all likely in this neighborhood, an ambulance had pulled up at the front of the church,
with the single circular emergency light turned on. The ambulance
crew came in and immediately began assessing the man's dire condition. They put him on a gurney and escorted him to the ambulance
while the girlfriend shared with them every detail of what happened.
Again, he coughed as they were taking him out. The congregation
went nuts with praise as they realized that this was indeed a miracle. Barring salvation, this was the first miracle on record at Miracle
Center.

Pastor Johnson noticed that the deacon's account of this story
was quite detailed. He had paid close attention to the description of
those involved, the stumbling over the raised place on the sidewalk
and other details, such as what the security guard said to the club
owner. He wondered how much of the story was actually true and
how much the old deacon had made up to make it sound better.
Then he decided to stop wondering and to ask the deacon a question
or two.

"That is a very compelling story, Deacon Bolden. You seem to have a lot of information about what happened that day. So tell me, who shared this story with you?" he asked.

"Nobody *shared* this story with me," the older man retorted, appearing to be the slightest bit offended.

"Oh? Well, you had to hear it from somewhere," he replied, folding his arms in anticipation of the deacon's response.

"Brother Pastor, I don't need anyone to tell me my own testimony," he replied with a gentle grin. "I share this because it is not only a part of our church's history but also a part of my story. You see, I was the one crouched down behind the building, I was the one helping carry the man to the church, and I was the one there crying and asking for forgiveness. Since that very day, I made a vow that I would dedicate my life to the Lord because I realize that it could have been me with a bullet inside of me. And since that time, we have witnessed miracle after miracle in the lives of so many people who have come and gone within this ministry."

"I'm sorry," Pastor Johnson apologized. "I shouldn't have—"

"There's no need for apologies, Pastor. You're young, and you have a lot to learn. Me? I'm not so young, but I still have a lot to learn. Let's agree to help each other to grow. That's how we do it here at Miracle Center. You don't know everything, and I certainly don't either. But we both know that iron sharpens iron. We also know that there are too many people out there who need what we have for us to waste time fighting each other.

"Listen, I want you to know that we're on the same team. You're the leader, and let me tell you, you won't find a better follower than me. You seem to be leading pretty well to me. Even just now, when you made a wrong assumption, you immediately apologized and attempted to make it right. That in itself is good leadership, Pastor! Now, I don't know a whole lot, but I do know that if you want to see the miracles stop, all we have to do is to set ourselves at odds against each other. But together—I said *together*—we can tear down the devil's kingdom.

"Now, you're God's man, and I can't tell you how to run this ministry. But if I could give you any advice whatsoever, it would be to do your best to squash any foolish bickering that tries to rise up among the members of the congregation, and by all means, don't let yourself get caught up in it. When we're unified, Brother Pastor, there's no limit to the miraculous power of God!"

Although it had transpired nearly five years ago, Pastor Johnson remembered this conversation as if it had happened yesterday. He thought about how God had given him three years with Deacon Bolden before he died, three wonderful years full of wisdom, faith, and servant leadership. Though the deacon was no longer with him, the man's wisdom lived on in his heart and mind. Aspen thought about the last thing Deacon Bolden said to him.

"One of these days, you're going to need somebody to carry on this work. Even before you're old and gray, you need to turn this ministry over to the next man or woman who will take it higher. Don't be like the last pastor, who took on too much responsibility. He was a powerful man of God, but he was spread too thin. Just think about what I'm telling you. Pray about it, and once God begins to give you understanding, don't play around with it, Pastor. Seek Him continually for clarity of vision!"

Pastor Johnson jumped when his wife called out, "Aspen, come on, let's eat, baby!"

"Uh, okay," he responded, grateful that she had helped him to snap out of his stupor. "Lord, You know that I need to be praying for this revival, and here I am, taking a trip down memory lane. Please help me to focus on what You want to do tonight. This is not the time to be reminiscing," he prayed aloud. As he stood to wash his hands for lunch, he thought to himself, *Deacon Bolden was right, Lord. While I would like to think that I have many wonderful years of pastoring left, it only makes sense to go ahead and begin praying about who my successor will be.*

Chapter 3

Pastor Johnson recounted the events of the previous night, putting special emphasis on little Kevin's miracle. He reported that he and Sister Johnson had gone to the hospital that morning to get an update and that, indeed, no cancer whatsoever could be found in the boy's body. He also reported that both Marvin and Big Ty had pledged substantial donations to the church, which was yet another miracle in itself, since the church had been praying for the money to industrialize their kitchen for the sake of maximizing their outreach ministry. Though he shared this news, he also downplayed it by saying he would talk about it in more detail during the upcoming church meeting, a more intimate setting. Furthermore, he never counted any pledge until the money had actually been given to the ministry, so although this was exciting news for the church, he didn't want to get everyone excited prematurely.

As a matter of fact, his true motive for sharing this bit of information was to encourage himself, as he was feeling very unprepared to preach, although the time was at hand. It was a feeling that he had experienced before, but never like this. He had such a spirit of expectation for that particular night of revival, and now that it was time for him to deliver the Word of God, he felt like he had not done his due diligence to prepare himself to preach that night. So although he was recounting to the congregation how good God had been on the past two nights, he was also scrambling, trying to encourage himself in the Lord.

His mind quickly drifted back to his time of preparation earlier in the day, when he couldn't keep his mind off the late Deacon

Bolden's statement to him about praying for a successor. Now here it was, time for him to deliver his sermon, and he was still thinking about that conversation. In this moment, he knew that he had to rely on his faith and not on how he was feeling. He closed his eyes and asked the congregation to join him in prayer.

"Less of me, and more of You, O God," he prayed over and over until he felt it down in his soul. By this time, the members of leadership who had discernment had begun to stand and pray for him too. Tara Heart, the assistant choir director, had been directing the choir that night. She rose to her feet and signaled the organist to cue the choir, most of whom had their heads bowed in prayer. She had them stand as she mouthed to them what they were about to sing, which was the final line to the first stanza of "Holy, Holy, Holy," "God in three persons, blessed Trinity."

As Aspen closed out his prayer, he said, "Father, we're believing for a miracle that would change Miracle Center and this community forever. We expect you to do something in our midst tonight that will be a blessing to us for generations to come. Let us experience Your power among us tonight like never before, in the mighty name of Jesus the Christ, we pray. Amen!" Immediately, Tara cued the choir to increase their volume, and they sang from their hearts as the congregation rose to their feet. "God in three persons, blessed Trinity," the choir sang a bit longer before bringing the simple melody to a close in an atmosphere charged with worship. This environment enabled Pastor Johnson to flow in the spirit like he really desired, and he began his message.

"The Spirit of the Lord is in this place tonight. Let me say that another way: the Creator of the universe…is in this place tonight. I need you to understand that the Holy Spirit is not some strange, distant being who is persuaded by the sound of organs, guitars, and drums to show up when the musicians begin to play. Rather, I need you to understand that He *is* God!" He paused to allow those last words to settle into the minds of the people, who were already starting to get excited. "I want you to stop and think about that for a moment. His job is not to make you dance and shout. He is the reason we dance and shout. Are y'all listening to me? Let me say it another way: if you praise the Lord, it is because you make a conscious decision to praise the Lord. In the same way, if you choose not to praise the Lord at all, it is a conscious decision. So you can't say that you don't praise God because the Holy Spirit doesn't move in you that way. By the same token, you can't say that you do praise Him because He made you praise Him. Who moved you to dance and sing when you went to the concert the other night? You did. When you were out there gyrating and shaking your rump, did God make you do that? No. You did it because you wanted to. When you went to the ball game the other night, God didn't make you clap, chant, and yell at the top of your lungs. You made up your mind to do those things because you were excited about the performance of the team you went to support, right?

"Well, when you come to the house of the Lord, who do you come to support? I just need to put that out there because I tend to believe there should be a reaction to the actions of the God we say we worship. I mean, is anything happening on the Lord's team that is worth getting excited about? Was it by chance that you got up out of your bed this morning, or was it God who allowed you to see another day? Are you in your right mind by happenstance, or did God have something to do with that? Who provided the food that you ate today?

"So now, when you experience the goodness of the Lord, there should be a reaction to His goodness, and we call that reaction praise. But whether you praise Him or not is a decision you're going to have to make. In other words, if you're gonna praise Him, it's going to be on purpose! So let me challenge each of you to think for a moment about the goodness of the Lord, and then give Him your best praise! It takes only a quick moment to realize that God is good, and a quick moment to make a decision to praise Him for His goodness. If you realize that God didn't have to do it, you ought to go ahead and praise Him because He blessed you anyway. Praise Him because He loved you anyway. Praise Him because He saved you anyway. Praise Him like you want to see miracles take place in here tonight. Praise Him like you believe that strongholds are going to be broken in our midst tonight. You might not praise Him like I praise Him, but everybody's got a praise! It's revival time!"

The church exploded into a thunderous atmosphere of praise. Even young Wesley Heart, who had been listening attentively, was now on his feet, clapping his twelve-year-old hands and praising God the best way he knew how. He clapped hard as he compared his mother's current clean bill of health to her cancer-ridden past. He clapped them while he thought about his parents' love for each other. He had a wonderful Christian family, and he was grateful. As he stood there clapping his hands and slowly shaking his head from side to side, tears began to roll down his boyish face. Wesley thought about making his way to the altar, intending to kneel and to pray, but his spirit began to pray before he could give that idea another conscious thought.

"Thank You, Jesus, for everything You have done for me. I gave You my life when I was nine years old, and You have never let me down. I am so happy now, and it's all because of You. So if praising You is a choice, like Pastor Johnson said, I choose to praise You…"

Since little Wes had come to know God and learned to pray, he had a very sincere way of talking to God, as if God were standing right there in front of him, as if he were having a conversation with a friend. He didn't realize it, but a very special relationship had begun to develop between him and the God of the universe. Sometimes he would have thoughts that would come into his mind so strongly as he began to pray that he would forget about his routine. He uttered child-like prayers that he'd been taught, but he would also begin to talk to God about whatever was on his mind. It wasn't until this particular night, however, that Wes began to understand this. God revealed Himself to the boy this night in a way that would affect him for the rest of his life.

"Thank You so much, God. I really appreciate You for answering my prayers. I mean, I believed You could do what I was asking and everything, but You do what I don't even ask You for. You bless me in so many ways. And it seems like whenever I do ask You for something, You find a way to make it happen. I never really thought about that, but now I see. I used to ask You every night to help me to understand You better. I didn't expect You to send me a new pastor, and I definitely didn't expect my old pastor to pass away. But now that Pastor Johnson is here, I guess…well, I guess this really is a miracle center, and I guess Pastor Johnson is just Your special guy, huh? I mean, since he came here, church makes a lot more sense. You used him to help Mama and Dad love each other more, and you've brought peace to our home like we've never had before.

"Thank You for sending him to us. He is really a special dude—uh, I mean a special man…a man of God. Jesus, when I grow up, I'm gonna look out for him like he has looked out for us. I ain't gonna let nothing happen to him. I'm gonna look out for him, God. I swear. I mean, uh…sorry, God. But for real, as long as You make me able, I'm gonna help him so that maybe he can help other people like he helps us. I'm gonna look out for him, I…I promise. So I guess that's all. That's what I want to do. You look out for me, and I'll look out for him. Amen."

Dazed and disoriented, Wesley opened his eyes. His lips were pursed, and he was now slowly nodding. As he gradually lifted his hands to wipe away his tears, one of the ushers placed tissue in them. Although he had never had assistance from an usher like this before, he realized that he was at the front of the church, standing right near the altar. He wondered how he had drifted so far from his seat without knowing it. He quickly remembered that he had made the decision to go to the altar to kneel and pray, but somehow, he never made it to the kneeling part. He now wondered how he could return to his seat without making an even bigger scene than he had obviously made getting to the altar.

Although he was only a kid, he was no stranger to being at the altar. However, he would normally go to the altar with his mom after the sermon, whenever she would go up for prayer, since his dad was often on duty as Miracle Center's head of security. For the first time since he could remember, neither his mom nor dad was able to attend revival. His mom, a nurse, was working a weird shift at the hospital, and his dad, a project manager at a pharmaceutical factory in the small town of Cayce, had also been working additional hours on a very important job. Without a doubt, this was the first time he had decided to go to the altar alone. To make matters seem even worse in his mind, no altar call had been given.

Revival was sort of a big deal to the Heart family, since normally Wesley and his two sisters who still lived at home would each invite a friend to spend two back-to-back weeks with them during the summer. The first week would be their revival week, and the next week, their vacation. This year had been different, however, since his parents' work schedules had gotten so turned around. In addition, Wesley's best friend, Jamar, was unable to come over this year because he was spending the summer with his dad in Montgomery, Alabama. So Wesley had come to church with his sister Amanda and her friend Charlesia and his sister Tara and her friend Lisa, who was also a very close friend of the family and likely to be at the Hearts' house pretty regularly. Each of the young ladies loved the Lord and had their own personal relationship with Him, although Amanda was a little rough around the edges.

Not really knowing what to do, he stood there paralyzed, waiting for the courage to move one way or the other. To make matters worse, he knew that God had given him some sense of purpose while at the altar, and he didn't even have the words to explain it. Young Wesley was overcome with emotion. Just then, a tall burly female usher named Sister Patterson was able to discern his confusion and approached him in an effort to guide him back to his seat. When she embraced him, he buried his face into her shoulder and began to sob uncontrollably. She embraced him and spoke gentle, comforting words. He heard her say something about how she could tell that he was having a real conversation with God and how that was probably his first encounter with Him in this way. He heard her say something else about how it was nothing for him to be embarrassed about but rather that he should feel special, given his age, that he was able to discern so much of God's purpose for his life. Whatever she was saying, it was giving him confidence and reminding him of the vow that he had just made to God. Before he was able to gain full composure, he said it one more time, speaking into the usher's shoulder, "I promise You, God. When I grow up, I will look out for Pastor Johnson."

After a moment, he stood up straight, dried his tears, and made his way back to his seat with a stern look on his face. There to welcome him were his two older sisters and their friends, and he dreaded facing them. What he didn't know was that his sisters and their friends had been praising God, too, and didn't even realize he was gone until things began to settle down. Then they saw him all the way down at the front of the church. As he approached his row, he thought about how he would be mocked and made fun of by Amanda for the rest of the summer, and to make matters worse, he remembered that she had been sitting right beside him before all this happened. He was expecting to be teased and to become the brunt of all their girly smirks, jokes, and jeers, and for this to especially intensify after church that night, with Amanda at the helm of it all.

None of that was the case, however, as Tara's best friend, Lisa Monroe, led the way. She stopped him as he attempted to scoot past her since she was now in his seat. She told the rest of the girls to move down a seat as she did so herself. She patted the end seat, instructing Wes to sit down. He didn't know what to think, but he was so grateful that he didn't have to sit beside Amanda. Tonight was not the night for joking around. Lisa put her arm around him and, without a word, gave him a squeeze of support as if to say, "I got your back."

As the music began to subside and the atmosphere shifted almost too abruptly from high praise to an expectation of what God was going to say, Wes's mind was back on what had just happened. He knew that God had put something in his heart that night, and he was going to commit his life to fulfilling it. In his boyish mind, being shielded from Amanda was a sign that God had already begun to move—a miracle within itself.

Chapter 4

After the revival service that night, Amanda drove everyone back to the Heart home. Amanda and her friend Charlesia were in the front seat, while Tara, Lisa, and Wesley sat in the back. It was early August, and the temperature in Columbia was still eighty-three degrees and very humid, even though it was 8:30 p.m. Everyone was overjoyed that Mr. Heart had agreed to let Amanda drive his 4Runner to church, since the AC in her Honda Civic had recently stopped working. Wesley also appreciated the extra legroom, especially since he always seemed to end up in the middle.

The plan was for everyone to go back home and resume the game of Monopoly they had started after church the previous night, and to talk about life, goals, dreams, and the like while feasting on sandwiches, microwave popcorn, and Kool-Aid. Surprisingly, the mood was kind of somber on the way home, and no one, not even Amanda, had much to say. Wesley had determined to take his mind off everything for the moment because he recognized that he was a little emotional about all that had happened in church. He resolved that he would just tell his dad about it in the morning to see what he had to say, but tonight would just be a night to chill. As he crossed his arms and relaxed his head on the leather headrest behind him, he prepared to zone out for the twenty-minute ride home.

Lisa's mind was also full of thoughts and emotions as she sat silently to Wesley's left. As she pondered how she even became acquainted with the Heart family, her heart was saddened, even though she had to acknowledge the hand of God in it. She leaned over slightly and placed her head on Wesley's shoulder. Wesley was momentarily paralyzed by her gesture, but after a moment, he decided to relax and take it all in. He was enthralled by the fact that out of all the girls that he knew, the one of whom he was the fondest had just placed her head on his shoulder. He wanted to know what she was thinking about, but he wasn't at liberty to ask her, because it would have drawn attention to them, and perhaps it would have caused her to move away from him. To him, her head fit perfectly on his shoulder, which was noticeably a bit larger than those of most boys his age. He embraced the gentle tickle of her hair on his face and neck. Her scent made him wish that he only had the ability to inhale.

For Wes, he was in heaven. For Lisa, not so much. However, she was grateful to have a shoulder to lean on as she found herself going down memory lane. She rehashed the time that she had been defiantly arguing back and forth with her grandparents about one thing after another for days. Unwilling to tolerate the disrespect any longer, her grandfather finally made her go to her room until she could calm down enough to be respectful. The problem was that there was so much anger and bitterness built up within her that "calming down" was just not possible, although she knew it was the right thing to do.

Knowing full well that it was not the right decision, Lisa stuffed a few items into her backpack and slipped out of the window in an attempt to demonstrate her frustrations to her grandparents. In actuality, it was a cry for help. Yet she was unsure how to voice her feelings about her life, her parents, her embarrassment, her pain. She did not know where she was going; she only knew that she was very angry. She ended up at the Heart residence when nosy young Tara, who was sitting outside, saw her walking and recognized her as the girl from school who lived across town in Nickelville. Although it was the end of their summer break, Tara wondered why this girl whose name she really didn't know was wandering through her neighborhood with a backpack on her back. Being the nosy person that she was, Tara decided to greet her and asked her if she wanted something to drink.

"Hey, uh…Lisa, is that you? It's Tara. We had psychology together. What are you doing out here in this heat? Is everything okay?" she asked.

"Oh, hey. Ah…I'm good. I'm just out clearing my head a little bit," Lisa lied.

"Well, would you like some water or tea?"

"Nah…no thanks, I'm good," she lied again as she continued walking.

Amanda, having heard everything, was making her way out to join Tara for tea. She, too, recognized Lisa and knew she was that pretty girl from Nickelville. Being her overly zealous self, Amanda joined the conversation.

"Girl, get over here and get something to drink. Now you know it's hot out here. You're sweating, which means you're probably thirsty and could use something cold to drink. What are you doing walking all the way over here, anyway? Don't you live in Nickelville?"

"Yeah, I live in Nickelville. Is that a problem?" Lisa asked rather defiantly as she stopped, surprising even herself.

Tara knew that was the wrong question for Amanda. While neither of them had a problem with the girl being from Nickelville, Amanda was not one to back down from a challenge, so Tara quickly spoke up.

"No, no one has a problem with that! If we did, do you think we would be inviting you over for tea? Listen, I apologize. This is my sister Amanda. You have to excuse her. She can be a little pushy. But I love my big sissy poo," she rattled on, attempting to disarm both of them.

"My bad," said Amanda. "Calm down, calm down. I didn't mean no harm, Ms. Lisa."

"We're cool," Lisa said, standing down. "Sorry to be so touchy. I just got some things I need to sort out in my head," she offered, heading down toward the deck. "I guess I could use something to drink."

"Great, come on up!" said Tara. When she walked up the deck steps, Lisa once again expressed her regret for sounding off at Amanda.

"It's okay," Amanda responded. "I should have minded my own business, anyway."

"Lisa, I can see that you've been crying," said Tara. "I heard you say that you wanted to clear your head. Listen, I know we don't know each other very well, but I am certain our paths didn't cross today by accident. Normally, when I see someone walking along here, of course I ignore them. I certainly don't invite them over for tea. So I guess what I'm trying to say is that, if you want to talk, I'll be happy to listen."

"Honey, let me tell you," Amanda interrupted. "Tara is the counselor in the family. She can drop some advice on you that will leave your head spinning. She won't judge you, and she doesn't care how serious your problem is. Trust me, by the time this is over, you're gon' feel like you've been touched by an angel. Straight up, you will feel like you can make it, girl—fa real! As a matter of fact, I'll go get that glass of tea for you, and y'all can just, you know…talk that thang out…heeey, talk that thang out, heeey!"

Amanda danced and sang her newly created ditty as she made her way back into the house, leaving Tara and Lisa snickering at her as they chose a seat and began talking. This was the beginning of their relationship, and by the end of the day, Tara had counseled, ministered, and on some level, prayed restoration and hope into the life of Lisa Monroe. Tara asked her dad to take Lisa back home so she wouldn't have to walk, and when they arrived, he knew that he should tell Lisa's grandparents what had happened to the best of his knowledge. It was Tara, however, who led the conversation. The elder Mr. and Mrs. Monroe were so impressed and grateful to God that they began crying and praising God right there in their front yard. They embraced Lisa, Tara, and Mr. Heart. Then they offered to cook them dinner, but Mr. Heart told them his wife would be arriving home and cooking dinner shortly. Lisa's grandparents shared that they had called the police once they realized Lisa was gone, but they couldn't really do much until after twenty-four hours had passed. They explained how, when they began praying, God gave them total peace, but they had still spent the entire afternoon circling the entire area over and over, looking for Lisa. They had come home for a few minutes to regroup and were planning to do the same for the rest of the evening when Lisa and the Hearts had arrived.

Mr. Monroe confessed, "When you pulled up, I said to Nancy, 'It's her, it's her.'" He turned to Lisa. "Baby, all we wanted to do was to wrap our arms around you and let you know that we love you. We don't want to fuss and argue with you, we just want to love you. We're just so happy and grateful to God for returning you to us," he said, putting his arms around the crying teen.

"I'm so sorry, Grandpa," Lisa cried. "You and Grandma have been nothing but good to me, and here I am, treating you like you've done something to harm me. I know Lisa from school, and as I was just wandering through their neighborhood, she recognized me and inquired about me walking in the heat. She and her sister invited me to have some ice tea. Then she sat me down and talked to me as if she were some kind of professional counselor. She talked to me about life and from a perspective that I never thought about. Like the fact that you guys are doing everything you can just to make sure that I have a normal life just like every other kid my age, but I can't even show you simple respect even though I'm living under your roof. She showed me how I am subconsciously so focused on being angry and resentful toward my mom, and even the dad I've never met, that I can't even express gratitude for the people God put in my life to take up their slack. I'm so sorry," she apologized through tears. "And I promise you, things are going to be different."

They all stood in the driveway as Lisa expressed through tears her remorse for what she'd put everyone through. As Tara chimed in that if all this hadn't happened, they would not have had the opportunity to make new friends, little Wesley hopped out of the running car and appeared out of nowhere in his martial arts uniform. Bouncing restlessly, he spoke up and said, "Uumm, excuse me, Daddy, I don't mean to interrupt, but I gots ta go to the bathroom." Everyone laughed heartily at the boy as Mr. Monroe directed Wesley to the bathroom.

It was truly the beginning of a beautiful, lifelong relationship. Lisa chuckled as she recalled Wesley's appearance that day. He couldn't have been any more than about seven or eight, but he was the cutest little fella. Lisa smiled as she thought about Wesley returning from the altar earlier that night. *He's still cute,* she thought. She

43

moved closer to him and kissed him on the jaw, causing his heart to flutter. "Shhhh," she whispered in his ear.

Tara broke the silence as they neared the house. "I really hope it's okay with everyone if we pick up our game late tomorrow morning. I think we all need to spend some time with our thoughts and maybe just having some serious one-on-ones as we prepare to get some sleep tonight."

"I didn't want to say it, but I was thinking the same thing," Amanda concurred. Everyone murmured their agreement as Lisa lifted her head from its resting place. Suddenly, Wesley spoke up.

"Wait a minute, who's gonna talk to me?" As if on cue, Amanda began with the jokes.

"The *Lord* is gonna talk to you! Y'all sho' had a good conversation going down at that altar tonight." Everyone, including Wesley, laughed at her statement. "But I'm gonna leave you alone tonight, because that was a serious moment. I can't even trip on that one."

Then Lisa spoke up. "Well, I really want to know what that was like, Wesley, so I'll talk to you while everyone is getting ready for bed."

"Well, I'm cool with that, as long as it's not a one-sided conversation," he returned, recalling something his dad recently shared with him about how to talk to girls.

"Aww, shucks now!" Amanda said as she turned onto their street.

"I'm just saying," he continued, "I don't want to just talk about what happened to me at church tonight. I mean, don't get me wrong. I don't mind sharing that, but I want to get inside your head too. I want a true dialogue, you know, a real conversation between a man and a woman."

"Whaaat?" Tara threw in, obviously surprised.

"Awww, sookie," commented Charlesia.

Lisa drew back, cocked her head to the side, raised her eyebrows, and folded her arms—all in true female fashion. "Okay, I hear you, bro, I hear you," she agreed.

Amanda's response had to be over the top, of course. As she pulled into the driveway, she tapped the brakes hard a couple of times.

"Boy, you gon' make me run into this house!" she yelled as they all laughed. Then, mocking him, she said, "Oh, I don't mind sharing my testimony with you, baby, as long as you understand that a man has needs. I expect that you will allow me access to the inner corridors of your mind, so that I may commune with the thoughts that resonate from the depths of your soul." Everyone was laughing wildly by the time she finished.

"Let me turn around and look just to make sure that I ain't bringing no stranger home from church." She turned around and looked at him and yelled, "Hey, big man! Who are you and what did you do with my little brother?" They all laughed even harder. "I might need to be in on this conversation," she continued hilariously. "Shoot! I need to know what happened at that altar too, 'cause if going to the altar will transform you like that, bruh, I'm going to the altar every time we go to church. I'm gonna just come in, greet the greeters and the ushers, and go straight to the altar. I'm gonna ask Dad if security will allow me to just put a chair down there—permanently!" Everyone exited the car, still laughing at Amanda's jokes.

They all trooped inside and headed off in various directions to get showers and prepare for bed. As promised, Lisa approached Wesley's bedroom door and knocked.

"Come in," he responded. She opened the door and found that his room was neatly organized and spotless. "I've never been in here before. You keep everything so nice and neat," she complimented.

"Yeah, I know it's weird," Wesley responded, "but I'm just kinda made that way."

"You're just full of surprises, aren't you? I'm still laughing about your last statement in the car."

Wesley smiled. "I didn't mean it the way it sounded. I was kinda glad when Tara suggested that we go our separate ways tonight and just maybe have some one-on-one conversations instead of playing our usual games, because that meant I could just chill and play my video games in my bedroom. At first, I was just kidding around with everybody and acting like I was sad because everyone had someone to talk to except me. But when you spoke up and said that you would talk to me, well, that changed everything for me. When you said that, I just wanted to make it clear to you that I didn't just want to talk to you but I also wanted you to talk to me. But you guys took that and ran with it, which was cool, because that *was* pretty funny."

Lisa chuckled. "Yes, and what made it funny is that we all knew you were kidding, but all of a sudden, you went from kidding to being very serious. And then when Amanda took over, of course it was a wrap then."

"No doubt," he agreed. "She's too much sometimes."

"That's Amanda for you. So just to be clear, you just said that when I spoke up and said I would talk to you, that changed every-thing. What does that mean? What if Charlesia had spoken up instead of me? Would your response have been the same?"

"Absolutely not," he said, probably too quickly and with too much certainty.

"Why not?"

"Uh, well, the short answer is, she's not you."

"What's the long answer?" she asked, somewhat coyly.

Wesley swallowed. "Uh, wh-why don't you come in and have a seat? You can hang out at least until my dad gets here about ten—that is, if we're still talking then. Just take your pick," he offered, pulling out his video game chair and buying a little more time before responding. "You can sit here, or you can sit on the bed."

Lisa sat on the corner of his queen-size bed. "Thanks. Do you mind if I take off my shoes?"

Girl, you can take off anything you want to take off, he thought to himself. This time, he almost blew his cover of smoothness as his thoughts nearly got the best of him, making him snicker as he responded.

"No, of course I don't."

"What's so funny?" Lisa questioned.

"Oh, nothing. I...I was just thinking that, uh, you certainly don't need my permission to take off your shoes."

"Okay, cool. So I'm waiting for this long answer of yours."

"Uh, the long answer is, I'm not into Charlesia. She's cool and all, but she's not nearly, uh...as cool as you are."

"Sooo...cool?" she asked. "Is that what you think of me?"

"You are very cool and very…" Wesley just couldn't do it. His pride wouldn't let him just come right out and say that he thought she was the most beautiful girl in the world and that he adored every single thing about her. "Very interesting," he finished.

"So what makes me so interesting?"

"Oh, that's easy. You're not like other girls. You're your own person. You have your own style, your own views and opinions, you will give your last to help someone out and never look for anything in return, you don't care what people think about you, and most of all, you love the Lord. Sooo…all those things make you a very interesting person."

"Whoa! That seemed too easy…like you've thought about that before now. I didn't know you paid that much attention to me. Have you been studying me or something?" she teased.

"I wouldn't say 'studying,' 'cause that's a little creepy. But I've noticed a few things about you, and uh, I can honestly say that I'm impressed." Wesley was satisfied with his answer and ready to hear from her.

"That's so sweet," Lisa said softly. "If I didn't know any better, I would think I had an admirer."

"Lisa, I'm sure you have lots of admirers," he replied, refusing to take the bait. "I want to ask you something. On the way home, you put your head on my shoulder, then out of nowhere, you kissed me and told me to keep quiet. What am I supposed to think about all that?"

"I hope I didn't offend you," she replied quickly.

"I was not at all offended. I just don't want to read more into that than I should."

"That's what I like about you, Wes. Instead of jumping to conclusions, you ask questions, even difficult questions, to get information. You are so far ahead of the game."

"That really was a hard question to ask. I hope it's not too hard for you to answer."

"It's tough, but I can handle it. Sometimes females have a tendency to be emotional."

"Sometimes?" he asked jokingly.

"You're not funny. But yes, we get emotional sometimes. When a person has been through something or when they have things on their mind, they look for comfort and security. I guess in the moment, you were able to provide that for me by letting me put my head on your shoulder. Then I thought about how you have been so precious from the day I met you. And in the moment, I just thought that a simple kiss was appropriate."

"So does that mean you were kind of using me in some way?"

"Oh, no," Lisa denied quickly. "I wasn't using you, Wesley, not at all. I told you that this was difficult to answer, and what makes it difficult is that a lot of guys just refuse to accept it. But if you learn this early on, it will save you a lot of confusion and misunderstanding with women. So here it is. I'm sure you already know that women and men are different. But you should know that so often, physical contact for women is far more about security than sex. That's why women always want to hold hands and have you put your arm around them and cuddle. It's often not about sex, Wesley, but about security."

"So when you say *security*, do you mean protection?" he asked.

"Yes, that's part of it, but not just protection. A woman looks for other things like acceptance, understanding, the freedom to be herself, and even provision for some women. What I probably shouldn't tell you at your age is that once they feel secure enough, they will be a lot more accepting of the idea of sexual contact."

"You sound like a teacher or something. That's a lot of knowledge for someone who's only sixteen. How do you know so much about all that?"

"Well, I love psychology, so I research and study this kind of stuff all the time. I guess I'm a nerd when it comes to that."

"I'm cool with that, but I'm still a little confused."

"I know, I know. You're not gonna stop until you get some answers, are you? So what happened in the car was about security for me, okay? Is that what you're confused about?"

"Yes. But you said it's acceptance, understanding, freedom to be yourself…how can I provide all that for you? I'm only twelve."

"Wes, stop it. You're just overthinking things now. Look, you can make virtually any girl feel secure. You listen, you're not judgmental, you let people be who they are, I mean, you got it, kid. But I gave you this information because I know you are very mature for your age. But you can't overthink it. Sometimes you just gotta flow with it, just like you did in the car."

"That makes sense. Thanks, Lisa. Thank you for everything."

"Of course. Like I said, I'm studying this stuff when most teens my age aren't thinking about school stuff."

"Well, not just for the information…thank you for putting your head on my shoulder and for kissing me. Okay, wait, I know that sounded weird. What I mean is, it feels good to know that you felt secure enough with me to do that. I mean…did that sound weird too?"

"Nah. I feel you. You're saying thanks for the vote of confidence, right?"

"Right. This is helping me a lot. Maybe we should talk more often."

"Uh, maybe not. You ask too many questions, dude," she said with a smile.

"I know, I know. I get that from my dad, who always tells me to make sure that I read and ask questions. He says that most guys try to act like they know everything when they really don't know much of anything. But why pretend to know when you can know for sure? He says that there are two sure ways to find out the answers to most of what you want to know—reading and asking questions. I try to do both as much as possible. As a matter of fact, most of what you've shared with me tonight was kind of familiar because I've read it somewhere along the way. I used to be really nervous when it came to talking to girls about certain things, but now they seem to flock to me when they want to have a serious conversation, especially about boys."

"Yeah, I *have* heard your dad say that a time or two. Tara certainly doesn't mind asking either. She'll ask you about anything, no matter how personal or private, and she's so professional about it."

"I do have one more question, though."

"Wesley!"

"It's simple. What about protection? Do you think I could provide that for you too?"

"Oh, please, we don't even have to talk about that. You know I trust you when it comes to that."

"Uh, excuse me!" Tara said abruptly, stepping into Wesley's room so fast that it startled both Wesley and Lisa.

"What's your problem?" Wesley asked casually.

"What do you mean what's my problem? The question is, What's *your* problem?"

"Tara, you come busting into my room like you're mad or something, then you ask me what's *my* problem? What's wrong with you?"

"Well, I come in here and Lisa's all cozy in your room, on your bed, where she really shouldn't be, and I hear you asking her if you could provide protection and her saying that she trusts you. Now somebody needs to start explaining what's going on, *right now!*"

"T, why are you acting like you don't know what's up? Y'all are best friends, and besties talk about everything. Lisa, you *have* told her about us, haven't you?" Wesley questioned, trying unsuccessfully to keep a straight face. Lisa burst out laughing.

"Boy, you're gonna get both of us jumped on in here! Ya know, on second thought, I don't know if I *do* trust you to protect me against a fuming, mad Tara."

As Tara began to better understand the context of their conversation, Lisa convinced her that she was just seizing the moment to have a conversation with Wesley as promised and that she would explain everything during their one-on-one after she showered. As she and Tara walked out of Wesley's room, Lisa turned around and slowly winked and smiled at him.

Chapter 5

Wesley's plan was to have a serious conversation with his dad the following morning, before reconvening with all the ladies to play Monopoly. He had two things that he wanted to talk about: God and girls. He explained everything to his dad regarding his experience at the altar, but that was as far as he got. His dad commended him for having the courage to be obedient to the pastor's instructions by praising God without regard for what others thought. He also gave him the assurance that everything was all right and about what the encounter could have possibly meant.

"Son," he began, "I think it's getting close to the time for you to start serving in the ministry. Now we can sit down with Pastor Johnson, perhaps after church Sunday, and get some insight from his perspective. But we should start exploring your gifts and skills to see where you would best fit. I don't want to jump the gun because, after all, you're only twelve years old, but hearing you explain your encounter with the Lord at the altar last night, I think you might be a good fit to begin training for the security ministry. You already know how to subdue a person without hurting them, you come to the training sessions with me most of the time anyway, and so you're already aware of a lot of the spiritual aspects of the position. But it's the anointing that's going to prepare you for service, son. It'll transform your entire life, if you stay in position. We can talk about that later, but let's talk to Pastor Johnson about it and go from there. Until then, I wouldn't focus on it too much. Let's just pray about it and see what comes of it."

As he finished that statement, the house phone rang, and the caller ID revealed that it was Pastor Johnson.

"Hey, son, this is the pastor calling now. Let me go ahead and take this call, and I'll let him know that you and I need to sit down and talk to him after church Sunday and see if that's okay with him." Mr. Heart might as well have told Wesley that they would finish talking tomorrow, since the conversation with the pastor was sure to be lengthy. Nonetheless, Wesley was excited because he loved the idea of serving in the security ministry. As he made his way upstairs, the sound of giggling girls reminded him that he had not had the other conversation with his dad. Apparently, that would have to be another conversation for another day. For now, he would have to put on his poker face and prepare to resume Monopoly with the ladies.

Later that evening, as Wesley sat in his aisle seat during the last night of revival, trying unsuccessfully not to concentrate too much on the encounter from the previous night, his mind began to take a journey of its own. As he thought about the commitment he'd made to look out for his pastor, he concluded that he had a much better idea of what it meant to "look out" for somebody after his brief talk with his dad. But what if there was more to this than just serving with the security ministry?

Ever since he was a little boy, his dad had always told him that he was expected to look out for his sisters, and to him that meant that he was to stand up for them, to protect them, and not to let anything bad happen to them as much as he was able. His dad, Rory Heart, a seventh-degree black belt in judo, would often teach self-defense tactics to Wes and his siblings. However, the Gulf War-era US Navy veteran who once took pride in training Navy SEALs in hand-to-hand combat could no longer practice the art as intensely as he used to due to occasional problems with his back. Nevertheless, he was well able to teach different self-defense techniques to his daughters, to the point of them being able to incapacitate an aggressor long enough to escape and get help.

Mr. Heart would always teach Wesley the "men's version," as he called it, instructing him on different throws, flips, and holds. He noticed early on that Wesley had a remarkable gift, a God-given instinct and a natural knack for the martial arts like none he'd ever seen. Wes was amazingly elusive and quick on his feet. The boy had such an ability to throw swift and accurate kicks and punches that it amazed his dad. In light of this, he knew that judo was not the martial arts style best suited to Wes, since it did not involve kicking and punching. So he determined to pull out of Wes what was already in him and to enhance it. He trained him like he had once trained the troops, attempting to instill in him the mental discipline needed to help him advance in whatever style of martial arts he would eventually choose, and hopefully to give him the discipline needed to excel in life.

"Listen, son," he would say. "I always train you like a man, because as a man, you are a protector. If you can't protect what God has blessed you with, then you ain't ready to be no man, son. So God has blessed you with three sisters and a mother. It's not your duty to protect them, it's my duty. But it's good training ground. Now you can't go around jumping on people, 'cause your hands and feet truly are lethal weapons, son. But if you ever see or hear of any dude trying to put his hands on them or anything like that, you have what it takes to put him on his back! Do you hear me?"

"Yes, sir," Wes would simply reply.

"Now I'm trusting you to look out for your sisters, understand?"

"Yes, sir."

The trust that Wesley's father seemed to have in him gave him the confidence to believe that he really could look out for his sisters. But he really wasn't sure how he was supposed to "look out" for a grown man like Pastor Johnson, who, in all likelihood, probably should have been looking out for him. He wasn't sure, that is, until talking to his dad that morning. At that point, he knew beyond a doubt that serving in the security ministry was exactly what he was supposed to be doing, and now, all he needed was Pastor Johnson's approval to begin training for it. *But is there more to it than that, Lord? Dad said not to think too much about it, but it's hard not to. Maybe you can give me some more answers as I listen,* he thought to himself. He made up his mind right then to stop allowing his thoughts to roam and to listen to what Pastor Johnson was saying.

"Understand that the Holy Spirit *is* God!" Pastor Johnson said, getting into the meat of his sermon. "As a matter of fact, He is just as much God as God the Father and Jesus Christ, the Son. Now, in Monday night's message, I shared with you the essence of who the Holy Spirit is. I showed you in chapter 1 of Genesis how He was there in the beginning, hovering over the face of the waters, preparing to do His part in the creation of the heavens and the earth. Then I took you to Psalm 33:6–7 and showed you more about the Holy Spirit's role in creation. We then took a look at Job 26:13, which re-emphasized how, from the beginning, the Holy Spirit has always been intricately involved in the plan of God.

"Last night, I took you to various accounts in the book of Acts and showed you how the Holy Spirit made His presence known to the disciples on the Day of Pentecost with signs and wonders. I showed you how He worked in the lives of the apostles and in the presence of other followers of Jesus Christ. We talked about how He worked great miracles and demonstrated great power throughout the lives of those who were serious about doing the work of the Lord.

"Well, on this final night of revival, my goal is to get you to see in the same way that the Holy Spirit's responsibilities did not end after the world was created, neither did His works recorded in the New Testament signify the end of His interaction with mankind. But I must get you all to see that the Holy Spirit is right here with us, right now, and that He wants to interact with you throughout the course of each day. It is when you come to this realization that you experience the transforming power of God and His Word like never before.

"So tonight, we want to focus on what the Holy Spirit produces in us. I want to slow down and teach on the fruit of the Spirit. Let me tell you something: this kind of teaching frustrates the devil. He would much rather we preach and teach about speaking in tongues and prophesying than about the fruit of the Spirit. But Miracle Center, we have to learn how to operate in the fruit of the Spirit.

"Galatians 5:22 teaches us that the fruit of the spirit is love, joy, peace, longsuffering, kindness, goodness, faithfulness, gentleness, and self-control [NKJV]. We must learn how to walk in love, how to abide in joy, how to live in peace. We cannot be so busy prophesying and speaking in tongues that we disregard the importance of faithfulness, gentleness, and self-control. How can we come to the house of the Lord and dance and shout all over the building but then leave the house of God and be so bitter and hateful, acting as if we don't even know God? We have nasty attitudes, we're selfish, we're lying, gossiping, lusting—I know you don't want to hear this, but I've got to tell you anyway. Come on and clap your hands and say 'Amen' with me tonight. If you can't say 'Amen,' just say 'Ouch,' but go ahead and clap those hands and say, 'Speak to me, Holy Ghost!'"

While the congregation shouted those words simultaneously, as strange as it seemed, Wes thought he heard a strange noise coming from behind him. Yet he was so interested in what Pastor Johnson was saying he quickly disregarded the childlike urge to glance over his shoulder and continued listening.

"You see, people are not too concerned about how well you prophesy. They are not concerned as much about your spiritual gifts as they are about the way you treat them, the way you carry yourself, how you react and behave when the pressure is on. Are y'all hearing me tonight? The Bible doesn't say that a tree is known by its gifts. It says a tree is known by its fruit [NKJV]. I need you to understand this teaching tonight. Don't get me wrong, we strongly believe in the gifts of the Holy Spirit. That's not going to change. They have a place in the kingdom of God, and as you know, we experience them here on a regular basis. But more than the gifts of the Spirit, the world needs to be able to partake of the fruit of the Spirit. Sinners need to see the *love* of God, in you. Those who are discouraged need to see the *joy* of the Lord, in you. Those who are in despair need to see the *peace* of God, in you. Are y'all hearing me tonight? People need to see *you* being faithful in the midst of difficult times. They need *your* kindness toward them. They get enough of people being rude and harsh—where is the kindness? They need *your* gentleness. They need *your* patience.

"I'm preaching the truth tonight, and somebody is going to be set free in this place. The devil doesn't like it, but it is truth that is going to make you free. Praise the Lord in this place. Praise Him for truth! Come on, Miracle Center. The more you grasp ahold of this, the more your ministry is going to experience increase. Miracles are going to happen as you apply what I'm telling you. I've come to tell you tonight that the greatest miracle—the miracle of salvation—is waiting for your family members. It's knocking on the door of your coworkers' hearts. It's at the threshold of your friends' lives. But you must let them partake of the fruit! I said, the fruit of the spirit that is in you. Find you a neighbor and say, 'Come on, neighbor, where is your fruit?'"

Again, Wesley thought he heard a strange noise coming from a bit farther back, but he neglected to turn around. He was caught up in the sermon because he knew Pastor Johnson was right, and maybe by uncovering the fruit of the Spirit within himself, he could figure out how to look out for Pastor Johnson, like he'd promised God that he would.

"Don't get distracted now. Y'all stay with me. Listen, I didn't come in here to tell you about resting from your labor one of these ole days. On the contrary, I came to tell you to get to work! I didn't come here to tell you about life over yonder on the other shore and about the sweet by-and-by. You learned that in the new members' class. But when I start teaching about bearing fruit, making a difference, winning souls, changing lives, people being delivered from bondage, breaking generational curses, pulling down strongholds... that's what the enemy has a serious problem with. You see, these are the miraculous outcomes that you are going to experience when you operate in the fruit of the Spirit. What do you think the apostles were preaching about when evil spirits would cry out in the midst of their sermons? They were preaching about things that were relevant in that day and time that were going to upset the devil's system. Listen, I've come here tonight to tell you to get to work! You need to be cultivating the vineyard of your heart so that you might produce more fruit.

"I have a question for you tonight. Does the Holy Spirit live in you? Let the record show that if you are a born-again believer in Jesus Christ, then He has taken up residence in your heart in the person of the Holy Spirit. So then, since the Spirit of God is in you, then where is your fruit? Ask your neighbor, 'Where is your fruit?' Ask your other neighbor, 'Where is your fruit?'

"I need you to understand that the fruit of the Spirit is inside of you. Oh, it's in there, but in order to see it produced in your life, you gotta put to death the deeds of the flesh. Listen to me right here. The same Holy Spirit that was in the beginning, hovering over the face of the waters…the same Holy Spirit that was so instrumental in bringing to pass the creation of the heavens and the earth…"

The musicians joined in. They played chords and beats in rhythmic succession with the ebb and flow of the preaching. Many people in the congregation were quickly on their feet. Although Pastor Johnson had originally intended to remain in teaching mode, he found himself being "puppeteered" by the Holy Spirit to dive headfirst into a different zone. He was suddenly preaching with fire like a good ole Pentecostal preacher from the days of his upbringing, and before he knew it, he was in tune and all as if he were a Baptist reverend. Despite all this, he recognized what the Holy Spirit was doing; there was no way that this message was going to be compromised by a man with an evil spirit, who the doorkeepers were addressing in the back of the church—at least not without a demonstration of God's power for all to witness. So while the ushers did their job, Pastor Johnson stayed on top of his.

"I said the same Holy Spirit that showed up in the days of Moses and caused the bush to burn with fire, yet to remain unconsumed… the same Holy Spirit that went down into the grave and raised up Jesus from the dead…I said this same Holy Spirit that showed up on the Day of Pentecost and appeared to the disciples as flames of fire, sounding like a rushing, mighty wind. I've come to serve notice to you tonight, that if you're a born-again child of the most high God, this same Spirit has taken up residence down on the inside of your very being. Hallelujah! Jesus is alive! And His Spirit is alive and well, down on the inside of your heart. I wish I had a witness in here. I said the Spirit of God lives inside of you. I've come to tell you tonight that whatever fruit you need to produce is down inside of you at all times. I said it's down…it's deep down in your heart. But tonight…"

Pastor Johnson stopped abruptly, evoking a reaction of celebration from the fired-up congregation. The organist and the drummer had begun to chirp right along with him, and when he paused, they played a few long, drawn-out chords that somehow seemed to produce an even greater measure of expectation among the people.

"Somebody missed that, so let me say it again. I said whatever fruit of the Spirit that you find yourself in need of at any given point in time, it resides, it lives, it has made its home, dooown…I said it's down, down. It's down on the inside of your heart. But tonight…"

Again, he paused. The pastor had mastered the art of preaching. And although he had transitioned to a teaching style over the years, he was in full "preach" mode tonight.

"Back when I was a boy, we used to sing a song that said, 'I've got the joy, joy, joy, joy down in my heart, and it's down in my heart to stay.' It went on to say, 'I've got the peace that passes understanding down in my heart, and it's down in my heart to stay.' But tonight…"

Once again, he paused, giving the congregation time to think about where he was going with this.

"I've got His love, down in my heart. But tonight…we've got to get it out of our hearts and into our daily deeds so that somebody can see it, so that somebody can feel it, so that somebody can know that God is alive. The Bible says it this way: 'Let your light so shine, so that men might see your good works and glorify your Father in heaven.' Somebody you know needs to *see* your joy. Somebody in the marketplace needs to *know* this peace that you have. Somebody right there in your own home needs to *feel* this love that you have tucked away down in your heart. It's time for you to be revived tonight. Shake yourself and say, 'Joooy! Oh, joy! It's time for you to wake up inside of me.' Say, 'Peeeace! Oh, peace! I need you to open up your eyes and wake up inside of me.' Somebody shout, 'Self-controoool! I know you're in there somewhere! Wake up! Wake up!'"

Both Pastor Johnson and the musicians suddenly stopped. The congregation was crazy with excitement and anticipation. Pastor Johnson lifted up his fists, and although one of them had the mic in it, he motioned as if he were shaking somebody. He continued preaching, and the musicians walked right along with him.

"'Longsuffering! Ooooh, longsuffering! Come on, baby, it's time for you to wake up, it's tiiime for you to go to work. Kindness and gentleness! Y'all come on outta there! It's time to move. It's time to share. It's time to minister. Come on, goodness! You've got to wake up. There are some people I want you to meet. Somebody needs you right now! Faithfulness! I know it's nice and comfy in there, but get up from there! I know y'all thought you were going to just hang out…to just ride it out in there until we get to glory. But I command you all, in the name of the Lord Jesus Christ, to wake up! Get up! Get up!'

"Somebody shake yourself and say, 'Wake up! Oh, wake up!' You've got to wake up the fruit of the Spirit tonight! Wake up the fruit tonight!

"I'm talking about the fruit of the Spirit. Where is your self-control tonight? The reality is, you *can* control your language if you want to. You *can* control your hormones if you want to. You *can* control your appetite if you want to. You *can* control your temper if you want to. The question is, Are you going to let God arise, or are you going to follow the influence of your flesh? Anybody can follow the flesh, but if the Holy Spirit lives in you, there ought to be some Holy Spirit *fruit* in your life! Give Him praise!"

When the Hamlin organ, drums, and shouts finally subsided, several of the people were on their feet, praising God, but a man's voice could be heard screaming from the back, "Nooooooo! Nooooooo! No more of this! No more of this!"

Pastor Johnson spoke once again. "Miracle Center, we are not afraid of any demonic influence. There is nothing to be afraid of. Bring him here to me. It's time for a demonstration of God's power. This man is going to leave here with some fruit of his own tonight. The peace of God is going to belong to him this very night."

When the congregation turned around, the same anointed usher who had assisted Wesley the night before was almost single-handedly detaining a disheveled man who appeared to be very angry. The other ushers gladly let him go while the tall lady walked behind the man, holding him by one arm. As he walked, the man yelled out, "Oh, I'm not leaving him! This is my house. I ain't going nowhere! No peace tonight! No peace for him, and no peace for you!"

At that moment, the demon-possessed man broke free of the usher's grip and began to sprint toward Pastor Johnson, shouting, "No peace! No peace!" The woman gave chase as best she could, along with a trail of other ushers behind her.

Instantly and without warning, young Wesley darted toward the man and slapped him so hard across his face that his hand was stinging. Before he even knew what he was doing, he had slapped the man two more times, sending him buckling to the floor right in front of the altar while saying, "Shut up! Shut up!" each time he slapped him. "You foul, troublemaking spirit! How dare you interrupt the flow of the Lord! This is God's house, and Pastor Johnson is God's man! In the name of the Lord Jesus Christ, do not say another word!" As these last words left Wesley's lips, he stepped back from the man.

Wesley felt no remorse after slapping the fire out of the demon-possessed man. As a matter of fact, he had never felt more right with God than in that moment. He held a martial arts stance, waiting to either defend Pastor Johnson or himself. Either way, he was prepared to light in on the man's head again if necessary—in Jesus's name, of course. His mind was flooded with thoughts of the promise that he'd just made to God the night before. He thought to himself that God had obviously kept His end of the bargain by giving him the understanding that he needed to look out for Pastor Johnson, so he was simply holding up his end. That was very real to Wesley, and that was what he would explain to his parents, to Pastor Johnson, and even to Amanda, who he was certain would use this incident to pick on him, probably for the rest of his life. A million miles a minute, these thoughts raced through his mind as he wondered what to do next.

Suddenly, Pastor Johnson spoke up. He explained to the congregation that although most of them were unaware, the disruptive spirit had been trying to cause a distraction from the outset of his sermon. "Sometimes," he continued, "you have to just be led by the Spirit and wait for His cue instead of jumping the gun and taking matters into your own hands. So tonight, we are going to see a demonstration of God's power, and I believe we've already seen the first manifestation of it as God has used a child to reveal His power tonight."

Actually, Pastor Johnson was amazed at the boy's ability to hear the Spirit of God and, more importantly, to obey. Through his obedience, he had silenced the demon spirit by commanding it with authority not to speak. As the man remained stunned on all fours, Pastor Johnson used what had just happened to cap off his teaching on fruit. He told the congregation to notice how young Wesley had not spoken to the man, but rather to the evil spirit, commanding it to shut up.

"The point is," he said, "this is God working here. This young boy could not know all this on his own. The power of God has moved through him tonight, and first of all, we're going to show love by letting him know that he has not made a mistake. He has been led by the Spirit of Almighty God tonight. No one is going to criticize him, no one is going to poke fun at him, not even his own siblings. He has done the will of God tonight, so let's give God some praise in this place."

The church exploded with praise and shouts. "Thank ya!" one woman shouted over and over. "Hallelujah! Amen!" a Nigerian man said repeatedly, with his hands lifted straight up in the air.

Wes was still standing there with his small hands raised. Once again, he was crying as his mind was now on the promise he'd made to look out for Pastor Johnson.

"I'm not going to tell him to stand down or to put his hands down," said Pastor Johnson, because God was working in this young man. "I'm going to let God keep working through him. That demon was coming straight for me, church. But God used Wesley to stop it in its tracks. This is my little protector here. So I'll let God tell him to relax when He gets through working on the inside of him."

The congregation gently laughed and began clapping in praise again.

"Now let's get this man his freedom." Pastor Johnson told the amazed congregation that it was important to realize that what this tormented man needed now more than ever was to witness the fruit of the Spirit that he had just finished preaching about. "Let's show him the love of God right now by asking God to free him from bondage," he encouraged, raising his voice again.

"Come on, church, let's pray together for his deliverance. Pray, church! Pray for the peace of God to flood his soul. Pray for God's joy to saturate his entire being. Pray for the power of God to rise up in this place once again. Come on, church, let's ask and keep on asking. Let's seek and keep on seeking. Come on, let's bombard heaven right now! Let's release our faith for it right now."

As the members prayed aloud for the man, he began to slowly regain his composure. While the congregation saw this as a sign that the man was getting better, Pastor Johnson recognized that the demon still had to be cast out of the man. Wesley was also still poised to strike as tears rolled down his face. Then Pastor Johnson began to pray aloud into the microphone.

"All the glory belongs to You, O God of heaven and earth. We seek no glory of our own, we only ask You to set this man free from the tormenting spirit that binds him. Now I speak to this spirit by the authority of Jesus Christ, come out of this man!"

Suddenly, the man stood erect and began to convulse as he stumbled backward a few steps. Two ushers quickly moved to assist him as he stilled and began to cry, but before anyone could reach him, Wesley abandoned his striking position and reached out to embrace the man, squeezing him with all his might. The man felt the love of God so strongly upon him that he was overcome with emotion. Instantly, he could feel the pent-up anger and hatred that he had toward his absentee father melting away. The shame and sorrow that he felt because of his own cruelty toward his wife were dissipating. His mind was racing with thoughts of how many wrong turns his life had taken over the years, but somehow he had an awe-inspiring sense of hope.

Unable to explain the love and forgiveness of God that he was experiencing, he began to sob uncontrollably. At first, he wrapped his arms around the boy's tall fairly robust frame, gently patting him on his back. After a few seconds, though, he lifted both his hands and his voice. His hands were lifted straight up in the air, but little Wesley was hugging the man and would not let him go! The man was crying aloud, and between sobs, he was saying something that sounded like, "Thank You, God, for setting me free. I'm so sorry, God. I've been tortured for so long! I'm free! I'm so glad to be free!"

When Wesley finally let the man go, he was totally free from all the evil spirits that tormented him. That night, the man asked Jesus Christ to come into his heart. His name was Leonard, and he went on to tell Pastor Johnson and the congregation about how he had spent most of his life in and out of trouble, jail, and bad relationships. He explained that tonight, before he'd come to church, he had been in an argument with his wife of three years. When things got heated, he became verbally abusive, threatening her, as was his normal behavior. Upset with her but mostly with himself, he decided that he was going to end it all that night. His plan was to get some marijuana, go back home to the little shed in his backyard, get high, grab his .45, and end it all right there in the shed.

However, after drinking and smoking for an hour and a half, he started hearing short siren bursts from police cars, which was pretty common in his neighborhood. However, when he heard police radio chatter close by, in his inebriated state of mind, he was thinking that he had actually hit his wife, that she had called the police on him, and that they were looking for him. In reality, there was simply a greater police presence in his neighborhood that night as the city had launched a campaign to better the relations between the police and the inner-city neighborhoods. Feeling uncomfortable, he fled and headed downtown mad, scared, and high.

As Leonard had walked down the sidewalk, he noticed that the church was open. He heard the Spirit-filled music and singing. Realizing that it was softening his heart, he began resisting it with all his might. As a way of expressing his resistance, he began to dance to the music right there in the church parking lot as if he were dancing at a nightclub. Yet the singing was still affecting him. It was starting to bring him down from his high, thus making him both angry and even more resistant to what God was attempting to do in his life. So he stopped dancing and said aloud, "Hey, God, I'll show You what I think about this religious stuff!"

With that declaration, he made a decision to take his own life right there in the church. But as he approached the front door, he reached for his gun only to realize that in his haste to get away, he had left it in his shed. In a fit of rage, he reached out and jerked open the door, but a tall burly usher looked at him and, with a big smile and an even bigger gap between her two front teeth, said loudly, "Wow, you must be *really* excited to be here! Welcome to Miracle Center. This could be *your* night for a miracle!"

He explained that from the moment he walked inside, something was telling him to disrupt the service. But each time he started down the aisle, the usher grabbed him and restrained him—for the entire service, until he was finally able to break free at the end. Leonard then said, "When that little boy hit me, I felt like I had been struck by lightning! I mean, trust me, I cannot tell you how many times I've been slapped hard before, but never anything like that! That kid can't be any more than, what, eleven or twelve? But there was so much power in his hand. And then, when he hugged me, it was like I was inside of a very hot fire and the fire was burning all the impurities out of me. But still, I felt so much love. Man, I'm telling you, I felt the arms of God around me, Preacher. I don't know if y'all know it or not, but there is something special about that young man!"

"I got one more thing to say," he continued as he began to cry. "I regret having to say this, but when I broke loose from the usher, that voice inside of me was telling me to attack, attack, attack! That little fella stood in harm's way for you tonight, Preacher. I'm telling you, there is something special about this kid. He has a very special gift!"

The church began to applaud. Wesley had relaxed his posture and was now just standing there as Pastor Johnson put his arm around him.

"He has a special gift, indeed," he said. "Let me tell you all something as we prepare to give our altar call tonight, because there may be someone else who wants to give your life over to Jesus Christ tonight. I noticed last night during the service just how strongly the power of God was upon young Wesley, and as I made my way home last night, I said to my wife, 'Wesley would be a good fit for our security ministry.' And here we are, just one night later, witnessing the power of God operating in him at the age of twelve. I want you to know that God wants to use you, regardless of your age, gender, skin color, or life story. He wants to save you right now, right this very second. He wants to clean you up and to use you to do His will. He's not going to use you exactly like He uses Wesley here. He uses Wesley according to the gifts and talents that He's given to him. But He has some gifts and talents that He wants to display through you, perhaps not necessarily at church, but in your home, on your job, and among your friends, or wherever you go. My question to you is, Will you give Him the go-ahead tonight? If your answer is yes, meet me and Wesley and Leonard at the altar."

Pastor Johnson was not at liberty to tell anyone—not even his wife—but he knew that night that he had found his successor in the person of Wesley Lamar Heart.

Chapter 6

Indeed, Pastor Johnson had grown tremendously over the past several years. Although he had developed a wonderful relationship with many families and members of Miracle Center, both he and Sister Johnson had become very close friends with Mr. and Mrs. Heart and the entire Heart household. Make no mistake about it; he was surely their pastor, and the boundaries were clearly established. But the closeness between these two families greatly exceeded that of any of the other families within the church. This wasn't planned or plotted by any stretch. Most couples or families have another family that they tend to hang out with more than any other, and for these two, they genuinely loved and celebrated each other with godly love.

Over the years, Pastor Johnson had become especially fond of Wesley and his very unique relationship with the Lord. His heart was pure, and he had a very strong desire to be used by God to do whatever God needed him to do not just on Sundays or while at church. At any given moment in time, Wesley considered himself an instrument in the hand of Almighty God. This was a gift from God, and both Pastor Johnson and Wesley's parents were fully aware of it. Even though Wesley's tendency was to downplay the gift, Pastor Johnson believed that it was his duty to help keep the boy grounded and to prevent him from becoming so inundated with the gift that he ended up neglecting to enjoy his youth and innocence. He had seen this happen far too many times in ministry, where a young boy or girl would be so focused on their gifting that it often consumed their youth so much that by the time they were in their early twenties, they were working backward, trying to recover the years of youthfulness they'd missed, supposedly in the name of the Lord. Determined that he was not going to allow this to happen to Wesley, he would often talk to both Wesley and his parents not about the calling on Wesley's life to minister but about his academic and athletic ability and about making sure that he didn't get sidetracked with things that were less important at this stage in life—the things that most kids his age did to gain acceptance.

Pastor Johnson knew that kids often dressed a certain way, talked a certain way, and even engaged in dating, dares, drinking, drugs, and a number of other activities not because they wanted to but because it was what every one else was doing. So he would always talk to Wesley about being his absolute best and being okay with not fitting into someone else's mold. Furthermore, he was likely to show up at the school to support Wesley's extracurricular activities in an effort not only to support him but also to emphasize how important these activities were in enhancing his overall development and the discipline he needed to succeed in life. While he tried to support as many of the youth in the church as possible, he and several other church members recognized that Wesley's athletic ability was something special to behold.

Wesley had just finished stretching and running a couple of warm-up laps alongside his friend Jamar in preparation for his two track-and-field events, shot put and discus. While he was certainly well above average in the shot put, he was unquestionably the best that South Carolina had to offer in the discus, even though he was only a tenth grader. He was expected to win first place at the state track meet since, as a freshman the year before, he had lost to a senior from Abbeville by only four inches.

Furthermore, Wesley had already broken his own record four times this season and was well-known on a national level in the sport. As a result, the news cameras would often show up at any given time to see if he was going to break his own record once again. As a matter of fact, it was solely because of Wesley that WXLT, the local news station, had expanded their sports coverage to cover exceptional athletes in the area who excelled in different sports other than football, basketball, and baseball. Because of this, Wesley was accustomed to being on the news since he was not only a track-and-field champion but also a state champion wrestler, and the first high school freshman in the state ever to hold this title. He was considered to be among the best in the entire nation—a status that had also earned him the nickname Slam.

The All-American sophomore was already being recruited by colleges and received a handful of letters weekly from schools all over the country, inviting him to come take a look at what they could offer should he decide to come to their school. Wesley loved the attention and was hopeful that he would ultimately make the right decision as to which school to attend. He leaned heavily on advice from his parents, and of course from his pastor, whom he loved and appreciated so much.

In addition to the national attention, he also loved the attention that he was about to receive from the crowd, just as he did every time he mounted up to throw the discus. The low roar from the crowd always served to signify that Slam was about to do his thing and that everyone on and around the field should be advised to watch out for a flying discus regardless of how far away one might be. The crowd was always silent while he prepared himself to hurl the flat piece of plastic and metal through the air at just the right angle so as to eliminate wobbling, but with enough strength to hopefully outdistance his last throw. Each attempt entailed the squatting and twisting of the boy's tall lean frame, followed by a loud growl and the simultaneous release of the discus. The crowd would then unleash a series of synchronized "Oohs" and "Aahs" as the discus hurtled through the air. They applauded, cheered, and yelled the moment it hit the ground. The attention that Wesley received gave him a sense of tremendous gratitude, knowing that all eyes were on him due to an athletic ability that was totally God-given as far as he was concerned.

These sports fans, however, were not the only group of eyes on him. Wesley Heart was nearly every girl's dream, not only from his school, Dreher High, but also from schools all over Richland and Lexington Counties. To be so young, he was very popular, and for a number of different reasons. His athletic skills kept his name listed at the top of the sports section in the local newspapers, and he was often interviewed and photographed by sports reporters who were certain to post pictures of him performing his sport.

Wesley was also known by a multitude of family and friends that he would often hang out with, thus giving him the opportunity to meet more and more people. This meant that more and more girls had their eyes on him. Most of the time, he was introduced to others as Slam or by phrases like, "This is my cousin Wesley, better known as Slam." Of course, such a statement would inevitably lead to questions about the origin of the nickname, and thus the stories began about how Wesley had broken the arms of two wrestlers and fractured the shoulder of another. One crazy story was told about the time Wesley wrestled a senior from Dutch Fork High School who decided to wrestle dirty by pinching and twisting the skin on Wesley's inner thigh. The referee ignored Wes's complaint, although this wrestler was known for being dirty. To make matters worse, the boy bit Wesley hard enough to make Wes spring to his feet and yell out in pain. When he tried to show the referee the bite marks, the referee's response was, "Boy, did you come to wrestle or complain?" Simultaneously, the Dutch Fork wrestler jeered at Wesley, "Aw, baby…awww. You wouldn't think the state champ would be such a crybaby. Waaa waaa waaa."

When the referee started the match again, the boy charged at Wesley, which was one of the worst mistakes of the senior's career. Wesley lifted the boy off the ground and stopped shy of slamming him hard to the mat. Nevertheless, he wanted him to know that he meant business. The crowd, most of whom had come to see Wesley wrestle, went crazy. It was already troubling to the senior that so many people had come to *his* school to cheer for his opponent. So he jumped up and asked the referee for time-out as his coach massaged his shoulder for him. As the referee positioned the two wrestlers to begin again, the boy spit on Wesley and pretended that it was an accident by coughing immediately afterward. Although Wes pointed at the blob of spit and complained to the referee, he was once again ignored and the signal was given to begin the match. Before Wesley could gather himself, the boy yelled and charged again. This was the second bad mistake of his career.

In even grander fashion than before, Wesley flipped the boy into the air, landing him on his butt outside the ring. Again, the crowd went crazy. But the boy was a glutton for punishment, because this time, he charged Wesley prematurely, even though, surprisingly, the referee tried to stop him by blowing the whistle repeatedly. Wesley simply sidestepped his charge and tripped him, pushing him to stumble to his face outside the ring. By this time, the crowd was laughing at the older wrestler, and the referee took a point from him for starting before being given the command.

Having lost so many points, the senior knew he would have to pin Wesley to win. This meant that he actually had to wrestle as opposed to using all the other dirty tricks that had not worked against the champ so far. He was doomed. As they began to wrestle, the boy tried to square up with Wesley, but somehow Wesley ended up behind his opponent. He lifted him in the air, performing a hard back arch, causing the senior to land on the same shoulder as before. This time, it broke.

Though he excelled in sports, Wesley was even more popular in another arena—the church. He worked security at his church, and he now served Pastor Johnson directly. Pastor Johnson was very well-known among religious and community leaders for his nontraditional approach to faith, which was often accompanied by signs and wonders, and for the work his church did in the community. Wesley loved serving in this much-needed area of ministry. He recognized that most churches didn't have a security ministry like Miracle Center. He was also aware that, in most places, it wasn't necessary as much as it was at Miracle Center, given the nature of the ministry. He had been taught that the enemy was constantly trying to find ways to disrupt the flow of worship since Miracle Center was so named for a reason. It was a place where the miraculous often occurred. In addition, about half of its members were people who had come off the streets and joined the church, and many of them were still in need of deliverance from various oppressing spirits. So there was a realistic need for security, and Wesley was absolutely the right person for the job.

After his slap-down encounter at age twelve, Wesley entered a period of training that prepared him to eventually serve Pastor Johnson directly. A portion of the training included detailed biblical instruction that pinpointed the need for those working in this area of ministry to remain pure and undefiled in order to remain effective. In light of this, Wesley had determined to downplay the wealth of attention he received from girls. However, there was one young lady in particular that he had been very interested in for a long time, and that was his sister Tara's best friend, Lisa Monroe.

Without a doubt, Lisa had the potential to be Wes's kryptonite. But thankfully, she never came close enough to do any real damage to the super boy. The problem was that she saw him more as a little brother than anything else, which, given his status among those of the female persuasion, was a real punch in the gut to his ego. Here he was, a sixteen-year-old who could have an audience with virtually any girl he wanted, yet the one that he was crazy about was not interested in him.

Lisa certainly thought Wesley was a very cool kid. She had always thought so, and she used to always tell his sister that if he were just a few years older, she would have him on lock. As a close family friend, she supported him and admired his amazing skills and high school success. She also recognized that he had a very special relationship with God. Lisa loved all these and many other characteristics about Wesley, and she knew that he was very mature for his age; still, the four years between them were just too much for her at this stage in life. She was a sophomore in college, and he was a sophomore in high school; thus, a relationship with him was simply a no go.

Wesley's pride wouldn't let him come out and say it, but Lisa's disinterest troubled him more than he wanted to admit, even though he fully understood. Nevertheless, his dad was fully aware of how much this bothered him. He had talked to Wesley about it on a few different occasions, given how often Lisa was at their house; most times, he would simply discourage his son from pursuing her. He couldn't explain it, but he believed that somehow, Wesley's charm had the potential to gently persuade Lisa to eventually change her mind about him, especially once they got a little older. He feared that anything more than the brother-sister relationship that Lisa had in mind presently might possibly lead to some "extracurricular" activities between the two of them if the opportunity presented itself, which he was not at all in favor of. So any discussion about Lisa became discussions about girls other than Lisa who were closer to his age and, more importantly, who were not spending the summer at his house.

Mr. Heart would talk to Wesley about how anything more than a friendship with Lisa might jeopardize the relationship that the girls and the rest of the family had with her. He would talk about how, although Lisa was a very sharp and bright young lady, Wes needed to remain focused on his future, which included maintaining his GPA and the continual training and development of his athletic skills. Mr. Heart would also attempt to make light of any "Lisa talk" by saying, "Son, what are you thinking? She's nearly twice your age!" He would laugh and give the boy a quick jab to the shoulder, but for some reason, although he valued his dad's advice, Wesley did not find much humor in the joke. Sure, Lisa was older, but Wesley knew that he often demonstrated a level of maturity that greatly exceeded even those of Lisa's age and older. Thankfully, he was able to talk not only to his dad but also to his pastor. He knew that between the two of them, he would surely get the wisdom of God on the matter, which he had been praying for. The consensus was that Lisa was out of his grasp for the time being, but if it was meant to be, then God would orchestrate it, just like He had done and would continue to do with every other facet of Wesley's life.

Chapter 7

"Good set, man," Jamar encouraged. "That second throw was dope, and that last one wasn't bad either. I'm telling you, if you keep throwing like that, you're gonna easily break the state record, bro."

"Thanks, man. I'm done for the night, but you gotta get ready for this relay. Come on, let's do some more stretching."

"Yeah, okay. Hey, Slam, what were you saying about the conversation you had with your pastor? You didn't get to finish telling me before you had to prepare for your events."

"Oh, I was just saying that I love my dad and I love my pastor, and I'm very grateful for them because some kids don't have anybody to talk to. But grownups get on my nerves sometimes. They just seem to have all the answers, but sometimes I just wish that I had never opened my mouth to ask. I mean sometimes, I just want to go ahead and do what I feel is right, then, after it's done, go back and ask them what I should have done."

"Okay, bro, help me get this stretching done, 'cause you ain't making much sense right now," Jamar replied as he lay on his back and lifted his leg for Wesley to stretch his hamstring. "I mean, if you know that they have the right answers, why would you not want that? I mean, you're the one always talking about how you want to be pleasing to God."

"I know, and believe me, in my heart that's what I really want, but it's hard sometimes. I'm still a sixteen-year-old with feelings and emotions, not to mention some very powerful hormones."

"Dude, wait!" Jamar exclaimed, pulling his leg out of Wesley's grip and sitting straight up on the ground. "Are you saying that you want to start having sex?"

"Come on, man! Who said anything about sex? I mean, don't get me wrong, I'm sure it will be nice when the time is right, but I'm not trying to get into that yet, bruh. I'm only sixteen, man. I have the rest of my life to do that with the right person."

"I'm just saying, bruh. I know how serious you are about your stance, but you're over here talking about how you want to just be disobedient sometimes and how you have these powerful emotions and hormones. So I just need to know where you're coming from. After all, you're over here talkin' crazy with *my* leg up in the air, bruh." Jamar and Wesley both laughed so hard that others began to notice, and their laughter was soon interrupted by the assistant coach.

"It's time to get serious, Jamar! Let's cut the horseplay and get your mind ready for this race, son."

"All right, Coach," Jamar answered, trying to appear serious.

"Hey, good set of throws today, Slam. Let's keep it up."

"Thanks, Coach," Wes replied.

"Wes, step over here with me for a minute," the coach instructed, motioning for Wesley to walk a few yards away from Jamar. As they walked away, he looked over his shoulder and ordered, "Jamar, keep stretching and get yourself focused on this race." He took a few more steps and stopped as he turned to Wesley and said, "Listen, I need you to help me out. I need you to start talking to individual team members about having the right frame of mind out here. I need you to start sharing with them about preparing themselves mentally. You know, like you were sharing with me the other day about seeing yourself exceed your personal best every time. Do you think you can help me out with that?"

"Oh, uh…anything for the team, Coach, but don't forget…I'm just a sophomore, ya know."

"Listen to me, son. You have the full respect of virtually every athlete at this school. They may not say anything to you, but trust me, your name is well-known not just here but all over the county as well, Wesley. I'm sure you know that you have amazing talent, but what you may not know is that you have incredible influence as well. Wesley, what other athlete do you know of that can opt out of training with the team because their personal training routine is so intense? Yet you still train with the team just for the sake of building a relationship with them? Trust me, son, you're a legend around here! Not only for your athleticism, but also for your character."

"But, Coach, the upperclassmen don't even talk to me. I mean, they speak, and most of them dap me up most days, but other than that, they don't have anything much to say to me, especially since I spoke up a few weeks ago to one of them about them calling me a name that included a cuss word."

"What? Who said that?"

"No worries, Coach. It's all good now. Big Gerald put an end to it pretty quickly."

"Okay, then, tell me about it."

"I'll tell you only if you promise to never mention it to anyone."

"Promise."

"Okay, so I was headed to the locker room after school a few weeks back, and I ended up running into the crew from Dogville and Lakeside waiting on their bus. I had to pass through to get to the hallway where the locker room is. Out of the blue, Dwayne Crosby yelled out, 'There he is, that—' Then he used a cuss word that rhymes with my name. I mean, I know it was more like a term of approval, but somehow it just got to me. I guess it's because I'm starting to really understand the power of words, and I just don't want to be referred to like that.

"So when everyone started laughing, I stopped and walked up to him and simply said, 'Hey, I would appreciate it if you would just call me Slam or just plain old Wesley.' Well, it quickly escalated into him trying to fight me, claiming that he can call me what he wants to call me. When I told him that I was not going to fight over that and began to walk away and make my way to the locker room, he proceeded to block the hallway entrance. At that point, I turned to go outside and all the way around the building to get to the back entrance of the locker room. Instead of letting me go my way, he grabbed my backpack, spun me around, and said, 'Some things you can't just walk away from, Slam.' Only he used that cuss word again. He kept on calling me that, but as I prepared myself to take him down without hurting him too bad, I kind of zoned out, and I don't remember what else he was saying. I do remember quickly removing my backpack and waiting for him to swing so I could make my move. I took my posture and locked my eyes on his, but I could see he was scared, even though he was trying to hide it.

"In that moment, Big Gerald yelled, 'Hold up! D, how are you just gonna *make* this man fight you? All he asked was that you stop puttin' a cuss word with his name. Just call him Slam or Wilford or whatever his name is.' Everyone started laughing, and some of the young ladies were telling him my correct name, but I didn't move. Big Gerald continued lecturing Dwayne, telling him that he was wrong and disrespectful. He told him that I was studying under a man of God and all I was trying to do was to get the respect I deserved since one day I would be a man of God too.

"I don't know how Gerald knew that, but at that point, I decided to stand down a little. I relaxed my stance, but I still had my eyes fixed on Dwayne. He spoke up and said, 'Aiight, aiight, I don't mean no disrespect. But Big G, you betta tell Mr. Future Preacher here to stop staring me down like that, 'cause in my eyes, that's disrespect too.' Big Gerald told him that he was only getting what he deserved for putting his hands on me.

"I was later told that a couple of the teachers finally noticed the commotion and came over to see what was going on. We all thought it was going to be over when Big Gerald started pretending to preach, 'He's trying to tell you…huh, my brother Dwayne. Huh! I said he's trying to tell you…huh, by fixing his eyes on you! Huh! That he can destroooy! Huh! And he will defeeend! Huh! Ain't he aaaalllll riiight! Huh! Say yeeesh! Say yeeesh!' The entire group was responding like they were in a church service. They were laughing as they pretended to be shouting, dancing, and praising God. So the teachers walked away, thinking that we were just a bunch of students being silly and having a good time.

"But as things settled down, Dwayne said, 'Well, all I know is that Mr. "I Can Destroy" is about to *get* destroyed if he don't fix his face. Ya know what I'm sayin'? Future Reverend Brother Slam here is about to *get* slammed if he don't stand down.' I held my gaze, just as I had since he spun me around. I could tell that he was hoping that Big Gerald or somebody would step in and just break it up, which was about to happen, until Dwayne jumped the gun. Big Gerald spoke up and said, 'I done told you, D, this man tried to walk away, but you put your hands on him. Now he feels threatened. So like a real man, he ain't going nowhere now. I ought to go ahead and let him take it to you, but both of y'all need to just shake hands and let it go.'

"Dwayne spoke up and said, 'Oh, it's like that, Big Gerald? You think he gon' take me? Naw, dog!' So he put his hands up and moved in on me. He threw a couple of wild punches, but I dodged them. The next time he threw a punch, I dodged it and countered with one of my own, hitting him hard in the gut. He bowed over, and I gave him a chance to just let it go. I put my palms up and said, 'Hey, just chill, man, let it go.' He was struggling to catch his breath but also unable to swallow his pride and accept defeat.

"As I walked away, I looked at Big Gerald, whose face was scrunched up in disbelief. I nodded and said, 'Much respect, brother, thank you.' He nodded and said, 'Respect.' I was going to get my backpack so that I could finally go to the locker room when Big Gerald spoke through the murmuring and said, 'Now just let it go, D. It's all good. He just landed a li'l gut punch. That ain't nothing to get suspended over. We good, bruh. Tomorrow, y'all gon' dap it up, and we good. Hey, y'all hear me? Hey, I'm talkin' to both of y'all. I said, tomorrow, we gon' meet right here and we gon' dap it up in front of everybody, no pride, no stare-downs, no rematch…nothing but respect.'

"I nodded again, but Dwayne was shaking his head side to side. I dropped my backpack when I saw him coming for me again. When he lunged, I used his momentum to send him hurling through the air. His body hit the huge window overlooking the seniors' commons area, and the glass bowed as if it was going to shatter. Thankfully, it didn't. Everyone said 'Oooooooh!' together. Big Gerald and a crew of guys came over and made Dwayne get up quickly. They signaled to the crowd to be quiet, and Big Gerald motioned for me to get out of there, and everyone dispersed as if nothing was going on.

"I was sure I was going to have to fight Dwayne the next day. When I showed up in the same place after school, he and everyone else were there, and Big Gerald motioned for both of us to come toward him. When we arrived, he told us to handle our business like we talked about the day before. I don't know what happened or what Dwayne and Big Gerald talked about between that moment and the moment we parted ways the day before, but to my surprise, Dwayne extended his hand and said, 'We cool, dog.' We shook hands, and that was it."

"Wait, what do you mean that was it?"

"We're okay now, I guess. He's never said another word to me. We just kind of say 'What's up?' to each other with a head toss now and then, but that's it. We've never exchanged another word."

"Wow, that's some story. Dwayne is not a small guy, ya know, and he is not at all the type to back down from a fight. If you guys had gotten caught, both of you would have been suspended, but he would have been done for the year. Coach Blair told me that he's on his last strike."

"So I guess I should be grateful for his sake too, huh? But getting back to my point, Coach, I hope you can see now that it's a little more complicated. How is it going to look for me to start challenging these guys about their thought life and routines when we don't even talk to one another?"

"Slam, listen to what you're saying. First of all, you silenced one of the biggest bullies in the school's history. The fact that he now greets you regularly, even though it's only in the slightest way, is more like an act of God than a mere coincidence. Secondly, how many underclassmen do you know who get dapped up every day by the most popular guys in the school? What you perhaps don't see is that you're one of them. And don't get me started on the females. How many of them have asked you out? Too many to count? No, here's a simpler question: How many seniors have asked you to the prom? Be honest, Slam."

"Uh, a lot, Coach."

"Mmhmm, but you're just a tenth grader, remember? And what happened in the courtyard during the promposal with the lovely Ms. Mackenzie Carson?"

"That was probably one of the most uncomfortable moments of my life, Coach."

"Tell me about it."

"Coach, can we talk about this later? I was helping Jamar stretch, ya know."

"It looked to me like you guys were just horsing around. So I'm listening."

"It was no big deal, Coach. She asked me to the prom in front of everybody. I really wish that she had approached me privately, but as it turns out, she had just broken up with her superstar boyfriend and felt she had something to prove. I guess going to the prom with an underclassman would have really been a punch to his ego. The average guy would have jumped at the opportunity to be her prom date, but I had a couple of things going on. First of all, I was not about to let her use me for her revenge scheme, and secondly, I had the opportunity of a lifetime planned for that weekend. My dad had arranged for me to attend a workshop in Charlotte that weekend with Olympic gold medalist Shawn Cathcart."

"Mmhmm…so what did you do, Slam?"

"Come on, Coach, I'm sure you've seen it already. It's all over social media."

"Humor me anyway."

"I picked her up and cradled her in my arms, at which point she squealed, dropped her promposal gear, and latched on to me. While I held her, I whispered in her ear, 'Whatever you do, don't freak out right here, but just go along with me.' Then I spoke up loud enough for everyone to hear, 'I am so honored that you asked me of all people to escort you to your senior prom. If I could, I would carry you there, just like this.' Her crew and the crowd that had assembled went crazy, which didn't help my cause. I thought I was going to pass out because of what I had to say next, so I thought carefully about how to phrase it to make it sound as important to everyone listening as it was to me.

"I said, 'I feel like I'm the luckiest man alive because I have been given the opportunity of a lifetime, twice!' When I said that, you could hear a pin drop. As I continued, I felt it necessary to add a little fluff just to help my cause. I looked her in the eye and said, 'The one person whom I personally deem to be the most attractive, the most popular, and the most desirable female at Dreher High is literally in my arms, waiting for my answer to her promposal, which is certainly the opportunity of a lifetime. Olympic wrestling gold medalist'—I said this with emphasis—'Shawn Cathcart has invited me to his training camp in Charlotte on the same weekend, which also is the opportunity of a lifetime.'

"As the crowd sighed, her facial expression followed suit. I had already made my decision. Barring some weird turn of events, I was going to train in Charlotte. But I didn't have the guts to say it to her, and especially with everyone watching and recording for their social media blasts. 'So is that a yes or no?' one of her crew shouted. 'It's definitely not a no,' I responded, and the crowd began to cheer. 'My answer is both a prayer to heaven and a request to the beautiful woman in my arms to give me a third opportunity of a lifetime by allowing me a little time to work all this out.'

"While the crowd responded with hopeful comments, I was convinced that she was preparing to slap me when, suddenly, Leroy Jamison spoke up and said, 'Aiight den, Mackenzie, so is *that* a yes or a no? Are you gonna give him time or what?' She and I looked at each other for a moment as if both of us were waiting for a response. In hopes of not getting slapped, I was about to remind her that we were being recorded when she reached up and grabbed me around the neck and kissed me. Instead of enjoying the moment, though, the only thing I could think about was that her ex was going to be coming for me after seeing that all over social media. But rumor has it he heard about my run-in with Dwayne and decided to move on."

"Slam, I have to be honest here. I already knew most of the details of the two scenarios I just asked you about. It's compelling to hear it from your perspective, but I wanted you to voice what happened in those situations because I want you to listen to what you're saying, not my version of it, but yours. Don't you hear it, son? Can you not see that you are a natural-born leader? You have a special gift, and you are a very unique individual. I've heard some people call it favor or grace or something. I'm sure with your training, you can describe it better than I can, but whatever you call it, the mojo, the vibe, or however you phrase it, son, you have more of it than anyone I've ever seen enter the doors of this school. You just gave me several accounts about how you silenced the school's biggest bully and how, of all the other guys here, you were asked to the prom by the 'most attractive, most popular, and most desirable female at Dreher High,' to put it in your words. On top of that, your response to 'the queen' was, 'Uh, slow your roll. Let me think about it, honey. I'll have to see if I can squeeze your li'l event into my schedule. You see, I've been invited to train with the greatest Olympic wrestler in modern history on that day, and quite honestly, my training is far more important than anything you have going on, Your Highness.'"

"Coach, you are trippin' hard. It wasn't like that at all," Wes said with a laugh.

The coach chuckled and continued. "Wait, there's more! In response to you telling Ms. Oh Most Beautiful in front of everybody that you need time to think about her invitation to the most important event of her present existence, she lays a kiss on you."

"But, Coach!" Wesley laughed.

"And then, instead of just taking it all in and enjoying this once-in-a-lifetime moment with the queen, the queen of Dreher High, you're thinking about the what-ifs of her ex-boyfriend. Son, that's not normal. And while, of course, I'm adding a little sauce to the story, you can take either one of these scenarios. These kinds of things just do not happen to normal people.

"You're right, I watched that promposal video for the first time last night. I watched it over and over, and I found it hard to sleep. You said you felt like the luckiest man alive, but what you have, that's not luck, son."

"You're right, Coach," said Wesley. "I don't believe in luck, but most people do, so I just used the word in that moment."

"Wesley, you're a truly blessed young man. You've been endowed by the Creator with something that most others just don't have, and as your coach, if I have any influence in your life whatsoever, I need you to take what I have to say to heart. It's time for you to take a more active role in sharing what you have with the people around you. The time is now for you to step up and take a serious leadership role, son. Look around at the so-called leaders around here. Now, mind you, Big Gerald is a cool guy and a leader in his own right. But at the end of the day, he is respected mostly because he is the alpha male among the people in his circle of friends, and no one is going to challenge him. But I have no doubt you would have challenged him, wouldn't you? What if it were him as opposed to Dwayne who put a cuss word with your name? Would you have approached him and asked him to just call you Slam or Wesley?"

"Yes, sir."

"So you're telling me that you would have just walked up to Big Gerald in front of everybody and checked him like you did Dwayne?"

"I wasn't trying to check Dwayne, Coach. At least not until he started messing with me. I just asked him not to call me that. But yes, I would have done the same with Big Gerald. Why wouldn't I? What's your point, Coach?"

"My point is that to you, it's no big deal. But there's no other kid in this entire school who would have approached Big Gerald, or even Dwayne, like that. So you're already a leader, whether you know it or not. I'm simply trying to get you to see it and to step into that role now, son. Here's why. The others around you need wisdom and guidance, and sometimes they can receive it better from a peer than from a coach like me. That's just the way it is. I can tell them all day to stop it with the junk food, but when they hear that a person like you will hardly ever have even a soft drink, the light tends to come on. Secondly, you need it, son. If you think you have media coverage now, just wait until you're a senior. You're going to need to know what to say so that it doesn't sound like it's all about you. That way, when some of the more prestigious schools take a look at you, they'll realize that they have more to work with than just a testoster-one-filled jock. Rather, they will see that they have the opportunity to have someone who is destined to be a difference-maker in society representing their school."

"Uh, well, like I said, I'll do what I can for the team. I'll give it my best shot, Coach."

"I appreciate it, Slam. I know about your relationship with the Lord and your stance on just doing the right thing. Some of these kids have never seen anything other than what the streets have shown them. I do what I can as a man to influence them and to present a different way, but when they can see it lived out through someone like you, it makes an even greater impact, and that counts double on the ones coming up behind you. We'll talk more about it soon, son."

"All right, Coach," Wesley replied. As the coach walked away, Wesley headed back over toward Jamar. "You about ready, man?" he called.

"Yeah, I still need a hand, though," Jamar answered. "So what's Coach talking about?"

"Oh, it's a long story. I'll tell you later."

"You always say something crazy like that, then you never tell me."

"I'll tell you after your race."

"Well, at least fill me in on what we were talking about earlier. So you said that you're not talking about sex, but you still didn't tell me what your pastor had to say," he said, switching legs so that he could get Wesley to help him stretch the other leg.

"Well, he had a lot to say, and it was a lot of the same things my dad had to say, although he took a different approach. He told me that he was so proud of me and that he wanted to see me excel and to fulfill all my goals and dreams. Then after I shared my true feelings for Lisa, he told me that he didn't realize it was so serious to me. He encouraged me to let her know how I feel and to trust God. He said if it's meant to be, God would work out all the details and that I had to be willing to trust His timing and to trust Him even if He says no."

"That's pretty heavy, bro."

"Yeah, that's Pastor Johnson for ya. I know he's right, but like I said, sometimes I just don't want to hear that."

"I know what you mean. I knew where you were coming from before—you just didn't sound like yourself. That was why I was questioning you like I was. Hey, Slam, man, I know you talk about her all the time, but I really didn't know you felt so strongly about this Lisa girl. She must be pretty hot, huh?"

"Oh, she is that, Tenderoni, man. I mean, everything I could ever want in a girl, she's it. She's absolutely beautiful, she has the smarts, she's independent, she has dreams and goals for a great career, a family, and an awesome future. I mean, it's all there, man. So much of what she wants is exactly what I'm looking for, and I just know that we would be great together."

"Bruh...," Jamar said, not knowing what else to say.

"What, man?"

"I guess I understand, but you...you're, uh...don't you think you're in kinda deep for a sixteen-year-old?"

"Yes. I know that in some ways I am," Wesley replied somewhat defensively.

"Slam, listen, bro. You can have virtually any girl you want. Why are you so stuck on the one you can't have? I mean, you're the one that all the ladies are after. You're smart, funny, at the top of your class. You're the state champion and rated number one in the nation in one sport and the top contender in the state in another! You, too, have big goals and dreams and desires for a family...all the things you said about her, plus you have this special God thing going on. And not to mention, you're an okay-looking dude," Jamar teased with a grin.

"You ain't funny," Wesley said. "How well do you like this leg? 'Cause I can probably break it, ya know," Wesley returned.

"I'm just saying, you have it all too, bro, so if she's not interested, maybe there's something wrong with her. Maybe you should see it as her loss, not yours. Besides, according to what you've always told me about her, she never said that she's not interested, only that you're too young. It just kinda depends on how you look at it, man. So my advice is for you to listen to your dad and your pastor. Just let it go for now."

"Hey, I really appreciate that, J. You have a valid point, and I appreciate you being a real friend to me. You're right, and I should take your advice. You know, there's something else that Pastor

Johnson advised me about, and I want to get your opinion on it. He told me that Reverend Seabrooks's daughter was really interested in inviting me to the prom."

"Who? Do you know her?"

"Yeah, I know her. We met at church a few years back. She's a cheerleader at A. C. Flora. I always go over to speak to her when we play them. You just don't know her because, of course, you're on the field during those times. Jamir and Kelvin and they have met her, though."

"Wait, do you mean the cheerleader from A. C. Flora that I met at a basketball game once? Does she wear braces?"

"Yeah, that's right! You did meet her. I forgot about that."

"Bro, she is hot, man!"

"Yes, she's really nice."

"I don't get you, man, I really don't. I mean, this girl is one of so many fine women who are chomping at the bit to go out with you, and you are just so nonchalant about all of them except one who is in a college three hours away in Greensboro, North Carolina. Come on, Wes, this girl Sade is a scorcher, bro! You're starting to tick me off, man. I need you to get over it already, 'cause you're starting to scare me a little."

"What do you mean I'm starting to scare you?"

"I'm really starting to wonder whether you have some kind of weird obsession with Lisa. What does the Bible call it, an inordinate affection or something?"

"Whoa, breaking out the Bible on me—that's impressive! I can't even get mad at you for that statement. Listen, I really do appreciate you saying that, because like I said, it shows that you're a real friend and that you really care about me. Actually, I've asked myself that same question, and I can honestly answer that it's not an inordinate affection. I agree that Sade Seabrooks is very nice-looking. I really like her, and in fact, we talk on the phone about once a week. My parents have met her at church functions, and I guess they like her. I've met her parents too, and they seem to be okay with me. Her dad is kind of, uh…weird, though."

"What? Weird how?"

"He's very…uh, you know what? I ain't even gonna talk about a man of God. He's just different."

"Nah, Wes, you know how I feel about that. You can't just start talking about something and say, 'Never mind.' Besides, it's not like you're running his name down in the dirt."

"You sound like church folks, bruh. Church folk be like, 'Let me tell you about Brother Willie so we can pray for him,' knowing good and well that the motive is not prayer but gossip."

"Whatever, just finish what you were gonna say, man."

"I honestly can't put my finger on it. He's just, uh, like he's so mean to her—it's almost as if he doesn't like her or something. But anyhow, that's just what I've heard from her, but like Pastor J says, there's always two sides to every story. I don't know what that other side is, and I guess it's not my business. For the record, it's not your business either, so let's just squash it and never talk about it again."

"Okay, cool. But aside from all that, how do y'all feel about each other?"

"We're really cool with each other. Neither one of us is looking for a serious relationship right now, and we're not into each other."

"Did she tell you that she's not into you?"

"Yeah. Well, I guess so."

"Either she did or she didn't."

"I love you, man, but sometimes I hate you. You don't let me get away with nothing! Look, she never came out and told me that, but she also never showed any real interest. So all I know is that she says that she's not looking for anything serious, and I'm not interested in her other than friendship."

"Mmhmm. Well, if she flips on you, don't be surprised."

"Nah, it's really not like that. We have the potential to have a really good friendship. It's just that we kind of keep things on the surface, and actually, I'm cool with that. She's a preacher's kid, so I don't know if I can handle anything below the surface with her. You know PKs can get kinda deep on you in a heartbeat."

"Bruh, quit trippin'. We both know that spiritual things are right up your alley. You love that kind of stuff, man. So either there's something you're not telling me or maybe the problem is not her, it's you."

"What do you mean by that?"

"Wesley, you told the girl that you are not interested in a serious relationship, which, first of all, is not true, because if Ms. *Lisa* told you that she wanted that, you would be all in. Am I right?"

"Oh, absolutely! You got me there. I stand corrected."

"Mmhmm, tell the truth and shame the devil!" He laughed. "But the point is, why would she look for more in a relationship if you told her that you weren't looking for that? Even if she was interested in more, a statement like that would most likely discourage her from pursuing it."

"Okay, so?"

"So Sade might actually be interested in more but she's afraid of rejection."

"Jamar, you're trippin', man."

"She's *so* afraid of rejection," he continued, "that she is even willing to ask her 'weird' father, who doesn't even seem to like her, to ask your pastor if you would be interested in being her prom date."

"Dude, you're killin' me. I don't even know that she went through her dad. I doubt it, as bad as their relationship is."

"Okay, well, her mom then. That's not the point. Come on, Wesley, get your head outta the sand, man! Why would Sade, as fine as she is, not have a prom date by now?"

"I don't know, Jamar. Why don't you tell me, since you know everything?"

"Maybe it's because the person that she wants to be her escort has had his eyes so set on Lisa that he hasn't been able to even think about a relationship with anyone else, and God forbid if you've ever mentioned your feelings about Lisa to her."

Wesley was silent. He found himself being a little upset at the moment, not as much at Jamar as he was with himself, even though Jamar was really getting on his nerves at the moment. Jamar was just doing what he did, being the voice of reason. He was more logical than anyone his age that Wesley knew. He always searched for a way to make things make sense, and if it didn't, he automatically concluded that there had to be some type of fallacy or lie or some other side to the story that he wasn't aware of. Wesley was grateful for Jamar's gift, but he was frustrated with himself at the moment. He would never intentionally hurt Sade, but listening to Jamar's reasoning, he concluded that he probably had done so.

"So have you?" Jamar asked.

"Have I what?" Wesley asked, needing to be reminded of what the question was.

"Have you talked to Sade about how you really feel about Lisa?"

The answer to the question was a resounding yes, but Wesley wasn't about to give Jamar any more ammunition.

"That's not important," he returned, scrambling to change the subject. He thought about his conversation with Coach Ernest. "What's important is that you mentally prepare for this race."

"Man, are you going to the prom with Sade or not?" Jamar blurted out.

"I'll tell you after your race. Now let's go. It's time to get warmed up. We gotta get your mind ready, Jamar! No more prom talk, Lisa talk, Sade talk. It's time for you to start breaking some records, man. Now, think about this: I want you to imagine yourself beating your personal best. Think about what it will feel like, think about the joy, the pride, the feeling of euphoria that you'll feel when you break it. Don't think about the speed, the strength, or the energy that it's going to take to do it, because those thoughts are reserved for your training and workouts. Right now, just imagine yourself breaking your own record. While you're warming up, don't think about anything else. Don't think about what lane you're gonna be in or who's gonna be beside you or how fast or slow they are. I want you to think about one person, about one thing—beating Jamar Perry's personal best."

Chapter 8

To both Jamar's and Wesley's surprise, Jamar had broken his personal best by listening to Wesley and taking his advice. Seeing his friend's success motivated him to continue capitalizing on opportunities to speak to his peers. Just as Wesley said, it wasn't Sade's father who contacted Pastor Johnson; it was her mother. She knew Pastor Johnson because he was so popular in church circles, and she knew Wesley because it seemed that he was always with the pastor at various church and community events. At first, she advised Sade to ask Wesley herself since the two of them were friends, but the more she thought about it, the more she could certainly see why Sade was nervous about asking him. She could also understand why her daughter was so interested in Wesley. He was not only tall, dark, and very handsome but also carried himself like a seasoned special agent of some sort. He was friendly, but he was very serious when it came to his responsibilities. He was always aware of his surroundings, and even as a teenager, he had an aura about him that was refreshing.

Because Wesley was often the only one available to travel with the pastor, his role became more of adjutant/armor-bearer than security. However, it didn't matter much to him, as long as he was able to fulfill his vow to the Lord, which was to look out for his pastor. His level of commitment to God, his pastor, and the work of the ministry, along with essentially everything about him, made him all the more attractive to Sade, who had spent her entire life in and around things related to the church.

Wesley was soon to discover that his friend Jamar was right about Sade. She had been crushing on Wesley for a long time but never said anything because he was always talking about Lisa. To him, any talk about other girls was not out of bounds because he and Sade were just friends who met through church. He was certain she felt the same way, even though they had never talked about it, but oh, how wrong he was. As a matter of fact, although she had been very careful to respect his decisions and choices, she cringed at the thought of hearing him mention Lisa's name during one of their Saturday-night phone conversations. She was almost at the point of not liking Lisa, although she really didn't know her very well, but she realized how selfish and childish that attitude was. The more Sade thought about all this, the more she realized how childish a lot of her thoughts and actions had been. She decided that she was going to call Wesley herself and ask him to go to the prom with her.

Thinking about his conversation with Jamar, Wesley was having a change of heart himself. He couldn't believe how blind he had been. He talked about Lisa to Sade all the time without regard for the possibility that he might have been offending her. He wanted to call her and talk about it; he wanted to get it out in the open and let her know that it was never his intention to be offensive. Each of them had some explaining and apologizing to do, but before she could get up the nerve to call him, he called her.

"Wesley! I was just about to call you," she lied.

"Oh, you were?" he responded.

"Well, I was trying to get up the nerve to call you, actually."

"Sade, why do you have to get up the nerve to call me when we talk every week? Do you have something to tell me?" he asked, as if he didn't know.

"Well, I have something to *ask* you. Wesley, I know it's very late notice, and I will understand if you can't do it, but I want to know if you will be my escort at my senior prom."

"Sade, I—"

"I know I should have asked you sooner, and I'm really sorry for putting you on the spot like this. It was very selfish and childish of me to keep putting it off."

"No, it's okay, Sade. You don't have to apologize. Actually, I owe you an apology, but first of all, just know that I would be—"

"Well, I do owe you an apology. It's not fair for you to have this kind of pressure on you, and if you say no, I promise you that it will not affect our friendship."

"Sade!" he yelled.

"What?" she yelled back.

"I would be honored to escort you to your senior prom."

"Really?"

"Yes. That's what I've been trying to tell you for three minutes," he responded with a laugh. "That's the reason I called you. Pastor Johnson contacted me about it, and I was calling to say yes and to find out why my friend felt like she had to go through all these channels to ask me to her prom."

"Wow, I figured you wouldn't talk to your pastor until Wednesday. But you are so right, and I am so sorry."

"Well, let's save our apologies for later—as in this coming Saturday. Do you already have your dress?"

"Yes."

"Well, I'd like to pick you up Saturday morning at ten to go shopping for my tux and a tie to match your dress. Afterward, if you have time, we can grab some lunch and hang out at Columbiana Mall for a little while. If that's okay with you, just call me tomorrow and let me know if your parents are cool with that."

"That sounds great! I'll run it by Mom, but my dad is out of town. Thankfully, he won't be back until late Saturday night."

"Okay, now, are you sure that your dad is okay with me being your prom date?"

"Oh, he's cool with *you!*"

"Really? I didn't know your dad knew me. I mean, I've met him a time or two at church here and there, but—"

"Oh, trust me," Sade interrupted, "he knows you, your mom, and your dad. He calls your dad 'the master' for something related to the military, and he thinks the world of you."

"Wow, I never knew that."

"The person he has a problem with is *me,* remember? That's the other reason it took me so long to ask you, Wesley. I—"

"Saturday, Sade," he interrupted. "Let's save all that for Saturday. We can get everything out in the open then. That way, when it's time for the prom, we can focus on having a good time."

"Okay, baby boy, I hear ya."

"Oh, now I'm baby boy. Just remember, you're the one asking baby boy to your prom, Granny." They shared a laugh. "So if you're sure your mom is okay, I'll see you Saturday at ten. Text me your address, and uh, I guess you'll need to bring your little dress-sample thing so we can match my tie to it."

"Okay. Oh my gosh, I'm so excited!" she squealed. "Thank you, Wesley."

"Thanks for inviting me. We're going to have so much fun, Sade. See you Saturday."

Sade's prom at A. C. Flora High School was only three weeks away. Wesley had had his driver's license for about six months. For years he had been saving his money from grass-cutting and other odd jobs, especially during his summer breaks, and he had purchased a 350Z from his brother-in-law Antonio. Amanda's husband had been assigned a new duty station in Germany and needed to get rid of the car, so with help from his oldest sister Patrice, who was an attorney in Spokane, Washington, he was able to get a super deal on the car, and Antonio was not left holding the bag.

As promised, Wesley picked up Sade from her house at ten on Saturday morning, and they made their way to a local tuxedo shop called Tommy Lee's Tuxedos. After they found the perfect tux and matching tie, they headed over to hang out at Columbiana Mall for a little while. They laughed and talked about some of the people they knew in common, about their plans for their future college careers, and about other surface-level subjects. Then he offered to take her to an Asian restaurant inside the mall.

"Wesley, let's just eat at one of the restaurants in the food court. I'm perfectly fine with that."

"Oh, I apologize, I should have asked if you even like Asian food."

"No, I love Asian. It's just that, I know that I asked you to go to my prom at the last minute, and I'm so sorry about that. I was just nervous, and I didn't know how you would feel about going with me. I guess what I'm saying is that I just didn't want to feel rejected if you said no. So I waited and waited until I finally got up the nerve to ask. Since I'm being honest, can I just tell you the whole story without pushing you away?"

"I'm all ears," he replied sincerely.

"I really hope you don't take this the wrong way, but I think you should know that I've been feelin' you for a very long time."

Wesley thought about his conversation with Jamar regarding how PKs can get really deep on you out of the blue. He knew he needed to respond.

"Oh, wow! Really?" he fumbled. "I...I'm flattered, I must admit. But I'm also totally caught off guard."

"Yeah, trust me, I totally believe you, because I've thrown every hint I can think of over the past year or so since we've been talking more, and you've been completely oblivious to it. Not to mention, you're *always* talking about Ms. Lisa Monroe. God knows I'm so tired of hearing that name. Then when I saw your promposal on social media and how you just respectfully declined Mackenzie's offer in front of everybody, I concluded that you are probably just so bombarded with girls trying to hit on you that you've most likely become desensitized to the subtle hints and cues that someone like me would throw at you."

"Uh, no, Sade, that's not the case. I really hope that you won't look at me in that way, because I...I'm actually not very comfortable when it comes to girls," he offered but immediately realized that wasn't really true. "I mean...what I'm trying to say is...my dad teaches me to try to give every woman the respect she deserves by just celebrating each one for who she is. My pastor teaches me to do the same, even with guys, and I've discovered that in doing so, I don't have to be nervous around women or intimidated by men. I can just be myself, and people can just take it or leave it. I'm not in competition with any dude, and I'm not pressured to come on to a girl just to make myself feel secure. So if she comes on to me, it's not because I provoked her in any way."

"Again, I totally believe you, because that is exactly what I've experienced with you. I probably should have just come on strong like Mackenzie did. But nooo, I'm trying to be all respectful, trying not to go too far too fast, trying not to be a stumbling block for such a man of God as you. If only I had the guts Mackenzie had."

"Sade, I really don't know what to say," he said helplessly. "The whole Mackenzie thing was not as it seemed. Look, the bottom line is that I'm going to *your* prom and not Mackenzie's. So what does that tell you?" he asked, realizing that he had just asked the wrong question.

"Good point!" she replied. "That tells me I should warn you."

"Warn me?"

"Oh, yeah. I should warn you to brace yourself for the time of your life!"

"And just what does that mean? I certainly hope you're still thinking along the lines of not too much too fast and not being a stumbling block and all that."

"You have nothing to fear, young man. While I wasn't kidding about what I said, it's not as intense as I made it seem. What I know and like about you is that you love God and that you are consistent in your relationship with Him. I know that you love serving in your church and helping your pastor. I know that you are a no-nonsense guy who has always treated me with respect and offered me sound wisdom and advice when I've asked for it. You're a top-notch guy, and you're one of a kind. So no worries here about too much too fast."

"I'm not worried, Sade. Usually, the level of respect that you show to others is what you get in return, and I'm certain that you, being a PK, are going to be respectful and honorable, or are you one of the ratchet PKs?"

"I don't know, I might be a li'l ratchet at times." She laughed. "Ya know, I had hoped that you and I would be a little closer by now so that I could feel more comfortable asking you to the prom. I could have asked someone else, and I have turned down several people who have asked me, but I didn't want to go with anyone else. So the truth is that I was either going with you or I was going by myself, because I'm not interested in going with just anyone."

"Well, I was honored that you asked me," he replied. *At least after Jamar helped me see how selfishly I was acting,* he thought to himself. "I know that I could have been a little more forward with you, but I also know that you are not looking for a serious relationship. At least that was what you told me. So I guess it stuck with me, and I made a mental note of it," he explained, choosing his words carefully.

He wasn't about to bring up Lisa's name, especially since so much of his inability to catch Sade's hints was because he was preoccupied with thoughts of Lisa. Nevertheless, in this moment, he was taking Jamar's advice and giving life outside of Lisa a try. He discovered that, so far, he was really enjoying himself.

"So about this restaurant," he continued. "I just want to thank you for a really fun morning and for spending the extra time with me today. I've truly had a great time with you, and I honestly am not ready for it to end. Now, if you have something to do, or if you are feeling uncomfortable in any way, then I understand. But if that is not the case, then let me say thank you for a good time by taking you to a decent restaurant, where we can continue our conversation without everyone from A. C. Flora and Dreher trying to holler at us in the food court."

"Okay," she agreed as she placed her hand inside the crook of the well-built arm he had extended to her. As they walked hand in arm toward the end of the food court, Sade wondered, *Is this guy literally going to escort me to the restaurant?* It appeared that he certainly was, and she was seizing the opportunity to take it all in. They had been silent for the short distance to the restaurant, but Sade was enjoying the silence, she was enjoying the escort, and she was enjoying the way her hand felt so secure inside the bend of Wesley's big arm. When they arrived, he opened the door for her and she entered the restaurant as he followed awkwardly behind her, since she didn't let go of his arm. Once inside, they stood side by side for a moment, waiting for a host or hostess to seat them. Sade took it upon herself to break the silence.

"You still didn't have to thank me by bringing me here for lunch. If it weren't for me, we wouldn't even be here at all."

Wesley turned his body toward her and looked down at her. She was still holding his arm as she looked up at him. She could have kissed him right there in the restaurant. God knows she thought about it as she mused to herself, *If Mackenzie can get away with it, why can't I? Playing second fiddle has gotten me nowhere. I just told him how I feel about him, so he really shouldn't turn toward me and look at me that way.*

Now that Sade had opened up to him, Wesley could feel it too, so he decided that he should reposition himself to avoid anything awkward or inappropriate.

"Sade."

"Yes," she answered, staring up at him.

"You can let my arm go now. We're here." They both laughed as she removed her hand and utilized it to gently slap him on the arm. He thanked God under his breath as he realized His divine intervention in that moment. He enjoyed the relief from the brief mounting tension and was even more thankful when he heard a very familiar, warm Southern voice come seemingly out of nowhere.

"I'm sorry to keep you folks waiting. Will it be just the two of you today? Oh, Minister Wesley! Hey, baby, lawd, we keep it so dim in here. I didn't even recognize you. How are you doing, young man?"

"Hey, Sister Patterson! It's always good to see you. I knew you were a restaurant manager, but I didn't know you worked here," he replied as he stretched out his arm for their usual side-armed embrace.

"Baby, I've been here since they opened, so for about seven years now." The tall burly woman looked down at Sade. Then she looked at Wesley again and asked in a very pleasant tone, "So who's the young lady? She looks very familiar."

"This is Sade Seabrooks."

Before Wesley could say anything else, the woman responded loudly, "Seabrooks! I knew you looked familiar!"

Sade was smiling with a friendly but slightly questioning grin.

"Honey, I remember when you were born. How's Reverend and Mrs. Seabrooks?"

"Oh, they're fine," Sade answered smoothly.

"Well, it's so nice to see you. You have grown up to be such a beautiful young lady."

"Oh, thank you."

Wesley interrupted, "Sister Patterson, you know everybody!"

"No, baby, I'm just very watchful. Like I tell you all the time, if you're gonna be the best at ushering, security, adjutants ministry, or anything like that, you've got to stay in prayer, you got to ask the Holy Spirit for discernment, and, honey, you *gots* to pay attention to everything," she instructed, seizing the moment to teach.

"Yes, ma'am."

"But y'all didn't come here for that."

"True, but you know I'm always open to wisdom, Sister Patterson. Actually, Sade invited me to her prom at A. C. Flora High School. So we've been out shopping for my tux, and I had to match my accessories to her dress. You know the drill. Anyhow, we came to the mall to hang out and decided to come grab some lunch."

"Aw, that's so sweet. Well, y'all be careful and enjoy yourselves. Make sure you both check in with your folks to let them know your whereabouts. It's good to see both of you, and I'll see *you* tomorrow, Preacher," she said as she motioned to the hostess to come seat them.

"Cut it out, Sister Patterson," Wesley said as they laughed and embraced once more.

"Rene, seat these young people wherever they want to sit," she instructed the hostess as she walked off. She threw back over her shoulder, "Y'all order whatever you want. Lunch is on me."

"Oh! Thank you so much!" Wesley called out to her retreating back.

"Thank you, Ms. Patterson," Sade added.

The hostess smiled as she said, "She's such a sweetie pie. Now, where would you guys like to sit?"

She seated them in a booth in the back corner of the restaurant, per Wesley's request. He didn't ask for Sade's input because he didn't want to make it more complicated than it had to be, but he didn't realize that the section he'd chosen was used only during dinner hours or to seat private parties. The hostess didn't bother to mention it, since the GM had told her to seat them wherever they wanted to sit. Once they were seated, he told her, "I just wanted to have a moment of privacy for a couple of reasons, so I hope you're comfortable sitting back here."

"This is just fine," Sade responded.

"First of all, I want you to know that I have a special surprise for you for your prom night. I want it to be a memorable night for you. You are a very special person, and I just feel that you should be treated in a very special way."

"A surprise? What do you have in mind?" she asked nervously.

He didn't tell her that he was planning to rent a limo, especially since he had already told her he would drive his car or maybe one of his parents' cars. Sade liked his car a lot and was actually excited about riding in it to the prom. A limo was not even a consideration for her, especially given that it was very late in the game and he was already spending a lot of money just to escort her.

"It's nothing for you to worry about. Let's just say that I think both you and your parents will be pleased and impressed," he offered in an attempt to put her mind at ease a bit.

"I can't wait to see what it is! Wesley, you are so sweet. You know, even as I sat here and listened to you talk about wanting to make me feel special, I thought your kindness is just so...so rare. No one has ever said anything like that to me. I know we talk just about every week by phone, but I'd really like to get to know you better—"

Wesley's phone rang.

"You know what? I'm not even sure what that means, so just forget I said it."

Immediately, Wesley remembered what Sister Patterson said to him about paying attention to everything. He didn't quite know how to proceed, but he remembered how Pastor Johnson always taught him to pay close attention to the thoughts that pop up in your mind, especially when you're in ministry mode. His phone rang again.

"Excuse me for just a moment, Sade. That's Mom's ringtone. Hey, Mom!"

Wesley began what seemed to be a very loving conversation with his mother. The ringing phone reminded Sade of how she and her family couldn't even go out for lunch or dinner without her father's phone ringing and interrupting their time with church business of some sort. Her mind drifted to how bad the relationship between her parents had gotten since she'd been in high school. Her dad had truly taken a turn for the worse. He was constantly starting arguments with Mrs. Seabrooks, making unkind comments about her appearance and the weight she'd gained. He also made frequent references to Africa, saying that he was going to send her to Africa so that she and someone he referred to as Reverend Kunta could start a new life together as missionaries. Sade had no idea what that meant, but when she would ask her mom in private, she would just say that her father was being silly, extremely immature, and disrespectful.

She did know that her mom had become really quiet lately and that, as opposed to arguing or even trying to reason with her dad, she would just let him argue and glare at him now and then, which only angered him more. In Sade's mind, he was now taking out some of his frustration with his wife on her by fussing more about her bad attitude. Their most recent argument had been over her iPhone, which didn't hold a decent charge anymore. He had promised her about two months ago that he was going to replace it. Since so much time had gone by, she had reminded him that it needed to be replaced. His response was to berate her for "calling boys and being fast," which was not at all the case. His attack angered her so much that she spoke up for herself.

"Daddy, I don't know why you treat us so bad. What have we ever done to you to make you think this is okay? And why are you always accusing me of things I am not at all guilty of? If you want to ask me something or talk to me about something, then act like you're my father or at least like a real man. Let's have a real conversation instead of you just making accusations and assumptions. Isn't that what grown men and women are supposed to do?

"Aren't you and Mom supposed to be able to communicate and have meaningful, adult conversation full of intellect and relevance? But all you guys do is argue and fuss, and you pick fights with Mom and me like you're in high school. I've lived with it for a very long time, and I've put up with you coming to my games and embarrassing me in front of my friends and other people. I've dealt with you showing up at our away games in the name of 'just making sure your baby is okay' when we both know you couldn't care less about me.

"I've dealt with your absenteeism as a father because you're on the road all the time and because you're constantly interrupted by church business even when you *are* around. I've watched you treat Mom like she's your worst enemy, and I've watched you act like two different people in public and in private. You're the loving, gentle giant when you're in the presence of your church members, and a vengeful ogre at home. I can't wait until I'm out of here, Dad. I can't wait until I'm out of your way forever!"

Mrs. Seabrooks had come down the hall and was trying to calm a seething Sade, who was aware that she had been truly out of control that night. She recalled feeling like she was having an out-of-body experience and that she was unable to calm herself. She recalled being frightened by that feeling. Had it not been for her mother, who somehow seemed to recognize that she needed to be protected and held, who reassured that everything was going to be all right, she was not sure what would have happened as she remembered the look in her father's eyes at that moment. Now she was sitting at the table with Wesley, nearly in tears. She had to snap out of her funk.

"Sade," called Wesley. "Sade," he said again, more loudly this time.

"Oh, yes, tell your mom hello for me," she responded, trying to seem with it.

"Sade, I was trying to tell you that Mom said hi, but you were in a daze or something. Are you okay? Do you need me to get our server to get you something to drink right quick?"

"Oh, no, uh, I'm fine. I was just in really deep thought for a moment. I'm okay now."

"Okay, cool. So I'm sorry, but I'm a little confused about what you were saying."

"Confused about what I was saying?" Sade asked, acting as if she had no clue in the hope he would let it go.

"Yeah, you said you want to get to know me better, but then you told me to forget you said that. What does all that mean?"

"Please, I don't want to argue," she begged softly out of the blue, dropping her head.

Where in the world did that statement come from? he thought.

"Sade," he said softly, extending his hand out to gently grasp hers, "I have had a wonderful time with you today." Then he demanded, "Look at me." When she didn't, he patted her hand and said, "Look at me, Sade." She lifted her head and looked at him sadly, almost fearfully. "I'm not going to argue with you. I don't like arguing. We've had such a great time today, and I don't want anything to change that. Now we're going to enjoy some good food. It's free, which makes it taste even better, right?"

She smiled.

"And we're going to enjoy each other's company, okay?"

Sade nodded and looked into his eyes as she murmured, "I'm sorry. I really am glad that you accepted my invitation to the prom, and I can't think of anyone else that I would rather have escort me. Today has been so much fun, and I appreciate you going the extra mile just to help me have a good time today. If the prom is anything like today, I know it's going to be very special, just like you said. I'm sorry I flipped on you just now. I do want to get to know you better, but I'm scared, Wesley."

At this point, Wesley was completely lost. He didn't know where she was coming from. On one hand, he wanted to say, "Look, girl, it's not that hard. You get to know a person a little better, and if you discover you're not a good fit, you move on. Now you need to get a grip!" On the other hand, he was a bit relieved that she was uncertain, because he really wasn't interested in getting to know her better. She was sweet and very attractive, but he was okay with just being friends with her. He was trying to practice the whole ministry thing, but he was starting to get frustrated. "God help me," he whispered under his breath. He was immediately surprised to hear himself ask, "What are you afraid of?"

Sade dropped her head again. She wanted to tell him the truth about her dad. While he was the good reverend to most people, she and her mom knew him as an absentee father and husband who put them through pure hell when he was at home. Sade had tried to maintain a normal life, especially in front of her friends, most of whom were cheerleaders. But her dad's Jekyll-and-Hyde ways had damaged her in many ways. She often just shut down when the time came to express her true feelings or to be her true self. When it came to Wesley, she hadn't lied to him; she had always wanted more out of their surface-level relationship. But aside from his constantly mentioning Lisa, the other problem was that she wasn't sure whether she was interested in him because of who he was or because he was likely the only person that her dad would have been okay with because of Wesley's reputation with Pastor Johnson and Miracle Center.

In light of all these things, Sade could never seem to find the courage to express her true feelings and to be genuine toward Wesley, because, after all, the good reverend, the man that she loved and wanted attention from more than anyone else on the planet, had demonstrated to her that the only thing she was likely to receive from a man was disloyalty, mistreatment, and a serious lack of support. While Sade didn't have the ability to fully know and express all that, she knew her dad probably needed counseling of some sort. She also knew that her parents' constant bickering and arguing was not at all what she wanted for herself. Yet it was what she had witnessed regularly, from as far back as she could remember. As unfair as it was to her, it had still shaped her thinking and perception of men and relationships.

"Okay, listen, Sade," said Wesley. "I don't know what you're afraid of, and that's okay. But I want you to know that you don't have to be afraid with me. If rejection is the issue, again, there's nothing to worry about. We're friends, Sade, and we have been for what? About four years now? I've already accepted you. Don't worry about our relationship going any further. That's God's business. If it's not meant to be, don't worry, God has someone better for you. If it's meant to be, you can't stop it, unless you just choose to walk away from God and start doing your own thing, of course. So let's do it this way. I want you to know that you can trust me. I want you to feel free to ask me any question about anything, anything whatsoever.

Here's the catch: until you're in a better place, I will only answer your questions."

"Well, that's not fair."

"It's fair if we agree on it."

"No, Wesley. And it's not that I don't feel comfortable with you. It's me."

"I understand that. Look, everybody at some point has some issues to work through. All I'm saying is, until you are at peace enough within yourself, you don't have to worry about me probing you with questions that may be uncomfortable for you to answer. So whether that's today, prom night, or this summer sometime, it's whenever you're ready. Cool?"

"Okay, cool."

"Great! So let's make a game out of it. I'm very competitive, and I don't like to lose, so this will help me to remember. If I ask you any personal question without your approval, while we're hanging out or on the phone, I lose, you win. But whenever we're together, if I make it through our time together without doing so, I win, you lose."

"Cool," she agreed, smiling.

He was still holding her hand. "Okay, go!" he said. Wesley was really thankful for the Holy Spirit's help. Again, he realized that he was only able to come up with a plan to help Sade to lighten up a little because of God's presence. He didn't know what she'd been through or what was going on in her life, but she obviously had some issues. He had already decided that he would do all that he could to help her out and that they were going to have a blast at the prom, but that was about as far as this relationship was going to go. Her first few questions confirmed it for him.

"My first question is, Are you really a minister?"

Really? That's your first question? he thought. "No, I'm not," he answered. "If you're referring to Sister Patterson calling me that, it's what she always calls me. It's kind of an inside joke between the two of us. So as the joke goes, when she calls me Minister Wesley, I'll usually tell her to cut it out, like I did today. Then she usually says, 'Well, I'm just calling it like I see it.' So I'll reply, 'So that makes you a prophet, then, right?'" Wesley laughed, hoping to evoke a laugh from

Sade. No laugh, no smile, nothing of the sort was returned. *Boy! As Grandma would say, she might be a tough nut to crack,* he thought. His thought made him laugh a little longer than he wanted to.

"So do you think she's right?" Sade asked.

"Do I think who's right?"

"Ms. Patterson. Do you think her assessment of your future is right?"

"Uh, well, first of all, she's not a prophet, she's a doorkeeper," he said teasingly, trying to evoke at least a smile. She didn't smile, but she did squeeze his hand and stare at him as if searching his eyes for information. Wesley continued, "So we have this minister's training academy at our church. The purpose, of course, is to provide instruction to those who feel they've been called and to teach them and train them the right way. So many preachers enter into ministry and they have no clue what they're doing. They are just doing what they see other ministers do. It leads to so many problems within the church, with the primary one being a sincere lack of growth in the lives of God's people."

Wesley was on a roll as he talked about what he'd heard Pastor Johnson teach regarding the purpose of the academy and the need for it. "So you have all these ministers out there who are supposed to be God's personal representatives. They represent Him in the pulpit, but outside of it, their lives are shattered. Their families are in shambles, their lifestyle does not represent God much at all, and their church members are often following suit." He drew a breath to continue, but he noticed a steady stream of tears flowing down Sade's cheeks, and she finally dropped her head.

"Sade?" Wesley said, letting go of her hands. He stood up and went to the other side of the booth and sat down next to her. He put his strong arm around her and just let her cry. With his free hand, he grabbed the napkin from the table and gently shook the silverware out of it. Then he unsuccessfully attempted to use the rough material to dry her tears. She opted to use his favorite Nike T-shirt instead as she buried her face in his chest. So he put his other arm around her and simply held her for a few moments as her body shook with weeping. Although this was not the time for games, the competitor in him remembered that he was not allowed to ask her any questions. So as she calmed down, he simply patted her shoulder gently in an effort to offer comfort.

God, please help me, he prayed silently. *I'm searching for the right words to say.* "I am so sorry, Sade. I guess I struck a nerve somehow, huh?"

To his surprise, she cleared her throat, sat up a little straighter, then grabbed the napkin and tried to fix her face.

"Wesley?"

"Yes, Sade?"

"You lose."

Wesley didn't know whether to thank God for such a quick answer to his prayer or to question Him regarding Sade's schizophrenic behavior. At any rate, although he wasn't sure how to proceed, he was glad she seemed to be okay for the moment. So he went with it.

"Okay, I'll give you that one. I guess that *was* a personal question, but I think we're going to have to create a couple more rules for our little game. I mean, you were obviously rattled there for a moment. It wouldn't be right for me to just overlook your emotional state for the sake of some silly game," Wesley countered, knowing he'd just done exactly that.

"Yeah, well, I guess you're right. It's also not right for me to pretend that I wasn't just bawling uncontrollably only to jump right back into some silly game. So I apologize."

"I accept."

"Wesley, I have a lot going on in my life right now, and I'm afraid that if I let you in on everything, you might run full speed in the other direction."

Girl, sho ya right! he thought. *Forget if you let me in on everything. I'm about to take off right now!* His silly thoughts made him smile. *I did not sign up for all this,* he thought. Then he heard a voice say in his heart, *I signed you up. Now get serious.*

Wesley cleared his throat and said, "Well, I'm no expert on love, but isn't that what makes it so special, Sade? I mean, maybe you're right. Maybe I will run away if you let me in, but suppose you're wrong. What if you open up and discover that you're not alone or that the other party is not shaken by the difficulties in your life? So you have to be willing to take a risk. But the wisdom is in *how* you open up. Some people open up and share their life stories with everyone they meet. But I advise that as someone earns your trust, you open up little by little, one step at a time to that person."

"Wow, you sound like a wise old man."

"Nah, I'm just 'baby boy,' remember?"

They laughed together as the waitress arrived at their table.

Chapter 9

Wesley was intent on going all out to make Sade's prom a very memorable night for her. Although he had no romantic feelings for her, he felt that she deserved to have a beautiful night and was committed to doing that for her. He discovered that it was a bit more costly than he had anticipated, so he asked his dad if he would be willing to help pay for a limo and was pleasantly surprised when his dad responded that he would gladly foot the entire bill.

The Saturday morning of the prom, Mr. Heart called him into the den and gave him five hundred dollars in cash for the limo. Wesley thanked him and told him that he really didn't mind driving his car but he wanted to make Sade's prom really special. However, he didn't want to put a strain on his savings. It was not a problem for Mr. Heart, since he never spent much money unless it was for something he wanted to get for his wife. Wesley was truly a chip off the old block; he was a bigger tightwad than his dad.

His savings had already taken a hit, but not because of any prom. It was due to the car he had just purchased a few months back. The boy had plenty of money, but he was not opposed to asking for help. His dad knew it, but he didn't mind helping, as he admired the way Wesley handled his money. And because Wes was trying to treat his friend with an extra touch of class, he also seized the moment to let Wesley know how proud he was of him and how he truly admired the fine young man he was growing up to be.

"Have a seat, son," he said. "I want to talk to you about tonight. I've noticed over the years that you have a sincere respect toward women. That is an admirable trait, son, and I certainly hope that tonight you'll be treating Ms. Seabrooks as if she were one of your sisters." In his own way, he was trying to talk to Wesley about sex. He was doing fine, but in his mind, he was failing miserably. "Son, whatever you do, just make sure that you are not inappropriate with her. Listen to me. I don't' know the young lady very well at all. I don't even remember her first name."

"It's Sade," Wesley supplied.

"Well, what I'm trying to say is that you have to be really careful and not let your flesh get the best of you. You're a young man with very strong hormones and desires. Sade is in the same boat, and even though these hormones and desires are God-given, if you're not careful, they can lead you to a place of temptation and passion that can be very difficult to get out of. So you have to be careful not to go too far with Ms. Sade. And even if she attempts to treat *you* inappropriately…I mean, if she tries to take things too far with you, uh…I mean…do you know what I mean, son?"

"I'm pretty sure I know what you're saying, Dad."

"Son," Mr. Heart said, changing direction suddenly, "have you ever been tempted by a woman?"

"Yes, sir."

"I mean *really* tempted to the point of having to make a decision one way or the other right there on the spot."

"Yeah, Dad, all the time."

"I mean, sometimes, a woman will just let you know that all you have to do is say the word and—"

"Dad," Wesley interrupted, "nowadays, people will even send you naked pictures of themselves. You've heard of sexting, right, Dad?"

"Sure, but I didn't think you were involved in anything like that, Wesley."

"I'm not *involved* in it, Dad," he replied soothingly, working hard not to smile as he saw the obvious surprise and distress on his dad's face, "but I have received some of them."

"*Some* of them? You mean, it's happened more than once? Wesley, what kind of friends have you hooked up with, boy?"

"Dad, it's nothing to get alarmed about. You know if it was something that was really troubling to me, I would talk to you about it, right?"

"Well, I'd surely like to think so, son."

"So first of all, to my knowledge, my friends don't go around sexting people. And, Dad, Sister Johnson taught us in vacation Bible school that young people who do things like that are generally not bad people. They are just curious young people with a bit too much freedom and a bit too little supervision, and when presented with just the right set of circumstances, they make decisions that they don't fully think through. She spent the whole week giving us scenario after scenario of bad decisions young people make, and she drilled us the whole week by breaking us up into teams and making us think through each scenario. She even gave us homework, and we had to contact our team members on our own time and prepare responses for class the next day. It was awesome, and the class grew larger every day because people were inviting their friends to come and participate."

Mr. Heart looked at Wesley with raised eyebrows.

"I know I'm taking a long time to make my point." He laughed. "But anyhow, that's when I really got to know Sade. I knew her from just seeing her at church events over the years, but I'd never really talked much to her. But that week, she and I and three other people had to work together, and the two of us somehow stayed in touch. We talk on the phone about once a week or so, and we're friends on social media, but we're not what I would consider tight. Most of the time, when we talk, it's about decisions we've had to make or decisions we're currently faced with. So far, we haven't talked about anything too deep, so we're really only friends. There are no romantic feelings involved. So the point is, you don't have anything to worry about, Dad."

"Mmhmm, well, she's not *sexing* you, is she?"

"No, Dad, and it's *sexting*, just like texting, but with an *s*. It's named that because the person is sending you naked or sexual pictures of themselves via text message. But just so you understand, Dad, most kids don't do that, even if they are romantically involved. Don't get me wrong, kids do some stupid stuff, but sexting is not a standard practice among my acquaintances. Usually when I see that stuff on my phone, it's from people I don't even know who have somehow gotten my number. I think I've been able to figure out who a couple of them are, though, because they start acting weird or trying to hold conversations with me when normally we don't talk much at all."

"So what do you do with the pictures they send you?"

"As soon as I recognize what it is, I delete it. Every time, Dad!" Wes said forcefully. *Now, if Sade's fine self decided to send me some pics, I might have to keep those for a few days,* he silently joked to himself.

"So what if Sade decided to start sexting you?" Mr. Heart asked.

Dang, was he just reading my mind or something? Wes thought. "Well, uh, I don't know, Dad. I might have to hang on to those for a while," he joked. "Just kidding, Dad," he quickly assured his father. "I would still delete it right away."

"I see."

"Seriously, Dad, I would treat it just the same as the others, and we would have to have a serious conversation about decisions, just like from the vacation Bible school days."

"And what if it was Lisa sexting you?"

Wesley was not ready for that question. He had been doing well with blocking Lisa out of his mind until now. He answered, "Well, I guess everybody's got a weakness."

"So are you saying that you wouldn't instantly delete those?"

"Dad, I would probably *never* delete those."

Mr. Heart was waiting for a "Just kidding," but it never came.

"Well, at least you're honest," he said. "I'm not surprised at all by your answer. I just wanted to see where your heart was with all the new developments—the prom invitation and the hype around Sade."

"Well, I've been trying not to think about Lisa. I've been doing pretty good until you just mentioned her."

"I apologize."

"Nah, it's cool. Like you said, you're just seeing where my heart is. So for the record, I'm still Lisa's for the asking."

"So if you were going to the prom with Lisa tonight, would I have anything to worry about?"

"No, sir. I would still treat her with respect, and I would expect the same from her."

"But what if things got out of control? What if things got heated between the two of you? Or what if that happens between you and Sade? That 'we're just friends' talk can only take you so far, Wes. I've been there, and trust me, what Sister Johnson taught y'all in VBS was right. All it takes is the right set of circumstances for friends to quickly become friends with benefits. That's the point I'm trying to make, son.

"You see, it's in those times when the pressure is on that you have to stand up and be a real man. Contrary to what you see on TV and in the movies, you don't have to give in to temptation, and you don't have to compromise what you know to be right. Not at all, son. In fact, it's in those times that *you* have to be the strong one. You have to be willing to say you're not ready for that, and the best strategy is to stay away from environments that leave the door open for foolishness to take place. I trust that you're going to do the right thing tonight, but this is bigger than tonight, and it's bigger than sex. That's why this conversation has to continue as time goes on. Does any of this make sense to you?"

"Yes, sir. I feel you, Dad, and I really appreciate you taking the time to talk to me about it. Some parents just assume that because their kids are in church, or because they've had this conversation once when the child was ten years old, they've done their due diligence. But we need to hear you guys say it. We need to sit down like we're doing right now and discuss situations and scenarios and ways to avoid these kinds of problems, even though it's a little uncomfortable to talk about."

"Son, I wish I'd had these kinds of talks with my dad, or with somebody who could have given me wisdom on it. When it came to girl talk, I was always taught to take advantage of what you can, if you know what I mean."

"Big Daddy said that to you?"

"No, Dad never said much of anything about it, and back in those days, it was not a subject that was addressed in the church, at least not in a practical way. So I was left to listen to what other guys around me had to say. Usually, it would be cousins or others from the neighborhood who were usually just a couple of years older, talking about their experiences and, of course, telling a bunch of lies. So I made a lot of mistakes when I was young, son. To tell you the truth, I made a lot of mistakes as a grown man. I haven't always treated women with respect.

"Don't get me wrong. Often, I was not even the aggressor. But one thing I've learned is that you have to treat *yourself* with respect. I can talk to you all day about respecting women. I've talked to your sisters for years about being respectful to men. But if you don't respect yourself, none of that matters because you can find yourself so flattered by someone's attraction to you that you eventually just give in to what they want, especially if you're insecure. But if you respect yourself, you're not going to compromise your values even if you're not as secure as you'd like to be.

"Some people get so caught up in sowing their wild oats and all that foolishness. But they don't realize that long after the fun is over, you have to reconcile not only with Almighty God but also with the skeletons in your own closet. Trust me, it's not a good feeling knowing that after all these years, some of those same women that you were involved with are still dealing with the pain, shame, and feelings of regret and rejection, and knowing that you played a role in that. I think about that sometimes, son. Then I wonder if I could have played a role in changing their lives for the better if only I had stood up and been a real man when the pressure was on, if only I had been man enough not to put myself in situations that encouraged sin. I thank God for the blood of Jesus, which removes the sin. Still, I sometimes find myself praying for those I hurt along the way. At sixteen, you're more of a man than I'll ever be. I just don't want you to start heading down a wrong path. I love you, son, and am so proud to be your father."

"Dad, you have always been there for us. You made sure that you were there for your family, providing for us, teaching us about the ways of life and how to trust God even when it didn't appear there was a way out of the trouble you found yourself in. You always made us laugh even though we knew you had been out in that shed, bawling and trying to figure out how you were going to make it happen for your family.

"We saw it, and Mom saw it. She might not have been so quick to let you off the hook, but while you were outside, conversing with God, she was inside, singing your praises, because she knew that you were a man of God. She would sometimes bring us over to the window and say, 'I want y'all to see what a real man looks like.'"

Wesley tried to continue, but both he and his dad were having a moment. Wesley stood up and went over to the window where he, his mom, Patrice, Tara, and Amanda used to stand to spy on their dad in the shed. He cleared his throat.

"Right here, Dad, was where we would see you out there reading the Bible. Sometimes we would see you out there on your knees, praying and crying out to God, or practicing some of your *tired* martial arts moves," he teased, trying to lighten things up. They both laughed loudly.

"Tired, huh?" Mr. Heart questioned, ready to defend himself.

"Just kidding, Dad. Everybody knows you were the man back in the day. I'll bet you could still hold your own even now if you had to."

"Yeah, as long as I can get to the body. But I can't be trying to fistfight no more. That never was my forte, anyway. Besides, I'm too old and too slow for that. I might have to call Brother G for help nowadays."

"Brother G?"

"Yeah...Glock!"

"Dad!" Wesley shouted as they both burst into laughter again.

He walked back over as his dad stood up. They embraced each other, and his dad said, "I love you, son."

"I love you too, Dad. Flaws and all, thank you for demonstrating to me how to be a real man. I'll take good care of Sade."

"I know you will."

"Hey, speaking of Sade, if you have another few minutes, I'd like to talk about something else."

"Of course, son," he said. "What about Sade?"

"Dad, please. Whatever you do, let's keep this between the two of us."

"Of course. Is something wrong, Wes?"

"Well, how can I say this? Uh, again, I can't thank you enough for talking to me about tonight, but I really don't think you have to worry about anything crazy happening between Sade and me."

"Let me make this easy for you, son. I already know you're gay."

"Dad!" Once again, both of them busted out laughing.

"That's what you get for calling my moves tired."

"All right, Dad, all right. Nice comeback."

"So what are you saying, Wes?"

"Well, come to find out, she thinks she's bisexual. And although she really likes me, she tends to lean more toward the female side."

"Wes, I really don't know what to say. How did you discover all this? When did you find out?"

"I didn't know what to say either. She told me a few weeks back, when I offered to let her go with me to pick out my tux. We went to the mall afterward, and we were having a great time. We had a moment, and, Dad, I'm telling you! She was about to kiss me right there in the restaurant. But like you were just talking about, I manned up and, by the grace of God, was able to shift the mood right there in that moment. We came really close because, truth be told, I wouldn't mind. I mean, I don't know if you've seen Sade lately, but she is a scorcher!"

Mr. Heart grinned and chuckled a bit. "Okay, hold on a sec," he said. "A *scorcher*? So is that what y'all say nowadays?"

"Well, you see, there're different levels of good-looking. I know that back in your day, y'all used words like *fine*, *bad*, *bad mama jama*, and all that. But when it comes to people like Sade, and not to mention Lisa, Dad, those are what you call scorchers, and if you really want to get nitpicky, Lisa is what you call a dime—she's a perfect 10!"

"Oh, goodness, I should have known that Lisa's name was going to eventually come back up. Anyhow, I'm listening. So you said you really wouldn't mind because she is a scorcher…go ahead."

"Oh, yeah, I mean I could have put one on her right there in the lobby of that place, but the voice inside of me said, 'Represent,

Wes, you gotta represent.' So instead we ended up laughing together at something I said to break the tension, and boy, was I so thankful because just then, Sister Patterson walked up to seat us."

"Sister Patterson? Oh, so you were at the Asian Escape, huh?"

"Right. Well, I didn't know Sister Patterson worked there, but I'm glad that she didn't walk up to me while I was smooching with Sade in that restaurant."

"Oh, you know she would have straightened you out right there on the spot, right?"

"Oh, yes, sir! She would have been so nice and sweet while ripping me apart from head to toe. But I introduced her to Sade, and we did our little minister joke that we always do. So we laughed together, she told us to sit wherever we wanted, and she even covered our meal. So I chose an isolated location because I wanted us to just be able to talk and get to know each other a little better. We talk on the phone sometimes. It's usually just chitchat, which has always been fine with me. But, Dad, she told me that she has a serious problem with her dad, Reverend Seabrooks, who is always very mean and strict. To make matters worse, he is rarely at home to be a real dad to her. On top of that, she has a problem with the church because she feels like, in large part, that's what took her dad from her, given that he is always either on the road, preaching at revivals or dealing with his church members' problems. She said there are even rumors that he is sleeping around with other women, Dad.

"And as if this story couldn't get any worse, she now has a problem with her mom, the only person she thought she could trust, because when she opened up and told her about her sexuality, her mom all but told her that she was going to disown her. Now, the good thing is that she and her mom are working through it, but she was so hurt by her mom's reaction that she's having a really hard time with trust.

"She even has issues with God because she feels like He's not doing enough to help her, or at least not fast enough. So in her mind, her dad needs counseling and maybe even medication because she said that when he was in the Marines, he got messed up during some kind of military operation in Panama back in the early eighties. Her mom, instead of loving her and being there for her through her most trying time, came close to rejecting her altogether. And the God that she thought she could trust no matter who else forsook her seems to be missing in action.

"It's just a bad situation all the way around. She's really messed up, Dad, and all I know to do is to pray for her. I'll even pray *with* her if she wants, but outside of that, I can only be her friend. I…I'm just at a loss for what else to do. Do you have any other suggestions?"

"Wow, son. That's a lot for a young lady to have to deal with and a lot for you to carry too. I'm glad you shared this with me, though, and don't worry, I won't tell a soul. I think you have the right strategy. Take her to her prom and show her that despite all she shared, you are committed to being her *friend*. I mean, make her feel like she's the most beautiful girl in the world and that you are so proud to be at the prom with her. Be sure to schedule another time after tonight when the two of you can hang out together. Let her know that she can call you anytime she's feeling low and just be there for her. The goal is to show her another side of life as she knows it. At this point, with her faith wavering like it is, she has to *see* the love and acceptance of God through someone other than those who have let her down. I believe in you, son. Ms. Sade the Scorcher is in good hands."

"Thanks, Dad," Wes said, smiling. "That makes a lot of sense, and I hope we can talk about this more in the days to come. I haven't told anyone but you, and I want to keep it that way."

"Of course. Like I said, we need to talk more anyway."

"Yes, sir. Well, I'm going to get a haircut, and Mom says I should get a manicure. She made an appointment for me to go to the shop where she goes at twelve thirty. She says I can't be decked out from head to toe and have hands that look like they belong to a lumberjack."

"Yeah, I've heard that one a few times myself. Just go on over there and get it done. Word to the wise, don't be late for your appointment, or you might be there a while."

"All right, Dad, I'm out."

Wesley backed out of the driveway and turned onto the main road that led out of their subdivision. As he made his way to the top of the road, he whispered a simple prayer: "Father, I really didn't realize it until Dad said it, but that really is a lot to have to carry." He shook his head, not knowing what else to say. "But You know what?" He suddenly spoke up as if he had an epiphany. "I ain't carrying nothing tonight! It's party time."

He turned on the radio in his car, which was tuned in to WFMV 95.3, a gospel music station in Columbia. "Sorry, Lord, but it ain't that kind of party right now," he said aloud, chuckling. He pressed button number 3, which was preset to an urban music station known as the Big DM. To his surprise, Bobby Brown's *Tenderoni* was playing. It was not the song he needed to hear, because it made him think about Lisa. As soon as he heard it, he hit the Power button. *I don't even want to hear that,* he thought. *It's not about you tonight either,* he mused, as if Lisa were there to hear him. He realized he hadn't thought much about Lisa since his conversation with Jamar, who had told him to give it a rest and move on.

Although he wasn't in love with Sade, he genuinely liked being with her, and subconsciously, he really liked the fact that she needed him. They had spent more time talking on the phone over the past couple of weeks, and Sade was opening up to him more and more. She was so glad that he didn't change his mind after she told him more about herself. She had taken full advantage of the game that he had created, asking him question after question about himself. She had even allowed him to ask her a few of his own, demonstrating that she was starting to trust him.

He wasn't 100 percent sure, but he was starting to believe that Sade actually was not bisexual, and he was certain that she was not sexually active. She was a virgin, and in his estimation, she really didn't like girls in a sexual way, but inasmuch as she was able to trust, she tended to trust her female friends more that she did anyone else. Wesley figured that when she told her mom she was bisexual, she was simply being rebellious and, in some way, actually reaching out to her mom for help. Mrs. Seabrooks's reaction, however, added fuel to the rebellious spirit that was already at work in the young teenager, and she was in a dangerous position. Wesley lacked the professional skills to articulate that to Sade or to anyone else. But he had a strong sense of spiritual discernment that gave him confidence that what he believed was right. For now, he was going to take his dad's advice and be there for her. He knew that over time, he could help her work through it, especially if she was willing to keep God in the picture.

When he arrived back home from his haircut and manicure, he was feeling like a million bucks. He was surprised to see that Tara had come home from college just to see him off to the prom. He got out of the car, ran up to her, and hugged her tightly. They walked into the house, exchanging small talk. She asked him how he had landed such a pretty girl as Sade Seabrooks. He told her about how it all went down, and she hounded him about how he must have thought he was "all that," being asked to the prom by a senior, given that he was just a sophomore. She continued to pick on him about being a heartbreaker until his mom headed off to her bedroom.

"Hey, T," he said, "I hope we can have some time to talk tomorrow. I need to catch up with what's going on in your life, and I really need to share some things with you as well."

"Bro, the only reason I'm here this weekend is you, so of course we can hang out after church tomorrow."

"Cool. Welp, I got to go get my shower so I can prepare to get dead clean! That tux *does* look good on me, if I must say so myself. The limo will be here at four, and we have a five thirty reservation at Halls Chophouse."

"Hold up! Wait a minute! You rented a limousine? You're taking her to Halls Chophouse? Bro, have you been playing the lottery or something?" she asked in a loud voice with a semiserious look on her face.

"You know how I roll, sis!" He laughed.

"Bro, I'm serious. So is she, like, going in half with you on all this?"

Wesley calmly replied, "No, she doesn't even know about the limo or where we're going to eat. It's all my surprise to her."

"What the h—Wesley!" Tara lowered her voice as she stopped short of swearing. "Boy, are you having sex with this girl?"

"No, Tara." Wesley rolled his eyes. "It's not anything like that. And did you just swear at me? I mean, I send you off to school and you come back acting like a heathen," he accused, laughing and trying to settle down his big sister.

"That's not funny, Wesley," she said. "Mom told me that you've only had two or three weeks to prepare for this prom. And you're telling me that you're shelling out somewhere close to seven hundred dollars in that short of a time frame. Either you're having sex or you're trying very hard to do so. Now, which is it, boy?" Tara demanded with gritted teeth and wide eyes.

Wesley could only laugh. He started to respond, but when he looked back at Tara's expression and pondered her question, he laughed even harder. She had a valid point, and he appreciated her sincere concern for him, knowing that he was far too young for anything like that, but her assumptions were out of line.

Wesley decided to tease her a little longer.

"All right, T, all right," he said, pondering his next words. "Well, I told you that I needed to talk to you. So we'll talk about all this tomorrow after church, okay?"

Tara jumped to her feet. "Wesley!" she shouted.

"Tomorrow, T," he promised, carrying out his prank to the full. "I'll tell you what? If you're still up tonight when I get home, we can at least start the conversation. It'll be kind of late, though. I mean, you know…"

Tara walked over to him and pushed him hard in the chest. The broad young man barely budged.

"T," he said calmly, resisting the urge to burst out laughing, "it's not that serious, girl."

"We gon' talk about this right now!" she growled. "Let's go!" she said, pointing to the front door.

Wesley couldn't hold in his laughter any longer. He laughed so hard at Tara, who had fallen for his prank hook, line, and sinker, that he fell to the floor. As he lay on his back, laughing, he began making a motion with his hands as if he were reeling in a fish.

At this point, their parents came out of the bedroom. "What's going on in here?" his mom demanded with mock sternness, though she knew both she and her husband had actually been listening to the entire conversation.

Wesley held his stomach as he announced, "Whew! Nothing, Ma. I just finished playing a prank on Tara, oh, oh…" Wesley burst out laughing again. "Oh, my stomach hurts!" he yelled.

"So what's this prank about?"

"Oh, nothing, Ma. Just having a little brother-sister fun."

"Well, obviously, only one of you is having fun, so what is this about?"

"Well, Ma, if you must know, Tara thinks I'm having sex with Sade, or at least trying to. I told her that it wasn't so, but since she didn't believe me, I played a prank on her."

His mother didn't say anything. She just stared at him, pursed her lips, raised her eyebrows, and put her hands on her hips.

"I'm not, Ma! Y'all know I ain't involved with nobody like that. I'm only sixteen, I'm single, and I am committed to celibacy—until I can do it God's way."

But if Lisa were down with me, I'd probably have at least two kids by now! That thought came out of nowhere, nearly making him laugh again.

"Look, what's wrong with a man treating a woman like she's special without expecting anything in return?"

Mrs. Heart straightened her head and softened her eyes.

"Dad told me that a real man will treat a woman with respect. He said that just because the temptation is there doesn't mean I have to give in to it."

Mrs. Heart looked at her husband, then back at Wesley with a smile.

"So as I follow the instruction of my father," he said sarcastically, "I'm going to take this young lady out tonight and treat her as if she were the only girl in the world. When I leave home, I'm going to leave here godly, and when I come back, I'm still going to be godly, because that's how real men get down. Now, if you all will excuse me, I'm going to get a shower. Thanks for caring, sis. I love you, and on a serious note, I really do appreciate your concern for me." As he headed off down the hall backward, doing the reeling motion again, everyone enjoyed one last laugh.

Chapter 10

When the limousine pulled up at the Seabrooks residence, the driver got out and opened Wesley's door. He stepped out of the car, walked up the porch steps to the front door, and rang the bell, with a corsage for Sade in one hand and a bouquet of fresh flowers for Mrs. Seabrooks in the other. The door opened quickly, and Mrs. Seabrooks greeted him warmly.

"Hello, Wesley!"

"Hello, Mrs. Seabrooks! It's a pleasure to see you again. I have something just for you," he remarked, offering her the bouquet of flowers.

"Aw, Wesley! For me? You shouldn't have. That is so sweet of you!"

"Well, I wanted to make Sade's last prom memorable for you too. So I figured a beautiful bouquet of flowers would be nice for a beautiful lady like you."

"Now, son, you're gonna make me cry," she warned as she hugged him tightly. "Thank you so much, baby. That was such a beautiful gesture—so thoughtful of you. Hang on just a moment. Have a seat and let me get Sade for you." She walked down the hallway, calling Sade's name. Wesley noticed that she was seriously crying.

"Whew, Lordy!" she said aloud as she purposely headed somewhere other than where Sade was. In just a minute or two, Sade came out of the first room on the right. When he saw her, he stood up, but he found himself rendered speechless by how beautiful she was. He simply smiled at her and finally managed to say, "Hey."

"Hey, you," she said, smiling back.

"Sade, you look amazing."

"Thanks. You really look nice too. I mean, you looked good in the tuxedo shop trying it on, but it doesn't compare to how great you look now," she said as she walked toward him.

"Thanks, Sade. So are you ready to go?"

"Sure," she said softly. She didn't move, however. She just stood there, right in front of him, staring at him. He wasn't sure what she was doing, but he was sure that she was acting weird, and he was even more sure that they needed to go. Smiling, he told her, "I have a corsage for you. Did your mom want to get some pictures of me putting it on? We really need to get a move on, because I have to show you your surprise."

Thankfully, that finally piqued her interest enough to cause her to move. She slowly turned away from him and called out, "Come on, Mom, we gotta go."

Mrs. Seabrooks came up the hall with her camera and said, "Let me get a couple of pictures of y'all. This young man had me back there bawling for a few. I had to pull myself together."

"Crying? For what, Mom?"

"He brought me a bouquet of flowers and told me he wanted your last prom to be memorable even for me. I just thought that was so special."

"Wow, that *was* very thoughtful, Wesley," Sade remarked. "You're so sweet."

"I have your corsage here. Let's get some pictures right quick. We really have to go. Our reservation is at five thirty," he reminded, removing the flowers from the container.

"Sade, it's really pretty, baby, isn't it?"

"Yes, it is, Mom" the young woman agreed.

"I'll just snap a few pictures right quick. Now, where are y'all going to eat? I have some money for you, Wes, to help cover some of the expenses."

"No, ma'am. I'm not looking for any money, Mrs. Seabrooks. I consider it an honor that Sade asked me to her prom."

"No, I insist, Wesley. It is so nice of you to be Sade's escort even though you only had a few weeks to prepare. But it costs money to get your tux, the corsage, gas and a wash for your car, a haircut, and it looks like you even got a manicure. That's a lot of money, and I insist that you let me help."

"Mrs. Seabrooks, please. I talked to my parents about this, and I explained what I wanted to do for Sade. They thought it was a good idea, so they gave me the extra money I needed. So I'm good. I promise, Mrs. Seabrooks."

"What do you mean by 'what you wanted to do for Sade'? Am I missing something?"

"I guess I can tell you now. Sade thinks we're going to Saluda's, but I'm taking her to Halls Chophouse."

"Halls Chophouse? Wesley, now that's just too expensive!"

Sade was caught off guard too. She was smiling as Wesley put the corsage on her arm. He smiled long enough to take a few poses for the camera. Sade retrieved his boutonniere off the shelf near the door and pinned it to his lapel, and they took a few more pictures.

He continued, "Yes, ma'am. I just want her last prom night to be special, so since our photos are being taken just around the corner at the statehouse, it only makes since. So I told her that I had a couple of surprises for her. Halls Chophouse was one, and another is, uh, right here. It's something for you and Reverend Seabrooks, but I see that he's not at home." He pulled an envelope out of his pocket. "It's a handwritten letter and a schedule that I printed out to let him know our approximate whereabouts at all times. It has my cell phone number on it. Either one of you can call me at any time. The letter states my commitment to take care of Sade tonight, to show her a great time, and to treat her with respect. It's signed and dated with today's date so that you guys will have a keepsake to go along with the pictures that you took." Once again, Mrs. Seabrooks was overcome with emotion.

"Come on, Mrs. Seabrooks, see us off," he encouraged, trying to stem the flow of tears.

"Wesley, you're amazing," Sade said quietly. "You got Mama crying again, and I'm not far from it myself. You have really outdone yourself, and I love my surprises. Thank you so much."

"My pleasure, Sade." He opened the front door for her as he asked, "Do you have everything? Where's your purse?"

"Oh, yeah, how can I forget that? Be right back." As she headed toward her bedroom, her mother went behind her.

"I'm sorry, Wesley," she said over her shoulder. "You got me all messed up, boy. I'll be right back." When mother and daughter entered the bedroom, Mrs. Seabrooks spoke.

"Sade, baby. I want to tell you something. I want to say that I'm so sorry for the way that I treated you the other week. Listen, you are my baby, and you will always be my baby. I don't care that you're bisexual. I mean, I do care, but that's not going to change my love for you. Do you understand me, baby? I just want you to know that I love you, and I will always be here for you, no matter what. So go and have yourself a good time with that fine young man, and we'll talk more tomorrow, okay? I've wanted to say that for several days, and Wesley reminded me tonight of just how precious life is and that we have to take advantage of the moments we're given to express our love to one another."

"I love you, Mama. I know I upset you the other day, and I really didn't even mean what I said. I'm not bisexual, Mama, and I don't even know why I said it. I just get so angry sometimes. Daddy is just never here, and when he is, he is so mean and distant. I was so glad that he wasn't here tonight, but I was sad at the same time, because I just feel so rejected. This is my second and last prom, and he hasn't been here for either one. He hasn't been here for much of anything important in my life. But let one of his church members need something and there he goes running."

"I know, baby, I know. But listen, this is your last prom. You can't spend it thinking about that kind of stuff. You've got a fine young man out there who's ready to wait on you hand and foot. You don't want to keep him waiting. Come on, let me fix your makeup right quick. Dry your tears now. We'll talk more tomorrow evening."

When they came out of the room, Wesley stood by the door, waiting, but he had a feeling something was going on.

"Are y'all all right?" he asked. He could tell Sade had been crying.

"Yeah, we were just having a girl moment," she said, revealing her pretty smile and shiny braces. There was a sparkle in her eyes—something Wesley had never noticed from her before.

"Okay, well, you *girls* are trying to make us late for our pictures. Now, come on so I can show you your other surprise."

"Another one?" Sade and her mom asked simultaneously. He opened the door again, and Sade's mouth dropped open.

"Wesley!" she exclaimed in shock. Once again, tears threatened, so she fanned her face with one hand as if that would keep them in check. Her mom, who had not noticed the limo earlier, came to the door and joined Sade in the tear fest as the limo driver exited the driver's door and opened the rear door for them to enter.

Wesley felt pleased that his plan was working. Sade was already blown away by his kind and thoughtful gestures. This would truly be a night she'd never forget.

"It sounds like you and your mom have done some making up."

"Yeah, she actually apologized to me. She said it's because of you that she realized she needed to seize the moments."

"Because of me?"

"Yes. You have really outdone yourself tonight, and I am so grateful to you. I can't believe you rented a limo for us. That is so special. I was just looking forward to cruising in your car tonight, but you really took it to the next level!"

"You deserve it, Sade. We're going to have a great time tonight. I hope you're hungry, and I hope you're ready to get your groove on, because we're going to dance the night away, and nobody's going to outdance us."

"Well, I can't wait. I love to eat, and I love to dance!"

The night played out better than Wesley could have ever planned. They were the envy of every couple at the prom and had gotten invitations to several parties afterward, none of which they planned to attend. As they were preparing to leave, Wesley's phone rang. It was Reverend Seabrooks.

"Hello?" Wesley answered.

"Wesley, this is Reverend Seabrooks. Is everything okay?"

"Oh, hello, Reverend Seabrooks!" he greeted, looking over at Sade to see her rolling her eyes. "Yes, sir, everything is just fine. The prom was so nice, and we really had a great time! We're actually a little ahead of schedule, Reverend Seabrooks, heading outside now to wait for our chauffeur. Did Mrs. Seabrooks give you what I left for you?"

"Young man, I need to speak to Sade," he demanded, ignoring Wesley's question.

"Oh. Uh, well, hang on just a moment." Wes extended the phone toward Sade as she shot him a scowling look.

"I'm so sorry," he mouthed as he handed his phone.

"Hello. Yes. I don't know, Dad. My phone has been in my purse. I apologize. I didn't hear it with the loud music and all...yes, I know...Dad, it was in my purse, and I didn't hear it....Hang on, I'm looking at it right now....I should have known, my battery died.... Well, Dad, I told you three months ago that something was wrong with it and that it wouldn't hold a charge....I'm not getting smart, Daddy, but I don't know what else to say. All I can do is either leave it on and wait for it to die or preserve the charge by turning it off.... Well, then, get me one that works, Daddy!...You know, that would be just fine with me because I never asked you for a phone, anyway. It was your idea....No, Daddy, I'm trying to be as respectful as I can. I just don't understand why you are making such a big deal out of this, especially since Wesley was thoughtful enough to leave you his number for that very reason....Scheme? Really, Dad? I don't believe you. This young man went out of his way to make sure that you had no doubt about where we would be and when."

When Wesley heard where the conversation was heading, he reached for his phone. He had wanted to retrieve it from Sade before this, anyway, because he didn't want her to have to deal with her dad's attack any longer. Nevertheless, he was surprised at how well she was handling herself. She wasn't out of control, and she really wasn't being very loud. But when her dad attacked Wesley, she changed almost instantaneously. And when he reached for his phone, she jerked her body away to signify that she was not ready to give the phone back to him. She spoke again through clenched teeth, and she was obviously seething.

"You know what, Dad? I'm not going to do this with you. I don't even care anymore. I know what you wanted, but I promise you that I am not going to let that happen. All you wanted was to ruin my prom, my last prom, Dad, but do you know what? I'm not going to give you that pleasure. Mom might have let you make her life miserable, and that's her choice. But I'm not Mom, and I am not going to sit back and let you control me like this anymore.…What? I don't care. I guess I'll just have to sleep on the porch. Better yet, I'll see if the homeless shelter has any vacancies, but you are not going to ruin my night, and you're not going to do this to me anymore.…Yeah, I know. I'm just so wicked and evil. It's very apparent that the straight As I worked hard for just to make you proud actually make me the scum of the earth. I didn't know that my perseverance and hard work to become the captain of the cheerleading squad and spending my Saturdays working with the church youth going to cause me to miss out on heaven."

Sade was letting her dad have it. She had had enough, and now she was on a roll. She had become a completely different person from the young woman Wesley had spent the evening with so far. At this point, Wesley wanted her to just end it. She had said enough, more than enough, to get her point across, but she had no intention of stopping despite his signaling and gesturing.

"Oh, sure, you're just so ashamed of me and so suspicious of my activity that you can't even let me enjoy my prom. Let me tell you something: I can't wait to be out of your life forever! Then it'll just be you and your wonderful church members. Oh, yeah, and your newborn in Charlotte!…Dad, don't even try to lie about that.… Disrespect *you*? Disrespect my *father*? *Really*? If I die tonight, I can stand before Almighty God with a clear conscience, but if He asks me anything about my father, I will let Him know with certainty that I never had one! I only had an insecure, controlling male who married my mom and donated the cell needed to get me here and spent his time trying to make us miserable."

As Sade pressed the End button, she could hear her mother yelling in the background. Unbeknownst to Wesley, she also pressed the power button long enough to shut off the phone entirely. And unbeknownst to them both, her mom had tried to call back to tell them not to come home but to go to her uncle's house instead and she would come get her tomorrow.

Sade turned to looked at Wesley, who was so full of mixed emotions. On the one hand, he felt so sorry for Sade and just wanted to be there for her. On the other hand, he was fuming mad at Reverend Seabrooks for ruining the special night he had sacrificed and had worked so hard to pull off for Sade. He had always respected Reverend Seabrooks and was still trying hard to be objective toward him, even after learning about his own daughter's disdain for him. He had been fairly successful with his objectivity until now.

Still, he couldn't focus on that at the moment. He made the decision to put his anger on hold and to just be there for Sade. She needed him more than he needed to be angry. Wesley reached out to her without saying a word and pulled her close to him and held her tightly. She wasn't crying at the time; she was too angry for that. As he held her, he looked around and noticed that none of the few people out there seemed to be paying them any attention. He also wondered about the total transformation he'd witnessed between the shy, timid Sade that he had taken with him to the mall and the Sade who was so bold and unafraid to stand her ground against her father, who had obviously pushed her over the edge. This, too, was something he had to push out of his mind for the time being.

As he held her, they stood silently outside of the school, waiting for the driver to come. Wesley pulled Sade away from him and looked her in the eyes. A couple of tears had actually begun to stream down her tan cheeks. Wesley took his freshly manicured hands and wiped her tears. He leaned forward and kissed her on the forehead. "I'm so sorry, Sade," he said. "I...I can't imagine how you must feel, but just know that I'm here for you. I'm not sure what I can do, but I can talk to my parents, and I'm sure they'll come up with something if you don't feel safe and need a place to stay tonight."

"Thanks, Wesley. I'll be fine. We've gotten into it before. It's never been this bad, but he'll get over it. This time, I'm done with him. He's a sorry excuse for a man and an even worse excuse for a father."

Just then, the limo driver pulled up. He got out and opened the door for them to enter. Sade got in first as the driver said, "Sorry I'm late, folks. You guys were ready a little sooner than I expected. Did y'all have a good time?"

"Yes, sir, thank you," Wesley replied. "Sade, please excuse me while I take care of the driver," he said, motioning for the driver to close the door. The driver, though taken aback, obliged. He looked over the night driving glasses he was wearing as Wesley stepped toward the back of the car and motioned for the driver to follow. Again, he obliged.

"Sir, can we take the scenic route back to the young lady's house? I promise there won't be any funny business back here. We just need a little extra time to talk some things over. I'll pay you cash for the extra time, and I'll give you a good tip to go along with it," he offered, thinking about the extra money he had since his dad footed the limo bill.

"I noticed the lady seemed to be a little upset. Is she okay? She should be enjoying her prom night, you know."

"Yes, sir, just a few problems on the home front. That's why I want to have a few moments to talk, that's all."

"The good reverend is at it again, huh?" the driver muttered disgustedly, catching Wesley off guard. "It's like he just tries to make that poor girl's life miserable," he whispered.

"Uh, how do you know the Seabrooks?" Wesley asked, whispering too.

"This here is my side business," he said, pointing his thumb toward the limo. "I work for the school. Ms. Seabrooks there doesn't recognize me in my chauffeur uniform and glasses, but she knows me well enough. I'll tell you what? I wouldn't want her to be uncomfortable, so if you can keep my identity a secret, I won't even charge you for the extra time."

131

"Wow, thanks. Okay, that's a deal." Wesley pulled out a fifty-dollar bill and said, "I still want to give you a nice tip, though."

"You're a classy guy, but save it, kid. I appreciate you looking out for this young lady. She deserves it. Just call on Harris's for your next prom," the man said, heading back toward the door. "I know you got a couple more years left at Dreher."

"How do you know which school I go to?"

"Are you kidding? Everybody who follows high school sports knows who you are, kid. I've seen you in the paper a couple of times, but I've heard about you slinging that discus, and I've seen you wrestle. When you slammed that big guy from Spring Valley High, I just knew you'd broken his neck! Thankfully, it was only his shoulder. I don't want to see any kid get injured, but when he spit on you, I got so mad...and for the ref to act like he didn't see it...man, I wished you had slammed him again."

"Oh, uh, well, thank you for the support, sir!" Wesley said aloud, disrupting the driver's temporary digression.

"Oh, sorry, son. I got off track for a minute, but anyhow, I got you covered tonight. Just remember Harris's."

"You bet, sir," Wesley promised, slipping the fifty dollars back into his pocket. The man opened the door for Wesley, who got in to find that Sade was okay. She had dried her tears and had a sober look on her face.

"What were you guys talking about?" she asked.

"Sade, I have another surprise for you. We're just going to ride around for a little while, if that's okay with you."

She folded in her lips, inhaled deeply, and exhaled. She slowly shook her head from side to side and said, "You never stop, do you? Tonight, you have treated me like I am the only woman in the world."

Wesley broke out in a huge grin, thinking of what his dad had said earlier that day.

"Mission accomplished. That's all I wanted to do, Sade. I just wanted you to have a night to remember. Hey, I'm so sorry that—"

"Don't even mention that situation," she interrupted.

"Okay, I understand. But I do need to know that you are going to be okay tonight."

"I promise you, I'll be fine. Now that we have a little extra time, let's enjoy it, just me and you. Thank you for a wonderful prom, Wesley. Just like you said, we outdanced everybody!" They shared a laugh.

"I knew you would have some sweet moves since you are a cheerleader. I know how it works. You learn all these dance routines, and then you add your own twist to them to make it seem like you're just a natural."

"You're so right!" She laughed. "I do know a step or two, but for me, it's not because I am a cheerleader."

"And you were the most beautiful," he said, stopping just short of lying. He had noticed a few girls there tonight that he had thought even better-looking than Sade. But his goal was to treat his date as if she were the most beautiful girl at the prom, and he had definitely done so.

"It's all because of you, Wesley. Over these past couple of weeks, you have made me want to believe again, and tonight, you made me feel so beautiful, so special! You treated me like a queen. You catered to my every need. You pulled my chair out for me. You brought me something to drink. Your focus was completely on me, and even when we were just sitting there, catching our breath and talking, you were holding my gaze as if no one else were in the room, just like you're doing right now. And you know what else? There were a couple of times I just wanted to stop and kiss you, just like I want to do now."

"Are you sure that's what you want to do?"

"Oh, I'm very sure."

"Well," he replied, smiling coyly, "I told the driver that there wouldn't be any funny business back here, ya know."

"Funny business?" She laughed. "First of all, where did you get that term, and secondly, kissing is probably not funny business."

"So first, you make fun of my terminology, then you turn around and use it. But if you are not familiar with the term, then how do you know that kissing is not funny business?"

133

"Oh, I have a pretty good idea of what it is," she said. "See, this is not funny business." She leaned over toward him and pecked him on the cheek. "Well, what do you think?" she asked.

Wesley was stalling, trying to use his wit in an attempt to gather his thoughts in regards to the direction Sade had just shifted the conversation. He really liked Sade, but he wasn't sexually attracted to her. What attraction might have been there was removed when she told him about her feelings of being bisexual. Although, at this point, he didn't believe her, he had yet to get over how he had felt when she said it—at least that was what he'd told himself. He simply wanted to show her a great time and make her prom night a very special night for her. He was confident that he'd done just that until Reverend Seabrooks called and upset her, which seemed to be a constant goal for the man.

As for Wesley, all he wanted was for Sade to be okay. He had pretty much concluded that if kissing her would help her to be okay, then he perhaps should go ahead and wet his whistle. If it became an issue, then he would just have to explain to her later that it was just a kiss.

"If *that's* what you had in mind," he said, "then, no, that's not funny business. But wait, are we really having a conversation about the definition of a term?" He smiled.

She tilted her head, pursed her lips, and continued, "I figured that this was a very important term to you. I said that I wanted to kiss you, and you started talking to me about some agreement that you made with the driver regarding something called funny business. So since it's so important, I just want to make sure that I have a good understanding of the term, that's all." Again, they laughed together.

"Okay, so do you want me to just define the term for you, or do you think you understand it now?" he asked, not realizing that he had just set himself up.

"Well, I may need just a little more explanation," she said, smiling and rolling her eyes. *Since you're obviously missing the point,* she thought. "Maybe it's you who doesn't understand what *funny business* is," she continued.

"Oh, I know what it is," he said confidently. Sade leaned over and kissed him—for real this time. Instantly, he leaned forward and turned his body toward her to embrace her. This kiss was what she was looking for. The way he was responding seemed to say that he certainly didn't mind either. It was the type of kiss that replaced unspeakable words with a physical expression of passion. She pulled away from him and rested her head on his shoulder. He leaned back in the seat and simply held her in his muscular young embrace.

"So?" she asked, smiling.

"Uh, that?" he said, obviously rattled. "That was close to monkey business."

"Wesley?"

"Yes?"

"Do you mean funny business?" They laughed loudly.

"Look, monkey business, funny business, whatever you want to call it, that was pretty close, all right? So are we on the same page now?" he asked, doing a poor job of regaining his cool.

"Well, I'm not sure. You said that you know what funny business means, but you are using words like *close* and *pretty close*. So that means that you either don't know what it is or maybe it's just not an exact science."

"Oh, I know what it is," he said again, being unwilling to back down.

"I'm not so sure that you do," she responded, removing her head from his shoulder and sitting up. "You said that was pretty close. I want to know, where do you draw the line?"

Before Wesley could prepare himself to say anything, Sade was on top of him. Quite honestly, she was simply trying to get the competitor in him to admit that he didn't have a solid answer. But as she now straddled his lap, sitting face-to-face with him, she took advantage of the opportunity to do what she had wanted to do all night, anyway—enjoy a heated moment of passion with the young man who had showed her such an incredible evening. She never had any intentions of going any further; she just wanted to be held in his embrace and absorbed in an undisturbed moment of passion with one person—Wesley Heart. Once more, she lowered her lips onto his, and they kissed passionately.

Immediately, the words his father had spoken earlier that day came to mind regarding self-respect and treating women with respect. For a split second, Wesley regretted that he had even had that conversation with his dad; he was thoroughly enjoying this moment. His mind ventured back to his conversation with Jamar at the track meet about how sometimes he wanted to just go ahead and do what he wanted to do and then go back and ask the grown-ups what they thought about it.

He knew that he had to bring this to an end, but he was in no hurry to do so. Wesley realized that his hands were much lower than they should have been. He quickly raised them by putting them on her back instead. He finally had his definition of funny business, and without a doubt, the way that he and Sade were conducting themselves was it! He brought his hands up farther and gripped her shoulders. He gently pushed her back, breaking their kiss.

"Well?" she whispered.

"Spirit of the Living God!" he gasped.

The teenager in both of them was fully exposed at this point. They laughed so hard that they found it hard to stop. "I think we have a definition!" Wesley shouted through his laughter as Sade resumed her seat beside him.

Their laughter was instantly interrupted, however, when the limo driver spoke through an intercom system and asked, "Hey, are you guys okay back there?" scaring both of them and causing them to jump. The short-lived fear was followed by another burst of shared laughter.

"Answer him, silly, so he won't think we're engaged in funny business. Or is it monkey business?" she asked through her laughter.

Still laughing, Wesley answered, "Yes, sir, we're good, we're good."

"Glad to hear you guys having a good time. Sorry to interrupt. We have about twenty more minutes."

Even that news couldn't put much of a damper on their spirits.

"Sade," he admonished, pulling a handkerchief out of his pocket and wiping her lipstick off his lips, "look at what you've done to me."

"You didn't seem to mind too much while it was happening," she teased.

"I have no comment."

"Oh, you've already commented loud and clear."

"Anyhow, I was just about to say that I will call you so that we can schedule a time to hang out, maybe at the movies or something. My sister is home from school, and I promised her that she and I would hang some tomorrow, but I promise to call you tomorrow to at least check on you. Are you sure you're going to be all right tonight?"

"Yeah, he's probably in bed by now. He's gonna be very angry after everything I said, especially the statement about the newborn."

"That is shocking news, I must admit, but don't worry, I'm not one to gossip."

"Well, I'm sure it won't be a secret for long, especially once his church family gets wind of it." Wesley noticed that she referred to the congregation of people as *his* church family and not *our* church family. He decided that he would inquire about that another time.

"How is your mom doing with that news?" he asked.

"Mama has been over him for a very long time. She's been telling me for a couple of years now that when I graduate high school, she's going to leave him. It's almost like she tells me that to try to gauge how I feel about it. I truly believe that she was about to make that move before I started freaking out on her. Looking back on it all, I guess she felt like making such a change at this point in my life could have made me behave even worse. So she opted to stay just because the environment is familiar, even though the relationship is very dysfunctional. Besides, he's not home much nowadays, anyway. I guess that was how he found the time to go screwing around on my mom. I always held out hope for him, but to find out that he's disrespected us like that…I'm done."

Wesley saw that Sade was getting upset again, and in a way, he regretted that he'd brought it up again. By the same token, he'd learned from his sister Tara that so many young people keep their feelings pent up inside because they don't have anyone they can trust to share them with, which leads to anxiety, depression, unhealthy lifestyles, and even suicide. He decided not to try to change the subject but to just let her talk. He grabbed her hand and gently squeezed it.

Sade continued, "I've never stood up to him like that before, and I'm certain that he thought Mom and I didn't know about the baby. He'll be upset, but he'll just have to get over it. He won't say too much since it's a Saturday night and he has to preach tomorrow. He'll be all diplomatic after church and will want to talk. I just don't have anything to say. I'm truly done with him. Mom is, too, based on what we've been talking about. I just hope they haven't been yelling and screaming at each other like they have been lately. Anyhow, thanks for caring, Wesley, and thank you again so much for a wonderful night."

"I would like it if we could finish this conversation over coffee next week," he invited.

"Pinky swear?" she asked, extending her pinky toward him.

"Pinky swear," he said, locking pinky fingers with her and smiling.

"Sade, I'm not sure I ever said thank you for inviting me to your prom. It has been my honor, and this has been an amazing experience for an underclassman like me."

"No, thank you, sir, for making my prom night one I will never forget."

Chapter 11

Sade hugged Wesley as the limo pulled up in front of her house. The driver got out and opened the door, and Wesley got out of the car and extended his hand to Sade. Once she got out, he placed her hand in the bend of his arm and escorted her to the porch. The motion light came on, revealing a sweaty and completely disheveled Reverend Seabrooks. At the sight of him, Wesley jumped and instinctively raised his hands as if to defend himself, and Sade, of course.

He barely recognized the man. His face was shiny with sweat, and his shirt was soaking wet. His hair was sticking up all over, and when his six-foot, four-inch body stood up, one of his hands, which was bloody, was visible to the two teens.

"Daddy?" Sade questioned, completely frightened and now trembling at the sight of her father, who was normally very polished.

"Don't 'Daddy' me!" he growled. "I'll deal with your li'l smart mouth in just a moment. But lover boy here got his hands up like he wanna get some of this too."

Too? What does he mean by that? was Wesley's first thought. *Did he hurt Mrs. Seabrooks? Someone else? I swear, I'll knock him out cold if he has hurt her* was his second thought. *Be diplomatic, Wesley. You don't know what happened yet. And remember, you're talking to a man of God here* was his third thought.

"Oh, no, Reverend Seabrooks," he said, lowering his hands. "It's just that...you startled me. I didn't mean any harm." He searched the preacher's eyes for any indication of what might have happened before they arrived. He was searching for remorse, fear, weakness, a wince, or a grimace that revealed pain or for anything whatsoever that would give him some type of clue about what had taken place and, furthermore, what action needed to be taken next. Although he had lowered his hands, the young boy was in full defense mode.

Reverend Seabrooks chuckled evilly. "Boy, your daddy has trained you well. I see you searching for cues, and look at you, your hands are down, but your body is ready. It's hard to slow that breathing down, too, ain't it? Don't worry. As you get a little older, you'll master that too, just like me. I've gotta give it to you, Heart, your daddy was the best of the best. He trained the world's most elite troops. Rumor has it, he even worked with a few of our country's top spies at one point. And I see that he has done a good job with you too. Look at you, boy, you're staring me down like a cat staring down its prey."

"Sir, you...you're bleeding. Is everything okay?"

Suddenly, a light came on in the living room, which seemed to surprise the preacher. "Ruunnn, Sadeee!" a scratchy voice shouted from inside the house. "Go to Tyrone's house, baby! Go to your uncle Tyrone's noooow!"

Reverend Seabrooks turned to enter the house. "Mama!" Sade shouted, trying to get around her dad to get to her mother before he did. Hindered by her heels, she grabbed the door at the same time as her dad. He grabbed her by her small arm and flung her backward, right into Wesley's arms.

"Go stop the limo right now, Sade, and get in it. I'll handle this," Wesley said loudly.

When Reverend Seabrooks heard those words, it angered him all the more. He turned around and said, "Oh, so you'll handle this, huh? So you think you can fight a grown man?" Seabrooks turned around and swung at Wesley, who quickly sidestepped the older man's punch.

"Please, Reverend. Calm down, sir. It's okay. I didn't mean any dis—"

Before he could finish his statement, Wesley could feel the wind as he sidestepped another of Reverend Seabrooks's punches, which in Wesley's eyes were amazingly slow. The reverend also realized his lack of speed. So he lunged at Wesley, which was a very big mistake.

Before he knew it, Wesley had easily performed some type of judo move, flipping the man through the air, off the porch, and onto the ground.

Wesley heard the simultaneous thud of the large man's back hitting the ground as he released a loud grunt. When Seabrooks looked up, he saw that Wesley was no longer on the porch but was instead on the lawn, standing over him at a distance. He was attempting to verbally calm him down. At this point, however, there was no calming. The big preacher's body felt like it had just been shattered into a thousand pieces. It was the shattering of his ego, however, that led to him slowly rolling over from his back to his side.

"I see how you wanna play, boy," he accused, mustering the strength to pull his knees under him and get to his feet again. This time, he charged at Wesley, who used another judo maneuver to lift him off the ground by using the big man's own momentum and sent him flying through the air to land on his back once again.

Sade, who had initially headed toward the limo, turned around to witness all this. The limo driver, who had just finished carefully backing out of the driveway, was startled to hear Sade yell, "Wesley, come on, let's get Mama!"

As Wesley turned to head into the house, the Seabrooks grabbed the boy's ankle and pulled it in close to his body, attempting to damage it. Sade turned around to see her dad and Wesley wrestling and fighting on the ground. She knew that Wesley was in his lane, but she was afraid of her dad, being unsure of what he'd done to her mother. Having no idea what to do, she froze.

Reverend Seabrooks rolled over, with Wesley's leg in tow. Writhing in pain, Wesley instinctively rolled with the big man to keep his ankle from being broken. The pain was shocking, and Wesley knew he had to do something. Now completely on the ground with his leg behind him, he extended his arm backward and was somehow able to put the Marine in a headlock. He squeezed hard. The more he squeezed, the more relief he felt on his leg. Finally, the preacher had to let go of Wesley's leg in order to try to free his head from the pressure. Wesley was so relieved when the pain in his leg stopped that he let go of the headlock. Now both he and Seabrooks realized the error of their ways—letting go too soon.

Simultaneously, both of them came to their senses and instantly sprang to their feet.

"Yeah, I'm gonna teach you, boy," the big man said. "You got some skills, but you've met your match tonight," he threatened, realizing that the opposite was true, but he was trying to get into the boy's head with intimidation tactics. "Oh, yeah, big boy, tonight we wrestle. I'm gonna let you be Jacob, and I'm gonna be the angel…ha ha ha! Mmhmm, especially if I get ahold of that leg again."

Wesley was fully engaged. He was *not* going to lose. "Sade, go get your mother now!" Those words infuriated the reverend again, and he prepared to lunge himself at Wesley. But before he could do so, they were both surprised to hear the voice of the limo driver.

"That's enough, Reverend Seabrooks."

"Man, if you don't get back in that car and get off my property, you gon' be next in line to get some of this!" he yelled.

"My name is Officer Scuffs, with the Richland County Sheriff's Department," the man replied, flashing his badge. "Now, get down on the ground and put your hands behind your head. You're under arrest for assault and battery."

"Officer Scuffs?" Sade exclaimed.

"It's okay, Sade," he calmly replied. "Come on now, Reverend. A simple assault-and-battery charge will soon blow over, but you don't want several other charges piled on top of that. That won't look so good when the media gets ahold of it. Think about it, Reverend. You don't want to put your family and your congregation through that."

"Family! Man, I ain't got no family!" Seabrooks blurted out. "Can't you see how screwed up we are?" he replied with a wicked laugh. "So what now, Scuffs? Whatchu gon' do now, bad boy, bad boy?" He laughed, mocking the officer.

"Calm down, Reverend," Officer Scuffs murmured as he cautiously took a step forward. He knew that his fellow Marine was unstable, but he needed to bring this to an end quickly. Wesley was still in harm's way, and God only knew what condition Mrs. Seabrooks was in.

"Reverend Seabrooks," Scuffs continued, "this is my final warning. Get down on the ground and put your hands behind your back. I can get you some help, but you got to cooperate."

"What do you mean get me some help? What are you trying to say, Scuffs? It seems to me like you're the one that needs help, trying to diffuse a situation like this by flashing your badge at me. Really? What are you, a chauffeur or a police officer? Where ya gun at, bad boy?" he mocked. "Hey, get your phone out and call for backup, because if you take one more step onto my property, you gon' need some help. You don't believe me? Ask Melissa in there. She'll tell you. I ain't one to be played with!" he yelled.

"No! Mama!" Sade screamed. She wanted to rush in and check on her mom, but she suddenly felt dizzy and light-headed at the thought of how Mrs. Seabrooks might look.

When the officer took a few more steps forward, Seabrooks suddenly lunged at Wesley, who had made the mistake of standing down a little prematurely. He grabbed the unsuspecting teen in a choke hold. Officer Scuffs lifted the jacket of his chauffeur uniform and drew his Beretta 9mm handgun, his weapon of choice for carrying off duty.

"There ya go, bad boy!" Seabrooks remarked mockingly. "Whatcha gon' do? Come on, you betta hurry up. This kid doesn't have much time. I know you got a laser on that thing. Pull the trigger! One shot, one kill, Marine."

Indeed, Scuffs did have a laser. But for some reason, the stupid thing wouldn't work. So the officer was not about to take such a risky shot, given the lack of light. He moved closer to Reverend Seabrooks and Wesley.

"Let the boy go, Reverend!" he shouted.

"Pull the trigger, Scuffs!"

He still didn't have a good shot, but he needed to do something, because Wesley was nearly unconscious. Noticing this, the reverend released the choke hold, holding the boy up with just one arm around his neck. Wesley was trying to determine his next move. He knew that he could incapacitate the reverend pretty quickly, but he couldn't seem to gather his thoughts due to the lack of oxygen to his brain. *If I can just get a few more breaths of fresh air,* he thought as he began to breathe deeply.

Reverend Seabrooks noticed the boy's deep breathing and knew exactly what he was doing. "I was trying to spare your life, boy!" He grimaced. "But you just don't know when to stop, do you?" He stuck his free hand into his pocket and whipped out his pocketknife, flipping it open all in one motion and putting the knife to Wesley's throat.

"How about now, Scuffs?" he yelled. "You better man up now! 'Bout to lose a fine young man here!"

"Drop the weapon, Reverend!" Officer Scuffs commanded again.

"Pull the trigger, Scuffs!" the deranged man yelled back.

Officer Scuffs found himself in a horrible situation. As badly as he wanted to save the young boy's life, he couldn't take the risk of firing his weapon without a clear shot. He was standing in the way of the limo headlights, and though he pressed the button over and over to turn on the laser, nothing.

Sade, who had been scared stiff up to this point, suddenly took it upon herself to do something. "Daddy, please don't hurt him!" she shouted as she darted toward them both.

In that moment, a red laser beam could be seen piercing the darkness. However, the beam was not resting on Seabrooks's fore-head. Somehow, the little red dot was on his back.

Pop!

The sound and flash from the discharge of a handgun and the simultaneous sound of shattering glass caused everyone to freeze in place. Even Wesley, who was quickly regaining clarity of mind, gasped at the loud and sudden noise. Reverend Seabrooks's large arm was still around his neck.

Terrified, Sade stopped dead in her tracks, screaming at the top of her lungs and shaking uncontrollably.

Pop!

The noise rang out again. Reverend Seabrooks fell over side-ways, carrying Wesley with him to the ground. The laser beam dis-appeared, and the motion light on the porch suddenly came on as

Mrs. Seabrooks staggered out of the front door with a swollen and badly bruised face. Her home and her heart had been broken for years. Her nose had been broken for just over an hour. But unlike Officer Scuffs, the one thing that wasn't broken was her laser, which was attached to her .38-caliber handgun, a combination that she had just utilized to ensure an immediate reunion between her estranged husband and the one who created him. Mrs. Seabrooks had just shot and killed her husband.

Chapter 12

The next few months proved to be difficult for the Seabrooks. Tyrone, Mrs. Seabrooks's brother, had solicited help from a couple of family members to get the money needed to get his sister out on bond. Still, both Mrs. Seabrooks and Sade had to undergo professional counseling to get help coping with the trauma they'd experienced that night. Had Reverend Seabrooks experienced a mental breakdown of some sort? No. He had simply danced with the devil for too long, not realizing that his dance partner was playing for keeps. Combined with everything else going on in his life, he was caught in yet another moment of weakness that pushed him right over the edge.

The night of Sade's prom was simply a moment in time where fate met opportunity for him. And being careful not to discriminate, Old Man Fate tried his best to seal the deal for Mrs. Seabrooks as well. Thankfully, it was an unsuccessful attempt.

That night, after Sade had hung up on him, Reverend Seabrooks began to get dressed.

"I'm going to put an end to this disrespect once and for all," he threatened aloud. Hearing this caused Mrs. Seabrooks's blood to boil.

"Now, Larry, that's enough!" she warned. "You just can't do it, can you? You find it impossible to let Sade go out and have an enjoyable night without doing your best to ruin it for her. This is her last prom, Larry. Can't she just have a moment in time without you finding fault in it, looking for something wrong, or worse yet, *creating* a problem with her so you can have something to fuss about? Do you not know that she will never forgive you if you show up at her prom tonight? She won't, Larry, and as a matter of fact, *I'm* just not having it. I refuse to let you go down there and ruin my baby's prom.

"Now, enough is enough, and I just am not putting up with your foolishness any longer! I'm tired of you treating Sade this way. I'm tired of all of your wicked and evil ways. I'm tired of you living a lie in front of the congregation of people that you are supposed to be pastoring, and I'm tired of you not even putting forth an effort to change. You get up in that pulpit every Sunday, and you put Jesus on the cross, bury Him, and resurrect Him from the dead with all power. But you refuse to access that same resurrection power to get some deliverance for yourself from that controlling, insecure, infidel spirit of yours. Sunday after Sunday you get up there lyin' and cryin', and while you've got most of the people fooled, you forgot that your first ministry begins at home.

"But what's going to happen when your own wife and daughter refuse to support your foolishness any longer? What are the people going to think then? Since they are all you seem to care about, how are you going to justify *that* to them? How good of a pastor are you going to be, Good Reverend, when they find out that you have a newborn baby with a woman who is not your wife? Not even those 'on-demand' tears of yours that you have somehow learned to produce at will can bail you out of that one.

"That's why we're done, Larry. Sade and I have thought about it, talked about it, and prayed about it for years. I have encouraged her to hang in there and keep praying. I've told her for years, 'Keep praying for your daddy, baby. You know he's been through this and he's going through that. You know he's got a lot on his shoulders. He doesn't mean any harm. He's going to get better.'

"But I apologized to her just a few weeks back, and I told her that I've advocated for you for the last time. She's done with you, and I am too. Twenty years are more than enough time for you to pull it together. I hung in there with you, praying and believing for you to get better and for me to get stronger. Well, I guess one of those prayers was answered, because somehow, by the grace of God, I've finally found the strength to stand here in your presence and do what I'm doing now, no matter the consequences. The other prayer? Either God didn't answer it or you were simply not willing to change. So go figure. When I tell you I'm done, I mean it. There's no room for compromise, no reason to negotiate, no time to reconsider. It's over—tonight! So go on and take care of your new, shallow-minded, gullible, insecure ho and your new baby in Charlotte. I guess you'll control their lives for the *next* twenty years, but one thing's for sure, you won't control ours.

"I'll take care of Sade while there's still hope that she won't give up on God. You don't have to worry about her or me anymore, because when she gets home tonight, we are outta here. We'll come back later and get enough of our stuff to survive. Better yet, you can have it. I'll talk to a lawyer and get everything written up. Don't worry, I don't want much. I just want a better life for me and my daughter, because contrary to how you've treated us with neglect, disrespect, abuse, empty promises, and betrayal, we deserve better.

"So there's no need for the 'big bad father' to go to the prom and teach his daughter a lesson in respect. It's too late for that. If she doesn't respect you by now, then I guess the 'big bad father' has failed. So try again with your new baby girl. But try spending some time with this one. Show up at her school to support her, not to embarrass her. And if ya gonna be with Ms. Don't Know No Betta, then show her love and affection, not condescension, control, and abuse. But what you're *not* gonna do is go down there and ruin Sade's prom tonight. I promise you that."

Mrs. Seabrooks had said what she needed to say. Indeed, she had prayed for years for the strength to endure her estranged husband's ways. Over the past couple of years, however, as his behavior became much worse, her prayer for strength to endure became a prayer for the strength to leave him and to deliver herself and Sade from him before their often verbally and emotionally hostile environment became physically hostile. That strength showed up that night when Wesley showed up. The way he treated her with the simplest of gestures warmed her heart. She was taken by his thoughtfulness and consideration toward her, and certainly toward Sade. She was awed by how he had spared no expense and at his unwillingness even to share the costs of the evening despite such short notice from Sade. His efforts that night spoke volumes to her. It was not a mere reflection of a fine young man but a reflection of the careful attention that his upbringing had produced. He was obviously a product of a village. Not just his parents, but a community of people had poured so much life into this boy that his mere presence communicated to her that there was so much more worth fighting for where her own daughter was concerned. Both her heart and her eyes were wide open to the fact that the care and attention that Wesley had been given were the very things that Sade had been denied. It was all that Mrs. Seabrooks needed to see, and it was the catalyst that caused her to be sensitive enough in her inner man to know that the time was near for her to make her move. Her husband's antics that night only served as a real-time indication that it needed to happen immediately.

Reverend Seabrooks had a host of problems, sins, and flaws. Nevertheless, he had come to master the art of preaching, and many immature Christians were drawn to that. He had the type of gifting that made a lot of men envious and a lot of women desirous. Prior to ministry, he had spent eighteen years in the Marines and had earned the nickname Aw Shucks Seabrooks for his no-holds-barred attitude and exemplary service during the Vietnam War. He had witnessed a lot of horrible things on the battlefield during his two tours in 1972 and 1973, but what he had managed to bury deep down within his soul many years ago came gushing back to the surface during the Invasion of Panama in 1989 and 1990, after which he was granted an early retirement due to mental health concerns. He was supposed to receive counseling services, but he refused to attend.

He was the epitome of a bad boy while he was in the military, and all the troops respected and even looked up to him. It was during his last few months of service, however, that he had come to know the Lord and displayed a true change of heart, a change that led to even more respect and admiration. He had been very sincere when he first began in the ministry. The problem was that he had always been received so well that he never put himself to the task of growth and development. So even though years and years had passed, he would preach messages that didn't have much substance, but they made the congregation feel good about being saved and going to heaven one day. His style of delivery was such that whether he was pulling on their heartstrings or stepping on their toes, it would only take him about twenty minutes to preach the congregation into near oblivion. He would then take his seat while leaving them on the edge of theirs. After each service, he would work the crowd like a seasoned politician, greeting each interested person with a huge smile accompanied by either a handshake, a hug, or both, visiting only for a brief moment before moving on to the next person. All this led to more and more doors being opened for him to preach in small-size and midsize churches in different cities and towns.

It didn't take long for the spirit of pride to set in, and he eventually began to think of himself more highly than he should have, thus rendering him unteachable—a very dangerous place for a minister to be. Had he known that the nickname Aw Shucks Seabrooks would become a personal prophecy to him, he would have quickly humbled himself to avoid the destruction that inevitably follows the spirit of pride. Little by little, he had fallen right into the enemy's plan and become so prideful that no one could correct him or give him any advice. It was going to be his way or no way at all.

Mrs. Seabrooks was kicking herself for not doing more. She felt like, over the years, as she watched her husband's slow fade, she should have been more assertive in her efforts to get him to a better place spiritually. She had prayed and prayed for him. She had urged him to get counseling or to at least talk to some other God-fearing ministers. But time after time he would accuse her of judging him or come up with some scheme in order to take the pressure off himself by putting it on her. Consequently, their relationship had so drastically declined over the years that missing him was no longer related to a lack of love and affection but, rather, of safety and protection.

Since he was rarely there to provide either, she had taken matters into her own hands and purchased a handgun. She was very familiar with handguns and how to use them, thanks to her older brother Tyrone, who had trained her well during her growing-up years. Never in her most vivid imaginations, however, did she see herself having to use the weapon on her own husband. The thought never crossed her mind, and while she knew that she and Sade were definitely going to leave him, her plan did not include violence of any sort.

Neither did she ever expect to see anything remotely close to what she witnessed that night. The man who attacked her was not the man with whom she had spent the last twenty years of her life. He was not a physically violent man; he wouldn't taunt or fight anyone, especially a child, nor would he hold them at knifepoint. And he certainly wouldn't attempt suicide by cop, being the borderline narcissist that he was. Whoever this man was who had broken her nose was not her husband. Whoever this man was who scowled at her with a look that conveyed that he probably wouldn't have stopped attacking her had he not tripped and crashed through the glass coffee table, badly cutting his hand, was not her husband.

Would her husband have gone to the prom to embarrass his daughter? He certainly would have, because for some reason, he seemed to love controlling Sade and making her life miserable, only to turn around and apologize a day or two later and spoil her with clothes, shoes, and the like. Without a doubt, he would have made his way to the prom, lied his way past any security to get her attention, and then just stared at her in a threatening way like he used to do in church when she would misbehave as a little girl. But now this type of behavior was utterly embarrassing, because it came across to her friends as weird, creepy, and inappropriate. Or perhaps he would have simply stood there and smiled at her with a grimace that said, "I'm going to teach you about respect right here, in front of everybody." Just like the time when she was an eighth-grade basketball cheerleader and he sat behind her squad, delivering an entire lecture while her cheerleading coach socialized with one of the teachers for nearly an entire half, not even caring that Sade was not cheering but rather being made by her father to sit there crying.

Or like in her junior year, when he picked her up from school before the biggest game of the year, claiming that he just wanted to spend some time with her; he took her across town to have dinner and drove around town until it was game time. When he brought her to the stadium, he told half-truths to the sheriff's deputies on duty regarding why she was late in order to gain access to drive right up to the ticket gate. He was even allowed to park in that area. When he pulled up to the gate, Sade jumped out of the car with her duffel bag and was allowed clearance to run through the gate and into the disgusting stadium restroom, where she changed into her uniform. Then, as an already-embarrassed Sade ran down the stadium stairs to where her squad was, her father embarrassed her even further by yelling, "Hurry up, Sade, hurry up!" making it seem as if it were her fault that she was so late. He was absolutely capable of this type of demonic game playing, but what in the world happened to him that led him to become the dark monster from the night of Sade's prom?

Mrs. Seabrooks wondered whether or not she was losing it. Her mind kept replaying the same scenarios over and over. Then, she would think about all the different times that she had tried to persuade her husband to get help. She recognized the pattern, but she couldn't seem to turn it off. She knew that somehow she had to pull it together for Sade's sake, but she just didn't know how.

She did know how to pray, however, and that was exactly what she did. As she fell to her knees to pray, it was as if she lost her ability to kneel, thus falling flat on her face.

"Lord Jesus, have mercy on me," she cried aloud. "Look at me, I'm an emotional wreck. I'm physically out of sorts, and my soul is in turmoil. I have this continuous cycle of thoughts that play over and over in my mind. I need You, Lord. All I have left to hold on to is You. I can't even hold on to my daughter, because right now, I'm just not able to do so. But she needs me, Lord. Can't You see me down here, holding on? I need You to step in right now and do something. I don't want to take these drugs that they've prescribed for me, because as soon as they wear off, I'm back to square one. But they are the only thing that seem to bring me some relief from this cycle of thoughts that continue to replay in my mind. But You are so much bigger than drugs, Lord. But I need something to help me put an end to these thoughts that continuously replay in my mind."

Mrs. Seabrooks realized that even as she prayed, she was using the same phrases over and over. She also recognized her overuse of the word *but*. Yet she knew that she had to keep praying as she believed that God was surely about to move in her situation. She could sense His presence. "God, help me," she pleaded through her tears. "I can't even pray right anymore. Will You help me?"

As she lay there crying herself to sleep, her mind bounced back and forth among all the times she had asked her husband to get some counseling. Time and again, she urged him to seek professional help, or for the both of them to go to marriage counseling, or for him to simply sit down and talk to her, or at the very least, for them to go to the altar and pray together—all to no avail. He was just not willing. He didn't see any need, and this spirit of pride ultimately led to his downfall.

In the midst of her mental rambling, Mrs. Seabrooks began to recall the last countywide revival as if it were yesterday. It was held every other year, and it was an event that was a breath of fresh air to so many pastors and churches. The evangelist for the week, Pastor Mahasta, had been invited by the association to be the revivalist. This was a slightly controversial move, since the minister was not the traditional-style preacher that most of the people of the Lower Lexington Baptist Network were used to. On the contrary, he was a missionary who spent about 75 percent of each year in some of the most remote parts of Zambia and Mozambique in Africa.

Although each Baptist association has its own rules, in the Lower Lexington Baptist Network, the moderator reserved the right to invite the revivalist of his choice, and he had invited Pastor Mahasta for all the right reasons. He knew that the seasoned missionary would come in with a fresh word. He also knew that he was not going to try to cater to what the people wanted to hear, but instead he would preach and teach with great authority and conviction. In addition, he had heard Pastor Mahasta on a couple of occasions, and he knew that miracles, signs, and wonders often followed his preaching. So he wanted the man of God to come in and be free to preach with that same fire and under that same burden-removing anointing that he ministered with while living in areas where modern medicine was scarce, where light and electricity were often insufficient, and where other basic resources such as food and water were available at times only on a hit-or-miss basis. In those types of conditions, faith was not optional. One couldn't rely on God only until the medicine kicked in, or only until the power company repaired the outage, as was the case in the States. Over there, it was trust God or nothing. Consequently, a seasoned minister like Pastor Mahasta was no stranger to the miraculous.

The moderator had expressed to the pastors during their meeting that he wanted to expose the association to a greater measure of faith and to a level of grace and anointing that he hoped would make them hungrier for more of God's power in their own lives and ministries. He told them he had prayed about it to the point of having peace with the decision he'd made. Most of the pastors and leaders were on board and excited. They welcomed the change and the potential for their members to experience greater levels of deliverance in their personal lives, which would ultimately lead to more impactful churches and stronger communities. However, there were always two or three who were just going to be oppositional, no matter who the moderator had chosen for the countywide revival, and Reverend Seabrooks, as usual, was the opposition ringleader.

On the first night of the revival, Pastor Mahasta made it clear that his message was geared specifically toward pastors and ministers. The title of his message was Charity Begins at Home. It was a very sobering message, bringing to light the understanding of how one can become so easily consumed with growing and building churches and ministries that they often do so at the expense of their own families. He spoke to pastors and to those who found themselves heavily involved in the ministry.

"Many of you feel called to lead a flock, and it is so wonderful to have this calling upon your life. Trust me, I know what it's like to have such a burden to do ministry in a particular area, whereby you feel like the calling is so vitally important, and in all sincerity, you just don't want to let God down. I also know that many of you over the years have lacked the presence of a true spiritual father, who could provide you with insight and understanding. This is a major problem in the body of Christ. The way you're responding leads me to believe that I'm in the right house tonight, especially since I haven't even begun with my message for tonight."

The congregation relaxed a bit with a little laughter.

"Boy, that really makes me feel much better, especially since while on my way to the church tonight, I informed the Holy Spirit for about the fourth time that I had no clue where to begin. You do know that you have to inform God of these things, right? If you don't tell Him, then how could He possibly know?" he asked ingenuously with shrugged shoulders and a huge grin on his face.

The congregation relaxed a bit more and laughed again.

"Of course, you know that I am joking, but it is good to hear you laughing. It is good, my brothers and sisters, to be able to relax in the presence of God. Can I talk to some pastors and leaders in here tonight? Some of you haven't shared a laugh with your congregation in a long time. You are so burdened down with the weight of ministry that your preaching is laced with stress and heaviness. Yet we say that we preach the 'good news.' I've come to set you free tonight by the power of God.

"If you have such a burden to do greater ministry, if you have such a burden to reach more souls, or to do more in your community, I've come to tell you that you are in a very good place! You are in a good place because Almighty God has put that desire in your heart, and He knows that if greater ministry, or reaching more souls, or having a greater community impact is going to happen, it is going to happen through you. However, God never intended for you to sacrifice your family in the name of the *burden* that you have to do great things for Him. I don't know where you got the philosophy that says, 'God first, then family, then whatever else.' I've come to let you know, it's all God. It's God first, God second, God third. When you get to the number 19, it's God nineteenth. When it comes to your career choice, it's God's position. When it comes to what to preach, it's God's message, not your version of what you heard someone preaching on TV. Say amen, somebody!

"When it comes to having time to yourself, you had better stop leaving God out! That's why you find yourself having fantasies and dreams about the person that you work with on your job. Watch how you carry yourself when it's just you and that other person in the office and stop pretending that God is not in there with you. That's why you've got a wife and a work wife. You have a boo and a work boo. But wait a minute, preachers, I thought we're God's personal representatives!"

By this time, the people were standing on their feet and clapping their hands and shouting comments at Pastor Mahasta.

"Y'all sit down, let me talk to ya," he said as if he weren't just wielding a two-edged sword. "We're just talking," he said. "What I am trying to get you to see tonight is that you don't just start out in those places. But when we fail to put God in His rightful place, we find ourselves slowly slippin', slippin', slippin'. Anybody ever found yourself slippin'? You're preaching good, but you're slippin', you're laying hands on the sick, but you're slippin', you're feeding the homeless, but you're slippin'. Well, calm down. You're in the right house tonight."

Pastor Mahasta slowed things down a bit. He read his theme scripture and delved into it, teaching the people about how to have balance in life even while doing the work of ministry in addition to working a full-time job, which was the reality of nearly every pastor in attendance. He talked about so many things that are of significant importance to pastors, but the entire time that he ministered, Reverend Seabrooks sat there with his arms folded.

After delivering an awesome message, Pastor Mahasta had an altar call just for pastors and their spouses. As they made their way to the altar, he asked the congregation to prepare their hearts to pray with him for these men and women of God. The altar was full of pastors, ministers, and their spouses from churches all over the area. Every single minister and his or her spouse who was in attendance was at that altar. Even the ones who were normally in opposition to the moderator made their way to the altar. Many came and fell on their knees. Others cried out to God in a loud voice, while still others wept, repented, and asked for forgiveness. These men and women of God recognized the error of their ways, and they wanted to be better; they wanted God's help.

Reverend Seabrooks, however, was utterly consumed with pride. There was no way that he was going to that altar. There was a very slim chance that he would have done so if he were alone. But to be on *this* side of the altar in front of everyone attending the countywide revival was not going to happen, despite the Holy Spirit's nudging. Mrs. Seabrooks stood to make her way to the altar. She grabbed her husband's hand as she stood, but he pulled his hand away from hers and remained in his seat.

As Mrs. Seabrooks recalled this scenario in her mind, she heard the still, small voice of the Holy Spirit say, "It wasn't just your hand that he pulled away from that night. He made a conscious decision to pull away from Mine. Rest assured, he didn't die because of you. He died because the time of his destruction was at hand due to his unyielding pride. Get up, Melissa. Your daughter needs you. Get up."

Chapter 13

Wesley was the quickest to recover, particularly since he had been only half-conscious when the most traumatic part happened that night. The rest of it was not as bad for him, especially having handled himself pretty well against such a large man as Reverend Seabrooks, who was also a Marine.

As for Sade, she wasn't recovering as quickly. Aside from the trauma, getting over the loss of her dad wouldn't be easy. His absenteeism, abuse, trickery, and games were over, and Sade was so relieved. The man who had made their lives so miserable was now gone, and truth be told, Sade was glad about it. But he left her without giving her the one thing she wanted more than anything else in life—his acceptance. She didn't care that her attitude was selfish; it was how she felt, and she was very much okay with that. But she wasn't okay with the fact that her father was still able, somehow, to make her so angry even from the grave. The therapy sessions that she attended were effective, until she stopped attending them. She simply refused to allow her father to dictate any longer for her what was mandatory or not. Sade was sinking into a pit of carelessness and hopelessness, and she needed help, the help of Almighty God. Unfortunately, she was not embracing God very much at that moment.

Thankfully, during the first semester of her senior year, Sade had acquired more than enough credits to graduate. She was taking two classes simply for the sake of getting a couple of early college credits. Her grades were so good that even if she bummed her final few tests and exams, she would still pass both classes. Each day, she would go to class, leave class, skip her counseling session, and drive home to isolate herself in her bedroom. She didn't have any friends that she trusted enough to talk to about something so serious. To make matters worse, the day after the shooting, she had received a text from Wesley stating that he was not allowed to communicate with her or anyone else who was present that night until he had started making significant progress in his therapy. Two weeks had passed since she had heard from him. She often thought about how he had proved himself to be genuine, how she loved his company, and how she wished she could be held in his strong arms again, if only one more time. If only she could talk to him, he was sure to say something that would help her to be reconciled to a place of hope and peace. Instead, she had very little peace, and very little hope. The little bit of hope that she had, however, she decided to hold on to it. In her heart of hearts, she knew that someway, somehow, God would come through for her despite her current disappointment with Him.

Mrs. Seabrooks had decided to put her house on the market and move in with Tyrone while she found another place she felt comfortable calling home. Tyrone's house was close to where Wesley and his family lived, and to her amazement, it was perfect for her, since no one she knew lived around there. She needed a reprieve from church members, coworkers, and other well-wishers, who all claimed that they knew how bad the situation had gotten and wanted to say something sooner but for a host of reasons they never said a word—until now, of course. Some of them were talking about things that they didn't really know about. Others were fishing for information.

The reality was that before that night, Reverend Seabrooks had never physically hit her. However, his verbal attacks could be so harmful that they were, in some ways, just as damaging. Not to mention, the verbal contention had become so intense that she feared his attacks could become physical at any given time. Furthermore, since she had been with him for so long, there were certain cues that probably should have warned her of the impending danger, such as some of the TV shows that he had started watching, finding a firearm in the glove box of his car, and finding that his phone was suddenly password-protected. Most of these signs, no one knew about. So she wasn't too keen on entertaining the rhetoric of those who claimed that they knew how bad things had gotten.

She and Sade were safe with Tyrone, as he was not one to fool around with. Had he known the details, he would have handled his brother-in-law the moment he learned that his sister and niece were in danger. Mrs. Seabrooks had given Tyrone's address to a few people, advising them of where she was staying. They would send cards and letters, but they were reluctant to go see her after it was rumored that he walked out a group of people from the church for asking too many questions. Indeed, the rumors were true, and thankfully, the visitors were from the church; thus, they were *kindly* dismissed. Knowing Tyrone, anyone else might have been thrown out butt first one behind the other.

One Saturday afternoon during the summer, Mrs. Seabrooks had a visitor show up. Tyrone, who worked a weekend shift on his job, was not at home, so it just so happened that the timing would have been perfect for a visitor, if only she had been expecting one. When she approached the door, she saw a pretty young lady standing there and immediately concluded that she was either at the wrong house or perhaps was involved in some type of door-to-door sales, which made her wonder why she was alone.

"May I help you?" she asked.

"Hello, my name is Tara, and I am the sister of Wesley Heart, the young man your daughter invited to—"

"I know exactly who Wesley is," Melissa interrupted. "How is he doing?"

"He's doing well, thank you for asking. Mrs. Seabrooks, I'm going to get right to the point. Wesley has been wanting to visit you and Sade for several days. During his first session, his therapist cautioned him about having interaction with anyone from the scene of the accident prematurely. The problem is that our mom was in the counseling session with him. She took the word of caution entirely too seriously and forbade him to talk to anyone who was involved that night. So I personally reached out to Sade for him, and she notified me of your new address. Wesley thought about simply sending you guys some flowers, but it just wasn't...I mean, he felt like that was not the same as…look, he's in the car, Mrs. Seabrooks, and he really wants to see you. He wasn't sure how you'd feel about it, so he asked if I would…"

While Tara was still talking, Mrs. Seabrooks opened the storm door and walked right past her as if she weren't there at all. She headed straight to the car, and as she did, Wesley got out and they met and embraced in the middle of the driveway. They held their embrace for quite a while, and they both were speechless. Tara, who had come down off the porch, stood silently by and watched the very moving exchange. Both Wesley and Mrs. Seabrooks were very emotional, and Mrs. Seabrooks was sobbing. Neither of them could explain it, but they had a need to see each other. Wesley needed to let her know that she was going to be okay. Mrs. Seabrooks's mind was flooded with the memory of the sincere kindness that Wesley had shown her on the night of Sade's prom. She had needed the flowers he gave her that night like she needed air to breathe. Then, the letter that he had written was indeed what she had been praying for—a sign from heaven that God was watching out for her and her daughter, no matter what she might have been going through.

Seeing that Wesley had come back to check on her caused her to be overcome with emotion once again. There was a sincere element of healing in their embrace. She invited Wesley and Tara in, and that day was one of the turning points in her journey to recovery. Tara seized the moment to work her magic by providing encouragement to Mrs. Seabrooks. Of course, she wasn't able to enter into any type of true counseling, but she was able to reach Mrs. Seabrooks by scratching the surface of some of the thoughts she was actually dealing with.

"Mrs. Seabrooks—"

"Please, just call me Melissa," she interrupted.

"Okay. Ms. Melissa, I know that you must have a whirlwind of thoughts going through your mind. You're probably wondering why you didn't do something sooner in your relationship that would have helped you avoid an outcome like this, or why no one else seemed to notice or even care, or whether or not *you* should even care. At the same time, you're trying to ensure the security of your future and Sade's. You're wondering whether or not she's going to be okay, whether she'll turn her back on you even though you did what you did to save her life and Wesley's. You may be a little put out with the church, or maybe even with God."

Mrs. Seabrooks had buried her face in her hands and was sobbing and nodding. Wesley, who had been holding her hand, stood to go find her some tissue. Finding none, he quickly returned from the kitchen with paper towels. He sat down beside her, put his arm around her, and pulled her over to his chest. He gave her the paper towels and held her as she attempted to pull it together.

Tara continued, "I just want to assure you that all these and the thousands of other thoughts you are experiencing are absolutely normal. It's okay for you to feel every bit of what you're feeling and thinking right now. If you weren't feeling anything, then there would be a reason for concern, but you are exactly where you need to be. God has you in the palm of His hand, and He's able to handle your thoughts, feelings, emotions, and even any anger that you may have toward Him."

Mrs. Seabrooks continued to dry her tears. She sat up, removing herself from Wesley's embrace. Before doing so, she put her free arm around the big boy, hugged him, and thanked him.

"Lord, have mercy!" she exclaimed. "I'll tell you the truth, young lady. You are voicing my thoughts as if you were living down inside of my soul. I go to counseling three times a week now, but what you have said to me in just a few sentences has uncovered more than we have talked about in two weeks of counseling. I guess I misjudged you. I know that you're very mature, but I thought you were rather young. Are you some type of counselor or something?"

"No, ma'am, not yet," Tara responded. "I'm a counseling major at South Carolina State with a minor in psychology. My ultimate goal is to earn my doctorate in clinical psychology from USC so that I can help people cope with and overcome traumatic experiences." While this was indeed the track Tara was on, the reality was that she had a God-given gift to reach the hearts of people through her words. She had been counseling her peers for a very long time, even as a teen, long before she ever took any courses on the subject. She continued to encourage Mrs. Seabrooks, and before she and Wesley left, she asked, "Mrs. Seabrooks...I mean, Ms. Melissa, I have a question: Would you be willing to come to church with us tomorrow?" She watched the older woman's body language and facial features, and she spoke up before giving her time to answer. "I was just thinking that I'll have some time after church if you wanted to grab lunch and just talk. I can imagine that you are probably not too keen on church right now, and that is truly understandable. But before you answer, I just want the three of us to pray together. You can decide later on. I'll leave you my number, and you can just let me know either way. No pressure."

Tara led them in a brief prayer, but by the time she finished, Mrs. Seabrooks was sobbing once again. Tara's prayer included a plea for confidence in the midst of judgmental people who meant her no good and for wisdom in knowing how to best help Sade to find peace and for her to be okay. She prayed for resolution to know that she did the right thing and that two young people were alive that day because of the action she'd taken. She also prayed for the strength for Melissa to overcome the accusatory voices from both inside and out trying to tell her that she was anything other than a child of the most high God.

This time, Wesley put his arm around her and said, "You're going to be okay, Ms. Melissa. I'll keep checking on you and Sade, and if there's anything I can do to help either one of you, feel free to let me know. You're going to be just fine."

"Thank you, baby. You're such a fine young man, and I'm so glad that you and Tara here came by to check on us. Y'all just don't know how much you've blessed my soul today. I know I'm going to be fine, but y'all pray for Sade. She's been skipping her counseling, and she doesn't have much to say to me these days. Our relationship was coming along okay before everything happened. We had opened up and committed to working on it. My counselor says she will come around after a while, but I have to admit, I'm worried about her. Maybe I can talk her into coming to church with me tomorrow. I know y'all over there at the Miracle Center have a way of getting through to God, and Lord knows I could use a miracle right now," she said, looking at Tara with a smile. "What time does the service begin?"

"We start at nine thirty on the nose, and I think that would be a great idea, Ms. Melissa," Tara replied.

"The way you two have helped me today, I want to experience the teaching and training that you all are getting," Mrs. Seabrooks remarked. "The one thing I know for sure is that I need to be in the presence of the Lord, but like you said earlier, Tara, I guess I am upset with Him right now. I wouldn't have put it in those words. I wouldn't have even had the courage to say that at all before you did. But despite my feelings, I still know that I need Him right now, and Sade definitely needs Him too. Maybe you can talk to her, Wesley. I don't want to burden you, son, but maybe she'll listen to you."

Tara spoke up to say, "I'll reach out to Sade, Ms. Melissa. Really, Wesley is not even supposed to be here right now. Our mother has told him not to talk with Sade, you, or Officer Scuffs until everyone has had time to go through therapy, and—"

"I'm fine," Wesley interrupted. "I'll be more than happy to talk to Sade, Ms. Melissa. I think my counselor would be fine with that at this stage, given my progress. And she will tell my mom the same thing."

"Wesley," Tara cautioned.

"No, sis, I think it would do me a lot of good to really talk to Sade and to find out for myself that she's okay. If you want, you can even supervise the conversation, but…I mean, come on. Her mother is standing here, pleading with us to help her daughter. We have the means. Let's help her, sis. Isn't that what Pastor Johnson teaches us?"

"I know, Wes, but—"

"Listen, Tara. Being here with Mrs. Sea"—he caught him-self—"with Ms. Melissa today has done me so much good. She has expressed to us how we have blessed her by coming, but I, too, have experienced so much healing by just being able to see her for myself, to hold her while she cried, and to let her know that I care. Don't you get it, T? That's healing for me. Everybody…" The boy dropped his head and began to cry, something that he hadn't done since the entire incident. Mrs. Seabrooks put her arm around him and began to gently pat him on the back. He wiped his face and continued, "Everybody doesn't heal the same way, T. That's what I've been trying to tell Mom, but she doesn't listen. I need this, Tara. I need *this*." He pointed back and forth between himself and Mrs. Seabrooks. "Sade needs it too, and having a conversation with her will most likely help her. I know it will help me."

Tara knew her brother was voicing his own need for help, and without a doubt, this was something that was going to help him. And she knew it. She knew it just like she knew that if she hadn't taken him to see Mrs. Seabrooks today, he would have gone on his own. So in the same way that she had just helped him to disobey their mother's orders by taking him to see Mrs. Seabrooks, she was about to be guilty of aiding and abetting, count two.

She walked over to her brother and put her arms around him and Mrs. Seabrooks.

"I just want to help, T. That's what's going to help me more than focusing on sports or writing down all my thoughts or anything else that's a part of my treatment."

"Okay, Wesley," she agreed. "If that's what you need, then that's what we'll do. But only if Sade is willing, okay? So, Ms. Melissa, if you would be so kind, please let Sade know that Wesley and I came by to see her and then just give her this number to call. Tell her not to dial Wesley's number but to call me at this number if she is willing, and I'll get Wesley on the phone. This will give me time to talk to our mother and to help her to understand what's going on."

"Oh, Tara, I don't want you all doing anything against your parents' instructions."

"No, Ms. Melissa, trust me, I will help Mom see the fallacy in her way of thinking. As for my dad, he already knows the deal. So just ask Sade to call if she wants to talk to Wesley, and everything will be fine. I'll be there, and Mom will likely be there, too, to supervise the call."

"I can't thank you two enough for this. You just don't know how much y'all have been my angels in disguise this day. I'll see you both at church tomorrow, and maybe I'll have Sade with me. Y'all keep your fingers crossed."

"We're trusting God," Tara and Wesley said at the same time. Pastor Johnson had taught his parishioners not to believe in things such as luck, crossing fingers, and the wishing-upon-a-star kind of thinking that many people, both believers and nonbelievers, espoused. Instead, they had learned that when they heard such comments, their response should be an expression of trusting God. Embarrassed that they had both said it at the same time, they looked at each other and back at Mrs. Seabrooks. They both were trying to think of something to say to alleviate the awkwardness of their joint statement when, as if they were reading each other's minds, they both spoke at the same time.

"See you tomorrow, Ms. Melissa."

Again, they looked at each other, shook their heads in disbelief, and walked to Tara's car.

Chapter 14

"Wanna go to the mall?" Tara asked.

"Sure," Wesley agreed. "Let me guess, you want to clear your head before you go home to fess up to Mom, right?"

"Only for you, li'l bro."

"Don't call me that, T. It makes me think about the love of my life...you know, the one who doesn't yet know that she's the love of my life?"

Tara liked where this conversation was going, because she recognized that Wesley, although he seemed okay, really needed to get his mind off everything, which was her real reason for suggesting a trip to the mall.

"Well, you might be surprised."

"What do you mean by that?"

"I mean, what if Lisa was actually interested in you too? What if she knew that you were serious about having a relationship with her and that was something she really wanted too?"

"Then I would think she has a funny way of showing it."

"Can you put yourself in her shoes for a moment?"

"Sure."

"Okay, imagine that you're a female."

"Okay, T, you know what? This exercise is over."

"Don't act so insecure, man. You know who you are. Just go along with me. Imagine that you're a female finishing up your sophomore year of college. You're preparing to pursue your last two years, to knock them out of the park and move on into graduate school, or into a career in your field, when all along there is a high school student who you know is absolutely crazy about you. And he's not just any high school student, he's the finest, most popular, and certainly the most likely to succeed. Still, he's in high school. Although you recognize that he's far more mature than most of the people you associate with, even in college, and you would love the opportunity to get to know him better, it's simply not a good move for either of you.

"Frequently, you think to yourself, *If he were just a couple of years older, there would be no question about having a relationship with him.* What do you do in a situation like that, Ms. Wesley? Do you disregard the obvious and go after the young man despite the fact that every voice within you is telling you not to, or do you resolve to understand that the logical and most ethical thing to do at this point is to simply walk away? I think you make up your mind to continue to work toward your goals while you earnestly pray that, one day, you will have the opportunity to pursue a real relationship with him. What do you think, ma'am?"

"First of all, T, I think you're crazy for trying to make me think like a woman. That is not based on any insecurities, but that is based on the fact that women and men think very differently. Secondly, I get your point, and I certainly understand your reasoning, but are you telling me that this is truly how Lisa feels, or are you just offering me a scenario?"

"I'll never tell."

"Oh, what was I thinking? You can't break the girl code, right?"

"Of course I can't."

"Well, I think you just did."

"No, I didn't."

"T, surely, you didn't just come up with that scenario off the top of your head."

"Boy, don't try to play me. You know good and well that I am very capable of doing that. Look, I'm just trying to get you to see that even if Lisa was into you, there's just no way that a relationship could be possible right now."

"Whatever, T. In time, I'll find out for myself how Lisa feels when I ask her out. So when she comes back telling you that she couldn't keep her hands off me, I'll see how strong your girl code is then."

"Oh, it's like that, huh?"

"Yep! By the time I finish wining and dining her and showing her how a real man is supposed to treat her, she's going to have a hard time trying to follow after that line of reasoning that you just supposedly made up."

"Line of reasoning?"

"Yeah, that entire scenario that you just made up with all those reasons why she can't entertain a relationship with me right now. You know, the scenario that led to you breaking the girl code."

"First of all, I did not break the girl code, and secondly, when did you become Casanova?"

"Hey, I'm learning from the best."

"Oh, and who might that be?"

"Dad."

"Dad! Boy, you're gonna make me hit this parked car!" she accused with a laugh as she parked in the mall parking lot.

"I'm telling you, T, Dad's been teaching me how to treat women. I think he knows his stuff. That's what got me in trouble with Sade."

Tara was almost regretful that Sade was back in the conversation. Still, she was feeling better about Wesley's disposition, as he was starting to unwind a bit. Any conversation about Lisa was sure to help, so she decided to tolerate a little bit of "Sade talk" in hopes of quickly bringing her girl Lisa back to the forefront of the conversation.

"What do you mean 'in *trouble* with Sade'? What else happened on prom night?"

"There you go again with your assumptions. You would think that you learned your lesson the last time."

"Don't try to avoid the question."

"Nothing happened, T. At least nothing worth telling. I'm just saying that after our time together on prom night, as well as the times we hung out together leading up to it, I think Sade will be looking for more than just a friendship, and I don't want that with her. Anyhow, I'm sure those feelings have been put on hold for now, given everything that transpired that night."

God, help me here. This conversation is headed in the wrong direction, she thought.

"Well," Tara responded, "just be a good friend to her, and if it becomes necessary, just tell her the truth about how you feel or what type of relationship you want or don't want with her. You know, you just have to be honest with her and embrace her as a friend, but let her know that you don't want to have the relationship go any further. And whatever you do, make sure that you don't muddy the waters by sending mixed messages."

"Or," Wesley teased, "I'll just tell her, 'Look, Sade, you're a nice girl, and you're really good-looking and all, but in comparison to Lisa, you don't even scratch the surface, so just back up, okay?'"

Wesley and Tara entered the food court entrance laughing at his nonsense. *Thank you, Lord,* Tara thought. *I think we're back on track.*

"She really is sweet, and a very nice-looking young lady too, Wes. So what makes Lisa so special?"

"Oh, that's easy. For me, Lisa's beauty is much deeper than her outward appearance. Don't get me wrong, she is extremely attractive to me. But the person on the inside amazes me. She will help anyone, she'll fight for you, she's independent, she's sweet and caring, and most importantly, she loves God. Sure, she's a little rough around the edges because she's been through a lot…from foster care to dealing with rejection from her mother to never knowing her father and having to be raised by her grandparents. But where she probably feels like those things makes her less lovable, to me, they only make her even more special because all those situations have worked together to help develop her into the person she is today.

"I love her rough edges because it gives her that spunky personality. Of course, I love her smooth curves too, but that's a conversation for me to have with another brother, not you. She's the perfect height, the perfect tone, and she has the perfect little gap between her teeth, which gives her the perfect smile. I love how when she gets upset, she tilts her head to the right and strokes her hair on that side, making sure that it stays behind her ear. I love how when she's excited, she puts her hands on her hips and smiles with her bottom lip tucked in, and how when she's focused, she tucks both lips in and lowers her eyebrows and looks so serious. I love everything about that woman."

"Wow! I'm almost sorry I asked!" Tara laughed. "You really pay attention, don't you?"

"Not to everybody, but I've paid a lot of attention to Lisa over the years."

"Well, if y'all did end up together, she would *never* let you go. Do you know how many women wish their men would pay just half that much attention to them?"

"I told you, T, Dad is the man. He taught me all this."

"When did Dad ever teach you anything about women, Wesley?"

"Since I was a young boy. We have always talked about stuff like this."

"So does he know how you feel about Lisa?"

"Of course he does. He just says that if it's meant to be, God has a way of working it out."

"Well, he's right about that. Just keep growing and becoming the man God intends you to be and see what happens in the future. Besides, once you're a little older, if your interest in her is still there, you can ask her out then."

"Oh, I'm going to ask her out in the near future!"

"No, you're not, silly."

"You'll see. Just give me a few more months."

Wesley and Tara enjoyed each other's company. They missed times like this when they would just hang out and not have to worry about much of anything. It used to be even more fun when Amanda was involved, as she kept them laughing all the time. They still couldn't believe that Amanda had gotten married and moved away with her husband, Antonio, to his duty station in Fort Hood, Texas, and from there to Germany. When he made the announcement that he had been called into the ministry, although none of the Heart family was surprised, given his kind and loving personality, they all got a big kick out of it, since Amanda was always the one making jokes and mimicking how people behave in church.

At any rate, once Amanda left, there was only Tara and Wesley, and Tara was often away at school. So they made it a point to hang out together as much as possible whenever Tara was at home. That evening, they hung out at the mall until about six thirty before concluding that they needed to go home and prepare for the next day. For Tara, that meant facing her mother, trying to convince her that she had somehow done the right thing, although she had directly disobeyed her and assisted her younger brother in doing the same. For Wesley, that meant trying to settle his mind as he anticipated seeing Sade the next day. Although his time with Tara was therapeutic, his thoughts and emotions were still brewing internally. He found himself out in the shed, fully engaged in a martial arts workout when his phone rang. It was Pastor Johnson.

Chapter 15

"Hi, Pastor J," Wesley greeted. He was panting hard from his workout, even though he was in optimal shape. He had trained with his dad until he became too big, too quick, and too strong for his dad to keep up. His normal workout was an intense hour, five days a week, outside of any time that he spent practicing his sport, weight training, running, or otherwise engaging with his team. He was stressed tonight, though, and he had been working out for over ninety minutes and had no intentions of stopping anytime soon.

"Wesley, it sounds like I caught you in the midst of one of your vicious workouts. You can call me back when you're done."

"No! No, sir. I'm glad you called, Pastor. I need to stop before my heart stops me," Wesley replied, putting his phone on speaker to avoid panting in the pastor's ear.

"Wesley, a heart like yours only begs for more. I have never in all my days seen anyone who is more dedicated than you. I declare, you're going to be in the Olympics one day."

"Well, Dad says…if I can just get a…full ride to a good school, that will be quite…quite an accomplishment."

"Son, with *your* gifting and dedication, you can go to any school in the nation for free, guaranteed. Set your sights on world-class competition. We'll talk more about that soon."

"Yes, sir," he responded, taking a few deep breaths in an attempt to slow his breathing.

"Well, I was just calling because you are on my mind. What's going on with you?"

Wesley took a few more deep breaths and began, "I meant to call you before I started working out, but I decided to wait, not intending to work out for so long. I just wanted to get your thoughts on something. If Sade and Mrs. Seabrooks come to church tomorrow, do you think it would be okay if I sit with them? I'm pretty certain Mrs. Seabrooks is coming. I'm just not sure about Sade."

"Of course, son. As you know, I advised your dad not to put you on duty to serve until I give the okay, but if you were on duty, you know that would be his call, not mine."

"Yes, sir. I understand."

"Wesley, I perceive that in the same way you need to talk to Sade, your friend needs you too. I meant to have a talk with your parents to see if they will reconsider their stance on keeping you away from her. I hesitated to speak with them about it last week, and now I wish I had followed through with the conversation. That raises the question, though: Have you spoken with the Seabrooks? I mean, how do you know they'll be at church tomorrow?"

"Well, I have been kind of disobedient."

"Kind of?"

"I know, I know, there's no in between. It's a long story, Pastor. Tara is in the house with Mom now, helping her to understand, and Dad was never fully in agreement with me being forced to stay away from them anyway."

"Yes, I'm aware of that. But it is still disobedience, so shouldn't you be in there, talking to your mother? Why is Tara defending you while you indulge in a workout?"

"Well, she was kinda…I mean, she was in on it too."

"Listen, I don't know what the two of you are up to, but I wish you well with your mom. If you guys survive the night, I will do my part to help you out, not with being disobedient, but I just believe that you and Sade, and perhaps Mrs. Seabrooks too, need to have a couple of conversations. I know your mom can go overboard sometimes, but still, when you honor and obey your parents, God will honor you. He knows how to deal with your mom, and he doesn't need your help, or Tara's. Anyhow, I will address the congregation in the morning, but in the meantime, both Sade and her mother need to feel the safety and security that our team can provide. I'll let your dad know to assign someone, probably Brother Elliot, to them. He can sit nearby, but his assignment won't be evident. That will give them an extra level of security just in case."

"Good idea, Pastor, just in case some crazies from the community show up and try to give Mrs. Seabrooks a hard time."

"Not crazies, Wesley. Don't refer to people as crazies, son."

"I'm just saying, Pastor, you know we have a lot of unsaved and unchurched people coming in every week, which is the reason that we have such a stout security ministry, anyway."

Pastor Johnson knew the boy was right. In any church gathering, people were likely to come there drunk, high, or otherwise not in their right minds. Miracle Center was not only a hospital for those who were sick in body and soul; it was also a temporary safe haven for people in any condition, and people were subject to show up just like that—in any condition—in hopes of getting some type of help, relief, and perhaps even a miracle. At times, the intercessors, doorkeepers, and security team had to work overtime to maintain order, yet it was never acceptable to mistreat anyone on account of their condition.

Pastor Johnson was surprised at Wesley's comment, and even more surprised that he had tried to defend it. He discerned that the protector in Wesley had gone into overdrive. The boy was determined to make sure that Sade and Mrs. Seabrooks were okay and that if any threat arose, he would resolve it himself. The pastor also discerned that the boy's way of thinking was out of balance. It lacked reasoning and judgment, and he needed to sit down and have a conversation with Wesley. In this moment, though, a phone conversation would have to suffice. He chose his next words carefully.

"That's true. Sometimes people come into worship who are not saved or who have no idea about church protocol or how to conduct themselves in worship. But let's refer to them as the unsaved and the unchurched, not as crazies. That way, if you or a part of the security team have to deal with them, you approach them from the perspective of love and mercy as opposed to manhandling someone in the spirit of anger and frustration. Even if an armed gunman showed up and tried to attack us, while the team is filling his or her body with lead, make no mistake about it, that led-filling is being carried out in the name of *Je-sus*," he joked, saying the name Jesus like one of the mothers of the church. Both Pastor Johnson and Wesley laughed, which was the pastor's goal. With the exception of the Holy Spirit, only three people could get through to Wesley like this: his dad, Pastor Johnson, and Lisa Monroe, who still didn't realize she had that kind of effect on him. Seeing that he'd made progress with him, Pastor Johnson continued, "Do you understand where I'm coming from, son?"

"Yes, sir. I feel you, Pastor. I just don't want anything else to happen to them, especially not…" He stumbled over his words. "I, uh, they've been through enough."

"Yes, they have, and by the grace of God, we're going to help them. If they'll allow us, we're going to be there for them to see them through to much better days than what they're experiencing right now, okay?"

"Okay."

"I'll see you in the morning, and I expect to see you right there by the Seabrooks' side. I love you, son. Good night."

"I love you too. Good night."

Wesley was breathing a sigh of relief, which was interrupted when his dad spoke up.

"'Especially not' what, son?"

Startled, Wesley spun around quickly with his hands up, prepared to defend himself. When he saw his dad, he dropped one hand to his side and put one on his chest while exhaling his response, "Whoa, Dad, you scared me!"

Mr. Heart's face was stern as he ignored Wesley's antics and continued. "I heard you tell Pastor Johnson, 'I just don't want anything else to happen to them, especially not…,' then you changed what you were about to say. My question is, 'especially not' what?"

"Oh, I…I don't know, Dad," he lied. "I think I said what I meant."

"Come on, Wesley, it's me you're talking to."

The boy dropped his head.

"Especially not on your watch? Is that what you wanted to say?" he asked, waiting for a response.

The boy nodded without looking up. "Yes, sir, it is. I have this pain in my heart that is just so hard to get rid of. I feel so out of control, Dad. I didn't just drop the ball, man, I crashed and burned. I let Sade down. I let Mrs. Seabrooks down. I just didn't…I didn't follow my heart that night. I heard Mrs. Seabrooks in there screaming, telling Sade to run to her uncle's house. That was my moment right there, Dad…right there! But I missed it. I keep asking myself what I was waiting for. I could tell by the sound of her voice that she was in serious trouble, but instead of moving in like my heart was telling me to do, I was still trying to respect this man's house because, after all, he was a man of God."

Wesley began to pace back and forth as his father looked on. Tears were streaming down his sweaty face when he stopped in his tracks, stared at his dad, and yelled, "Forget all that! He was no man of God! What kind of preacher would treat his family like that, leaving them for days at a time without so much as a phone call to make sure they were okay, no protection, no prayer, no covering? He broke his wife's nose, Dad! I'm sorry, but that ain't no man of God," he said, dropping his head. He stood there and wiped his tears as Mr. Heart listened. Wesley lowered his voice and continued.

"And then he'd show up days later after he'd been out screwing around on her?" He looked up at his dad and raised his voice again. "And he claimed he was doing it all in the name of the Lord, Dad! He was running revivals and preaching to the lost while his family was left hanging in the balance. There they were, the preacher's family, open to the attack of the enemy because the one who should have been covering them…oh, he was covering, all right. He was out *covering* some other woman's body, giving away what belonged only in his own house!" Wesley was in a zone that his dad had never witnessed before, but he knew that he needed to just let the boy talk through his thoughts and feelings. Thinking that he had gathered himself, Wesley continued.

"And not to mention Sade," he said, getting even louder. "He treated her as if his life's purpose were to make her miserable! She couldn't even enjoy her prom, Dad! Her last freakin' prom, man! And here I was, being the nice one, giving him the respect that he so-called deserved, when I knew I should have stopped him! I missed my moment three times, Dad! When he flung Sade, I should have handled him right then, but I didn't. Then when I heard Mrs. Seabrooks screaming and he went in after her, something was telling me, 'Move in, Wesley, grab him, stop him,' but there I was, frozen. And then when I finally had to put him in a headlock, like an idiot, I let him go! I should have choked him out!" the boy yelled, using an expletive, which was totally out of character.

"And then what, Wesley?" his dad asked, yelling back. "You choke him out, and then what? He eventually wakes up and it's business as usual for the Seabrooks family. Except now it would be worse because housed inside of that choked-out body, there's an ego gasping for air, trying to bully its way back to its previous status. Listen, son, it sounds like you've learned some really good lessons about what it means to be a real man. I thank God for that, because I haven't always been the best example for you. But the one lesson that you don't seem to get yet is the very first lesson: *you are not God*! Do you hear me?

"I know that you have been given a gift from God, son, and I know that you have all these abilities that most people don't have, and trust me, I pray that you will use your gifts to protect the people you love all the days of your life. But you got to understand, son, you are not God! Let me tell you something. Reverend Seabrooks is guilty of all the things you accused him of, and I'll tell you something else: it has been going on for a long time. But our duty has always been to pray for him and to let God deal with His preacher. He is the one who called him, and He knows how to handle him."

"Take a look at the end of the story, son, and listen to what I'm telling you," Mr. Heart implored, now preaching to the boy, evoking the use of slang. "You didn't choke him out 'cause you didn't have the authorization to do so. That's why in that moment, when you felt the pressure ease up on your leg, you didn't just release that headlock because it was the nice thing to do. Ya know why you did it? 'Cause your authorization expired! Is you listenin' to me? Listen to what I'm tellin' you! When God is on the scene, not even the policeman could take him out! He had the right equipment, and he even had the authority to shoot without one single charge being brought against him, but at God's command—do you hear me?—I said at God's command, son, even the officer's equipment malfunctioned because, in that moment, God removed the authorization. Is you listenin' to what I'm tellin' you?

"Because what you need to see is that God has a way of dealing with the people that He calls in a way that you and I cannot understand. Now, I don't know why Mrs. Seabrooks had to be the one God used to bring forth these results, but take a look at the outcome! The outcome, I tell ya! I said the outcome! The problem is gone, and although it might take a little while, Sade and Mrs. Seabrooks are going to be okay. And I'll tell you something else, son, she gon' get off scot-free.

"But now, what if you had gone up in that house that night, trying to be Big Billy Bad, huh, son? You would be in jail right now! And with your big, overgrown self, you know they would charge you as an adult. I can see the headlines now: STATE-CHAMPION HIGH SCHOOL WRESTLING STANDOUT ARRESTED FOR ASSAULTING A LOCAL PREACHER. Is you listenin' to me, son? So you got to understand this…that God is God and you are not. And when God gets ready to take care of what's His, there's nothing you can do to alter it and nothing you can do to stop it.

"Now, Wesley, it's in your best interest to stop judging what God has done. Stop replaying it in your mind. Stop saying, 'If only I had done this or that,' but lift up your head and say, 'To God be the glory for the things that *He* has done.'"

He made is way over to his son, who was standing across the shed. He repeated his words as he walked toward Wesley, who was nodding and wiping his final tears.

"To God be the glory for the things that *He* has done," Wes's dad said again. He extended his arms toward his son, and they embraced as they repeated together, "To God be the glory for the things that *He* has done."

Chapter 16

Sade never called Tara's phone that night. As it turned out, Wesley and his dad were not the only ones who had a very intense conversation. Sade and her mom did too. They talked about how life had been over the years, and Mrs. Seabrooks told Sade that her husband had become more and more threatening and verbally abusive over the past couple of years. What *was* a total surprise to her, however, was Sade's response.

"Yeah, I know, Mom," she confirmed. "I've watched and listened to y'all for a very long time. I've also listened to your phone conversations with him, and I know how bad the situation had gotten. Mom, I never told anyone, but when things started getting so bad, I used to think about ending it all." Ms. Seabrooks's heart fluttered, and she immediately began to cry. "Mama, please don't cry. I'm okay now, and I'm only sharing this with you because we're putting everything out in the open, and I want us to have the loving, trusting relationship that we deserve to have with each other. You've cried enough for both of us over the years and, God knows, over the past few days. But we're going to be okay."

"Sade, I want to make sure that you're okay, baby. Please, let's go together and talk to a therapist."

"Mama, please! Just listen to me. I don't mind talking to a therapist, but not about that. Those days are behind me now, okay?"

"But how can you be so sure, Sade? How do you know that something can't trigger those thoughts again?"

"Because the person who was triggering those thoughts is gone, Mama. He's dead, and I...I won't say I'm glad he's dead, but I'm glad that he is out of our lives! I hated him, Mama! I hated him for the way he treated you, and I hated him for the way he treated me. I even hated the church!"

"Sade!"

"I did, and for a long time, Mama! And I didn't like feeling that way. One day I prayed about it, because I knew it wasn't right. After doing some real soul-searching, I discovered that I actually liked most of the people at church. It was the pastor I had a problem with. So since the pastor happened to be my dad, my disgust carried over to the church. I know that *hate* is a strong word, but I also know that I shouldn't have had to be terrified of my own father. I shouldn't have had to look over my shoulder, wondering what kind of scene he was going to make at one of the games. I shouldn't have had to worry whether I was going to come home one evening to find that the two of you had been in an argument and that he had injured you in some way.

"So the more I thought about it, the more my thoughts moved away from suicide. I made up my mind that if he ever put his hands on you, I was going to kill *him*. I knew that each of you had a gun, and I knew yours was in your bottom dresser drawer and his was in the glove box of his Escalade. I researched how to use each one, where to shoot a person, and how many times."

"Oh, Sade!" she gasped. "I'm so sorry I put you through that. I should have left him years ago. I just had so much hope that things were going to get better. I never imagined that they would get so much worse. I never thought I would ever kill anyone…much less, God forbid, my own husband. But what was I to do? Was I to let him cut Wesley's throat or harm you? So I did what I had to do. I'm still dealing with all my feelings and emotions about everything, but I'll get through it. I just know I would never forgive myself if I had let something happen to you or that young man, who is such a beautiful soul."

"Okay, Mama, you know what? Let's change the subject. I can't do any more intense stuff tonight. I don't know how else to end a conversation like this, and like I said, you've done enough crying for a while. Furthermore, we are not going to put an angel like Wesley into a conversation with…well, you know. So like you said, I need to keep my therapy appointments, and uh, you can continue yours."

"That's a good decision, baby. A good therapist can help you to heal so much better and faster—the kind of healing that takes place down in your soul. Of course, a good dose of Jesus can too, ya know. And speaking of Wesley, I couldn't tell you earlier because you were so distraught when you came home, but he and his sister came to see you today."

"Mama!" Sade exclaimed, trying to be upset with her, but her teeth just wouldn't stop shining through the huge grin on her face.

"I was going to tell you as soon as I had the chance, but we needed to have this talk tonight."

"We did, but you could have…why didn't you…Mamaaa! I've been wanting to see him so badly.…I want to apologize to him, and hold him…just to let him know how much he means to me…and to you…but his mom…his…Mama, I-I…"

Sade stopped speaking. Just that quickly, she was crying and trying to figure out where her words escaped to and why she couldn't breathe. She couldn't tell whether she was overjoyed or upset or both. She felt like she was losing it, but she was actually in the midst of a panic attack and had begun hyperventilating.

Her mother rushed to her side and grabbed her daughter's hands and put them up to Sade's mouth. "Cup your hands and breathe into your hands, baby," she instructed. "Shhhh…calm down, baby," she said softly. "Just breathe into your hands, like this," she demonstrated. "It's okay, I got you. Let's get your breathing under control, then I'll tell you the good news."

Hearing that there was good news, Sade worked hard to control her breathing so she could hear what else her mother had to say about Wesley. Mrs. Seabrooks hurried into the kitchen to find a bag for Sade to breathe into. Once Sade had calmed down, her mother talked to her about her visit with Wesley and Tara and how it had helped her so much.

"Listen, it's okay. You can see him tomorrow. They invited us to come to church, all right? No talking right now. Just breathe. I know you're excited to see him. You've got a lot to tell him, and he has a lot to say to you too. But right now you gotta calm down so that you actually get to see him in the morning. Shhh…breathe in, breathe out. That's good, just breathe in and out. Slow, calm breaths. Okay, that's good. Nice and calm. We got to get our clothes together, get our showers, and get our beauty rest. That's better." She held her daughter tenderly and rubbed her back. Sade was better, but she was enjoying being in her mother's arms again.

"I love you, Mama," the young woman whispered.

"I love you too, Sade. Whew, you had me scared for a minute, girl. That fine young man has you over here about to pass out on me." She chuckled.

"You are not funny."

"I'm just trying to get you to smile, sweetie. He was in tears today too, ya know. He wants to see you just as much as you want to see him, and he is not wanting to talk about the details of that night, do you hear me? That's what therapy is for," she said, giving Sade a stern look.

"Okay, that's cool. I don't want to talk about any of that either."

"Good. Now, come on, it's getting late. We gotta get you ready. You are going to be the sharpest thing in that church tomorrow."

"Mama, they don't dress up like that at his church."

"Well, *you* can still be sharp. Now, come on."

Perhaps it was just the night for intense conversations, because by the time Mrs. Heart got through with Tara, the word *intense* had a new definition! Thankfully, Mr. Heart and Wesley went back in the house after Wesley apologized to his dad for his language. He explained that he wasn't even sure where the words came from and that he had never used them before, except in his head. Mr. Heart jokingly told Wesley that, thanks to his father, the language was unfortunately ingrained into his DNA, but he was glad to see that Wesley regretted it.

Once they were inside, Mr. Heart spoke up for Tara. He simply told his wife that she had gone overboard with Wesley and that the restrictions she had imposed on him, which limited his contact with Sade and Mrs. Seabrooks, should have been mandated by his therapist and not her. He told her that both Wesley and Tara were out of line and they recognized their error, but she was taking things way too far. In actuality, Tara had already defended her own case, and her mother knew that she had been extreme. But she wasn't willing to back down so easily to Tara, until Mr. Heart came in. After he addressed the situation, she looked Tara and Wesley up and down and said, "This conversation is *not* over," as she headed toward her bedroom.

"This conversation is very much over," Mr. Heart contradicted. "Now, everyone go get cleaned up and ready for a wonderful worship service tomorrow. As a matter of fact, come on, all of y'all. Let's pray. Come on over here. We can't let the sun go down on our wrath." Mrs. Heart, though she rolled her eyes, turned around and came back into the living room to pray.

Wesley's dad had a tendency to use scriptures, songs, and repetition when he prayed. It wasn't the vain repetition that Jesus criticized in the Bible but the type of repetitious praying that expressed sincerity and the true intent of his heart. He prayed for each one of them, asking for forgiveness and for the mending of the broken breeches. "Blessed be the tie that binds our hearts in Christian love and fellowship," he prayed. "Father, we repent of the error of our ways. For each one of us has sinned, and sometimes we fall short of Your glory. We want to do things our way and to carry out our own agendas. But that's how we end up making a mess of things, it's where we find ourselves getting into trouble. But, Father, we have found You to be a very present help in the time of trouble, so we turn our hearts back to You. We turn our hearts back to You, Father! We lay down our own agendas, and we turn our hearts back to You. And as we do so, I believe that we will discover that the Seabrooks family situation is far more important than our little agendas."

As Mr. Heart continued to pray, he lit in on the Seabrooks "situation." He prayed for them both individually, then he asked God to unify them like never before. By the time he finished praying, he had prayed over Mrs. Heart, Tara, and Wesley too, and all of them were in tears as they apologized to one another, acknowledging their shortcomings and asking one another for forgiveness. Mrs. Heart was in awe of this man who ruled his house with God-given authority and grace. Tears threatened when she thought about the person he used to be versus who he had become. God had truly done a work in this man of hers, changing him from the inside out.

Chapter 17

The plan for Wesley to sit with the Seabrooks might not have been the best idea. It drew attention to his guests, revealing their identities even to most of the congregation who did not know them personally. He had not been on duty to work security since the incident happened. Rather, he had sat with his parents and was careful not to entertain any questions, as both his therapist and Pastor Johnson had instructed. Most Miracle Center members had known about the situation since the Sunday morning after it happened. Pastor Johnson had given a brief overview to the church and told them that he wanted them to hear the truth and not to entertain rumors. He had the gifting to communicate such news in a way that was extremely supportive of each victim involved while simultaneously exposing the foiled plan of the enemy and victorious hand of God. He had managed to get a verbal commitment from the members of the congregation who were in attendance to refrain from gossiping about it but rather to pray.

Now, only a couple of weeks after the incident, Mrs. Seabrooks and Sade were actually in their church, worshipping with them. Pastor Johnson knew that he had to address the congregation again, so he seized the moment immediately after praise and worship to provide a blanket address to the congregation regarding treating people with respect, love, and mercy. He talked to them about how Miracle Center was a place for people to be able to come and find that love and mercy and how it was not the place for gossips and busybodies, and if that ever changed, then they might as well lock the doors, because that was not what Miracle Center was intended to be.

Worship that morning was a beautiful experience. Pastor Johnson took his time with the Word. He preached about how love has more to do with action than mere words. He talked about how God demonstrated His love toward man as opposed to just talking about it. He used this to make his point about how Christians, too, are expected to demonstrate the love they say they have for one another. As he preached his sermon, he had Sade's full attention.

"In John 14:15, Jesus said to His disciples, 'If you love me, keep my commandments.' In other words, if you love me, the way to prove that love is by demonstrating it. Don't just tell me that you love me and then talk about me behind my back. Don't just tell me that you love me. If you see that I'm hungry, you can at least make me a sammich or two," he said, evoking both "Amens" and laughter from the congregation. "If you really love me, you won't treat me just any old way. Love has far more to do with action than it does mere words."

Pastor Johnson continued his teaching on love and how it must be demonstrated and not just spoken. As he preached, Sade listened. She was so in awe of God's presence during the course of the worship service. Pastor Johnson's teaching was so clear and concise too. It lacked the fanfare and hype that were always present when her dad preached, but the impact of his teaching made her feel as if she were being cleansed down in her soul. As she listened to the Word of God being taught, she thought about how her mother had always been there for her and gone out of her way to make sure that she had everything she needed and most of what she wanted. More importantly, her mother had done her absolute best to teach her how to love people and to always believe the best for them.

This led to thoughts of her deceased father. As she thought about him, she tried to reason that he really did love her in his own way. But Pastor Johnson shifted to 1 Corinthians 13 and blew that line of reasoning out of the water. He was teaching about the different characteristics of love. "Love suffers long and is kind; love does not envy, love does not parade itself, is not puffed up, does not behave rudely, does not seek its own." The more he read and taught the Scriptures, the more Sade became convinced that her dad didn't really love her after all. She tried switching her mind back to the happy thoughts about her mom, as she was determined that her dad was not going to control her from the grave, but she found it difficult to make the switch.

Eventually, her mind landed on Wesley and how it was so obvious that the love of God was in him. He was always good for her. Now, she simply wanted the service to be over so she could spend some time talking to him and telling him what was on her mind. When she came to herself, Pastor Johnson was asking everyone to stand, and she recognized that it was time for the altar call. She knew that she needed prayer, and as she stood up, she was nervous and undecided about whether or not to go to the altar for prayer. But before she could get settled in her nervousness, she noticed that four people had already made their way to the altar even before the full invitation had been given. Although this was the norm for Miracle Center, it was not normal for Sade. It warmed her heart that there were people who were so moved by the presence of God and by His message that they were eager to get to the altar for prayer. They came, knelt, and began to pray as the ushers and a couple of ministers came to assist them and to pray with them.

Not knowing what to do with the mix of emotions she'd just experienced, Sade began to zone out. It was as if she were having an out-of-body experience. She saw herself crying and slowly walking down to the altar as Pastor Johnson extended the invitation to all. She saw Wesley join her, as well as her mother and Mr. and Mrs. Heart. She saw herself fall to her knees, praying to God in a way that she had never prayed before. She prayed both through her sobs and her pain as a female altar worker joined her on her knees and held her while she prayed. As she looked on, she could tell that it gave her great comfort to know that she was not alone. She had several people in her corner, including a complete stranger, holding her and letting her know that everything was going to be all right.

But Sade was not all right. This vision she was experiencing was just something that her mind had created. She was still standing there in the same spot, and when she came to herself, her mother was placing her arm around her and whispering in her ear. "Come on,

Sade," she said. "It's okay, baby. We're just going for prayer. Come on."

As she listened to her mother's gentle nudging to come with her to the altar, she realized that she had obviously been out of it for a few seconds, as her mother seemed to be trying to convince her to move. She was almost embarrassed and thought for a split second that she was going to have another panic attack. She took a deep breath and looked to her left at Wesley. He noticed her mom's arm around her, but he was not at all aware that she had been trying to convince Sade to go to the altar for prayer. With a sincere smile on his face, he spoke aloud to Sade as if they weren't in church and said, "I don't know about you, but I sure could use some prayer right now. Wanna go with me?"

"Uh…yeah," she agreed. "Come on, Mama." Dumbfounded, her mom grabbed her hand as Wesley led them to the altar for prayer. When they got to the altar, Wesley said, "Pastor, I'm here with my friends today, and each one of us is in need of prayer." Right on cue, Tara directed the choir to sing louder. Pastor Johnson greeted Mrs. Seabrooks with a smile and a hug. He seized the moment to remind her that he and Sister Johnson were there for her and Sade and that if they or Miracle Center could be of service to them at any time, all she needed to do was to reach out to them. He also greeted Sade. He told her that she was a beautiful young lady and that, in spite of every-thing she was going through, God had her in the palm of His hands. He told her that he had been praying for her and that he had some instructions for her if she was willing to receive them. He instructed Mrs. Seabrooks to listen in as well.

He first told Sade that it was not a coincidence that they were at church today because he had already told Sister Johnson that they needed to pay Sade and her mother a visit today. He continued by saying, "God is so faithful. First, He confirmed the importance of what He wanted me to tell you by giving me a sense of urgency. Then He didn't even give me time to get through this service and over to your house—He sent you to me. So indulge me for a moment as I share what the Lord wants to communicate to you. He wants you to know, first of all, that you are not losing your mind. When you find yourself zoning out and running different scenarios through your mind, do not allow those times to overwhelm you. That's the time for you to pray and stand firm on what you believe. God said to tell you not to let your mind just do its own thing but to use the power of Jesus's name to command your mind toward what is good and wholesome. Does that make sense, Sade?"

"Yes, sir, it does," she replied.

"The next two instructions are related to the first one. God has empowered certain people to help you on the road to recovery. These people have been given special power from the Lord to help you. We call that power the anointing. Are you following me?"

"Yes, sir."

"One group of people are the professionals that He has put into your life, such as your therapist. It is very important for you to attend your therapy sessions, take any prescribed medications, and follow the instructions your therapist gives you, because this person has been granted a measure of authority by Almighty God to minister directly to Sade Seabrooks. Understand?"

"Yes, sir. Honestly, I haven't been going, but I will start back. I promise," she assured him as tears came to her eyes.

"That's okay, Sade. It's good that you recognize you need to get back on track. God wants you to know that He has already prepared another therapist for you, in the city that your college is in, and that your current therapist will be the one to connect the two of you. God has also anointed others to help you, like the two people on either side of you. Now, your mother has been anointed to take care of you since the time that you were a mere embryo in her womb. She's done a great job so far. Don't you agree with me?"

"Yes, sir, I agree with you 100 percent," Sade said, squeezing her mother's hand and looking over at her. Mrs. Seabrooks, who was already crying, began to cry harder, although she was trying hard not to. Sade released her mother's hand and gripped her in a full embrace as the ushers stepped in closer to assist them. "I love you, Mama," she said fiercely, "and we're gonna be okay."

"Yes, we are, and I love you too, baby," Mrs. Seabrooks whispered, pulling herself together. She was grateful for the ushers' comforting presence and even more grateful to see that Mr. and Mrs. Heart had also joined them at the altar for support.

"Now, here's the key, Sade," Pastor Johnson continued. "Your mother doesn't lose the anointing to take care of you just because you reach a certain age. Granted, a part of her responsibility in taking care of you is teaching you to spread your wings and fly on your own. But listen to what I'm telling you. Even when you are fully grown, living on your own, and able to sustain yourself, she will always have wisdom for you that can help to keep you grounded and pointed in the right direction, because she has been anointed specifically for you. So honor your mother, Sade. Listen to what she has to say and be obedient. Are you still with me?"

"Yes, sir."

"Now, as for people like Wesley, God puts such people in your life to also be there for you. This young man is one of a kind. If he has made up his mind that he's going to be your friend, he's going to be there for you, no matter what. So be mindful of these relationships, Sade, and don't push these very special people away.

"Finally, you must keep your spirit fed. Go to church, engage in fellowship, read the Word of God, and make sure that you are praying on a very regular basis. This will keep your spirit strong. It will help you to make sound decisions and to maintain an attitude of faith and confidence in God no matter what may be going on around you.

"Furthermore, if you keep your spirit strong, your flesh will not be able to just do what it wants to do. You see, as a human being, you are made up of spirit, mind, and body. Certain attributes are spiritual attributes, such as faith, hope, love, power, joy, peace, victory, and the like. Other attributes are connected to your flesh, such as sensuality, anger, doubt, confusion, passions, inordinate appetites, hatred, lust, and the like. Well, your mind, which is sometimes also referred to as your soul, is a neutral component. It is going to be led by whichever is stronger—the spiritual or the physical—and that is determined by whichever is fed the most. So that is why you have to feed your spirit on purpose. The natural man, the body, is fed automatically by all the negativity around us at all times. But feeding the spirit man has to be done intentionally. It is not automatic, it's intentional, Sade. Are you listening to me?"

"Yes, sir."

"Do you understand the instructions?"

"Yes, sir, I got it."

Wesley knew what was coming next. He had been listening attentively and had already prepared himself to assist Sade in answering his pastor's inevitable next question. Without skipping a beat, Pastor Johnson asked, "What did I say?"

"You said that I have to be intentional about feeding my spirit by going to church, reading my Bible, and praying throughout each day. I have to truly value the people that God has given the anointing to take care of me in one way or another, and I have to take authority over my mind through the power of Jesus's name and not let it just have free reign."

Wesley was both relieved and impressed by Sade's accurate response. It meant less work for him to try to help Sade recall all that Pastor Johnson had said.

"You got it, Sade!" Pastor Johnson said. "Just follow those instructions and you will be just fine. Follow the instructions, now. Are you listening to me?"

"Yes, sir," she assured the man of God.

"What did I say?"

"You said if I follow the instructions, I will be fine," she confirmed with a smile.

Pastor Johnson put his hand in the air for a high five, and Sade slapped it with authority.

"Well, I want to pray for the three of you. I've been praying for each of you, but the Lord, in His infinite wisdom, gave me specific instructions only for Sade. The good thing is that He knows what He's doing. Do you trust Him, Wesley?"

"Yes, sir."

"Sade?"

"Yes, sir."

"Ms. Melissa?"

"Oh, yes. I trust Him with all my heart."

195

"All right, let's pray."

As he led them in prayer, Mrs. Seabrooks was so overwhelmed with joy that she couldn't help but cry. She tried to control it, but she was just so grateful for all that God had done to bring them to this point in time, from sending Wesley and Tara to her house, to the sermon, to the prayer itself. Though it was normal for Pastor Johnson and the people at Miracle Center, it was mind-boggling to her for God to have given such accurate and specific instructions to Sade through Pastor Johnson.

After church, the Hearts, Johnsons, and Seabrooks went out for dinner at Rebecca's Cafeteria. Mr. and Mrs. Heart found a new friend in Mrs. Seabrooks. She was a beautiful soul, and they were glad to have the opportunity to sit down and dine with her. It was there that Mrs. Heart and Mrs. Seabrooks discovered that although they didn't really know each other, they had actually attended the same college, North Carolina A&T, during the same time for a full year before Mrs. Heart had to leave to change duty stations with her husband. Mrs. Seabrooks shared how happy she was that Sade had been offered both an academic and a cheerleading scholarship there and that she had accepted.

While everyone was congratulating Sade, she seized the moment to relish in the fact that the people around her in that particular moment were genuinely proud of and happy for her, with no strings attached and no ulterior motives, like being celebrated as a show-piece, the kind of crap her father had always done. Rather, this was a pure moment of celebration of her and for her, and it felt good. She was not used to this, and it reminded her of how she felt on the night of her prom when Wesley treated her with so much attentiveness. She looked at him and smiled as she reminisced.

"Oh, so when were you going to tell me, Sade?" he asked, smiling back.

"I wanted to tell you, but I haven't been able to talk to you."

"Well, I can't argue that," Wesley agreed.

Mrs. Heart heard the exchange but acted as if she hadn't. She continued talking to Mrs. Seabrooks about people they knew in common and other aspects of life. She really wanted to hug Mrs.

Seabrooks and thank her for being so courageous, to let her know that she fully realized that it was quite possibly because of her actions that her son was alive today. She wasn't sure if this was the right setting, nor was she sure of exactly what to say. She really didn't know whether she should say anything at all about it. She did know that it probably wasn't a good idea for her to say anything about it as long as Sade was sitting nearby. As if reading her mother's mind, Tara spoke up.

"If you'll excuse us, the young people are going to carry our conversation outside. We have some catching up to do among ourselves."

Mrs. Heart was both glad about and upset by Tara's statement. She was glad because the timing was perfect, considering her recent thoughts that she could have a more meaningful conversation with Mrs. Seabrooks without Sade present. She was upset because she felt as if she wasn't fully prepared to have the conversation. Mr. Heart, however, unknowingly came to her rescue. Since he had given his life to the Lord, he had become the type of person who believed that if God places something in your heart, there's no use beating around the bush trying to word it perfectly or figure out what should or shouldn't be said. He'd much rather ask for forgiveness than permission, and in most cases, he was very much in tune with the Holy Spirit, because his intentions were pure.

"Ms. Melissa," he began, "you have to be one of the most courageous people I've ever met. You have done a bang-up job raising Sade. She's a beautiful young lady inside and out, and I know it's because of the role you've played in her life. I wish we all could just wrap our arms around you and make everything all right, but we all know that life is not that simple. Truth is, Ms. Melissa, we can't even imagine what you must be going through, but I want you to know that we are here for you.

"Now, I'm sure that Pastor Johnson wants to say a few things to you, but I don't want us to go any further without offering you an apology on behalf of my wife and myself. We made a decision that we thought was right by putting some distance between Wesley and you and Sade after...well, you know, after everything happened. But it was absolutely the wrong thing to do. Actually, we didn't know *what* to do in a situation like this, and it was as if we were trying to feel our way through the dark. If you really want us to tell the whole truth, we still don't know.

"Ms. Melissa, we owe you not only an apology but also a thank-you. Our son is alive and well today quite possibly because of your actions. But when we look at what saving our son cost you, we don't even know if saying thank-you is appropriate. But our goal is to let you know that we want to do right by you, and if we have offended you or if we happen to offend you in any way in the future, please know that it is not intentional. We need one another, Ms. Melissa. We are much stronger together, and whatever we can do as a family to help you on this journey, I want you to know that we are in your corner."

The conversation inside continued. It was a sincere time of healing and reconciliation for Mrs. Seabrooks, who had been dealing with her own feelings of bitterness and resentment not only toward her deceased husband but also toward herself. She still hadn't fully forgiven herself for ending her husband's life, and even after the events of today, she realized she would still need to continue the therapy sessions she had been faithfully attending. But today represented a huge step in the way of progress because she had not been attending church until today; aside from her brother, she had not had any real fellowship with anyone, and she had not seen Sade being so vibrant and present as she had been today. Thus, she was taking full advantage of the show of love and support evidenced today.

Outside, Wesley and Sade seized the moment to catch up as Tara gave them a little bit of space. Somehow, their conversation made its way back to the night of the prom as Sade reminisced about how well Wesley treated her. "Wesley, can I ask you a question?"

"Have you forgotten, Sade, that you can ask me anything?"

"So today marks three weeks and a day since we last saw or even talked to each other. If things hadn't gone down like they did with my dad, where do you think we would be in our relationship?"

Relationship? he thought. *Oh boy, here we go.*

"Uh, I'm not sure what you mean, Sade."

"I mean, do you think that we could be in a real relationship by now?"

Oh my gosh…no! he wanted to shout. Instead, he smiled at her.

"Sade, I consider you a very special friend, and I think you and I are better for each other as just that…friends."

"So are you saying that you don't want there to be anything between us?" she asked, realizing that she was showing too much attitude. "I mean, I've been thinking a lot about how much attention you showed me, not to mention how much money you spent just for me. Guys just don't do those things unless they want something in return. I want you to know, Wesley, I'm ready to give you what you're looking for. Please don't think I'm trying to rush you into anything you're not ready for, but I do want you to know that I am ready for 'us' and that I am more than okay if you want us to go slow and take our time."

Okay, Sade, please just stop talking right now, he thought. *And furthermore, where is Tara when I need her?*

Wesley tried to gather his thoughts, which seemed to be playing hide-and-seek at the moment. He recognized that he didn't need to leave too much space between her statement and his response, but he was at a loss for words.

"Sade, I…uh…can I have a hug?" he asked, not knowing what else to say in the moment. In his mind, he prayed frantically, *Holy Spirit, I need You. Come on, help me out here. This is harder than I thought.* Immediately, he thought about Pastor Johnson's sermon on love and how it was something that needed to be demonstrated and not just spoken. He knew that he had to tell her the truth but also that he had to be careful about how he said what he needed to say.

"I love you, Sade."

"I love you too," she returned as she gave him a squeeze.

He then pulled away from her and said, "Let's go for a walk."

"All right!" she agreed excitedly.

He noticed that Tara was just around the corner and had probably been listening to their conversation the whole time. He gave her a thumbs-up as they walked around the parking lot. She hesitantly returned a thumbs-up.

"I've been thinking about your prom night as well. I had the time of my life. I can't think of anyone else that I would have had more fun with at a prom."

"Who are you kidding, Wesley?" she asked. "What about Mackenzie Carson? Based on what I saw on social media, it appears that you two would have hit it off pretty well," she said with a teasing smile.

"To that, I'll just say, things are not always as they seem."

"So it *seemed* like she asked you to the prom in front of everyone, and you picked her up and cradled her in your arms, and in front of everyone you basically said, 'I'll have to think about it.' Then, in response, she sticks her tongue down your throat! You rock, Wesley Heart!" The two teens laughed.

"You sound like my track coach," he responded. "That's *not* what happened. I mean that is what happened, but it was not like that."

"You sound confused, man," she said, laughing at him. He couldn't help but laugh along with her. As he tried to explain himself, she kept interrupting.

"You sound as confused as you were about funny business. Sooo wait. What you and Carson were doing, was *that* funny business? Oh, no, wait, that was probably more like monkey business."

Wesley was so glad to see Sade in such a good mood that he stopped trying to defend his position and just let her enjoy this laugh at his expense. Tara, who was watching them, could also hear them laughing and having a good time. She was also glad to see this from Sade. As the laughter came to an end, Wesley used it along with the reference to funny business as a segue to get back to the matter at hand—Sade's crazy proposition.

"Anyhow, all that reminds me of the awesome time I had with you at your prom. Not Mackenzie's, yours. But the way that I treated you is just a result of who I am."

"So are you telling me that you would have treated Mackenzie the same way?"

"What I was trying to tell you when I was so rudely interrupted was that I wouldn't have gone to the prom with Mackenzie even if I didn't have anything whatsoever planned for that evening. She's not my type."

"But isn't she, like, the queen of your school?"

"Yep. But she's not my queen."

"So who is your queen?"

My queen's name is Lisa, he thought.

"Uh, I don't have one," he lied. "I'm just not ready for that. I'm very focused on my future, my grades, and my athletics, and since everything happened, I have become even more focused."

"Do you mean since the night of the shooting? It's okay to say it. That *is* what happened that night, and I've had to come to terms with that. My mother shot and killed my dad. Now, I'm not glad that my father is dead, but I'm glad that my mom took the necessary action that possibly saved your life and mine. She did what she had to do. She did what any good mother would have done, and I am thankful."

Not knowing how to respond to that, Wesley just rephrased and continued, "I agree, so yes, since the night of the shooting, I realize just how precious life is and how all I have is what's in my hand at this moment. You are a beautiful person both inside and out. You are about to enter into college, and you need to be focused on your studies. I am entering my junior year of high school, and I am so focused on getting into the right college I really don't have time for a relationship, even though, I have to admit, a relationship with you would be very interesting, Sade. I just don't think it will work, though. You'll be in North Carolina, and I'll be here in Columbia, selfishly engaged in getting better and studying hard. You would break up with me before we ever got started good." He said this in an attempt to bring a little levity to the situation.

"Yeah, I guess you're right. I really wasn't thinking about all that. I was just thinking about how nice it would be to have a future with a guy like you. I guess I was being a little selfish too. That *would* be kind of weird if I'm in college while you're still in high school."

Wesley was thankful that this conversation wasn't as difficult as he had anticipated, given the way it began. "If a relationship is what you're looking for," he continued, "I'm sure you won't have any problem at all being discovered by a nice guy at A&T. Trust me, they're going to be scoping you out from day one."

"I've never had an issue with guys coming on to me," she returned. "I just feel like, if you're going to approach someone, you should have something to offer."

"True, but we're talking about high school kids, Sade. Most of us don't have anything to offer anybody."

"I'm not referring to material things. I'm talking about the basics, like bathing and brushing your teeth, getting a haircut, or at least combing it, ya know! But don't be up in my face and your breath smells like pimento cheese and beer and your hair smells like you washed it in marijuana-scented shampoo."

"Whoa!" He laughed. "You mad, sis?"

Sade laughed. "I'm just saying, a sista needs to know that you at least care about yourself before you start trying to invite her into your world. Take you, for example. I didn't say anything on prom night, but I noticed that even your hands were soft and your nails and cuticles were clean and trimmed. I mean, do you get manicures or something? Women notice that kind of stuff, man."

"Well, my mom made me get one for the prom, but, Sade, some people can't afford that kind of stuff, ya know. I'm grateful that my mom makes decent money as a nurse and my dad has a really good job, plus he's retired from the military, but that's not everybody's story."

"That's bull crap, Wesley! While there are some people who are truly struggling, the way I see it, if you can afford Jordans and every video game ever created…if you can afford to get high and drunk every other day, you can afford to pay better attention to your personal hygiene, dangit!"

Wesley had stopped walking, causing Sade to stop too as she finished her rant. "Whoooo weee!" Wesley muttered. "I think we struck a nerve over here! What happened to the quiet, reserved, smooth Sade?"

"Look, all I'm saying is, people can spend their money on whatever they want to. Just don't be up in my face if you can't come correct. Besides," she continued as they resumed walking, "even with the cool guys, as long as my dad was in the picture, I couldn't have a meaningful relationship with anyone unless it was like super secretive."

"Super secretive?"

"Yes. Super. He checked all my text messages and social media accounts. He insisted on having all my passwords. You name it."

"I guess you never really know what a person is going through."

"You don't even know half of the story, man. He made my life so miserable. I was so shocked when I told him that I wanted to invite you to be my prom date and he didn't seem to have a problem with that. He just said, 'That boy is going to be famous in a few years,' and walked out of the room. He was the reason it took me so long to ask you. I just knew that he was going to come back and veto the whole thing, but he never did. And when we were at the mall together, he was the reason I was so distraught. He and Mama had been arguing for days, and I just knew that my phone was going to ring and he was going to tell me that I couldn't go with you. I was trying so hard to take it all in and enjoy my time with you that day. I was even going to try to sneak in a kiss right there in the restaurant lobby because I just wanted to be selfish for a moment in case he called and abruptly ended everything. I know that I was being very forward. Trust me, I've replayed all these things over and over in my mind, and I apologize if I have offended you in any way. It's like I'm coming out of a big hole that I have been trapped inside of for so long, and now that I'm out, I have to learn how to live on the outside with balance and discipline. That's what my therapist was trying to show me before I stopped going."

"That's a lot to have to deal with, and it sounds like life outside of this hole can be dangerous without the discipline and structure that your therapist talked about."

"Yeah, but I think I'm pretty balanced."

"Are you?" he asked.

"Yeah, don't you think so?"

"I'll answer you only if you can handle an honest response coming from a true friend."

"Shoot it, friend."

"Okay," he agreed. He knew that what he had to say was going to be a little rough. He stopped walking again and faced Sade. He grabbed her hands and held them firmly in his. He looked her in the eyes and said, "You're talking to me about the idea of us having a relationship, knowing that you're headed off to college. You're refusing to attend your therapy sessions, which is a form of self-care, yet you're talking about other people who don't care for themselves. And you know full well that this is the same kind of mental health care that your father needed and refused, but here you are, doing the same thing. So no, I don't think you're balanced, Sade, not because you're a bad person, but because you *just* came out of that hole your therapist talked about. And the circumstances that led to you coming out were very tragic and traumatic for you. I don't think *anyone* could be balanced after going through what you went through just a few short weeks ago. And when you add to that the way of life you were accustomed to before that horrible night, it's going to take some time for you to achieve balance, my friend."

"I guess I'm pretty messed up, huh?"

"No, you're not messed up. If we were talking about strength, I would be calling you a beast right about now! But becoming balanced after all you've been through, well, it's just going to take some time…and of course, the other intentional things that Pastor Johnson expressed to you today. But you need to take care of your mental health. Listen, I had a long discussion with my family just last night, and I have to admit, I had to repent of some things too."

Before she could ask him what it was and find out that he was being a little hypocritical regarding his feelings about his therapist, he quickly resumed his lecture. "So when we see ourselves in error, we have to repent and fix the problems. It's when we refuse to do so that we end up all messed up."

Tara had noticed how serious the conversation seemed when she saw Wesley stop and grab Sade's hands. When Wesley looked up, she was heading toward them.

"Sade, I promise to always be your friend. I'll support you when you're right and tell you when you're wrong. I need you to be strong and to keep working to find that balance. I hope you will make the same commitment to me."

"After what we went through together, I think that would only be right," she said.

"And please, let's stay in touch with each other, because I really want us to have a very strong friendship. Can we promise each other that too?"

"I promise, Wesley."

Sade had that seal-it-with-a-kiss look on her face, and Wesley recognized it instantly. *Stop it, Sade. Did you not comprehend anything we just talked about? Just stop,* he thought to himself.

"So uh...pinky swear?" he asked quickly, extending his pinky toward her.

"Uh...yeah, sure. Pinky swear," she replied disappointedly.

Chapter 18

As promised, Sade resumed her counseling sessions. She made significant progress, and by the time she was ready to begin college, her therapist had found another therapist that she trusted, located near A&T in Greensboro, just as the Lord had prophesied through Pastor Johnson. She and Wesley remained in touch with each other, and she jokingly reminded him on occasion that if he ever changed his mind about having a relationship with her, she would be ready, even if it meant breaking up with whomever she might be dating at that time. Although she was mostly kidding around with him, she knew deep down that her statement was actually true. She also knew that chances were slim to none that they would ever end up together.

For now, she was enjoying her freedom as a new college student, her freedom as a young woman with her entire life ahead of her, and her freedom from the control of her dad. She had never felt more liberated in her life. Her mom was doing well, and she fully supported Sade, encouraging her to make the most of her college journey. She also encouraged her more than anything to find a church to attend and stay connected to God. While she respected her mother's advice, her church attendance was normally not as strong as she often reported. In general, however, she was doing okay, taking life one day at a time. After her first year of college, her communication with Wesley also became less frequent due to both of their schedules being busy. She missed him, but she was good with occasional communication, as long as their friendship was intact.

As a high school junior, Wesley was fully focused on being the best student athlete possible. He had taken his coach's advice from a few months back and was on his way to becoming a true leader in his school among athletes. His leadership journey had begun not long after his conversation with his coach last spring at the Shawn Cathcart Camp for gifted wrestlers. He met a senior wrestler there from Greensboro who was struggling to catch his breath after a conditioning session, which he knew was indicative of poor training and preparation outside the ring. He took time to talk to the guy, whose name was Roquan. He showed him a technique that helped with the breathing, then he talked to him during the lunch break about the importance of putting his heart into his training. He reminded him that he had not been invited to train with an Olympic gold medalist by happenstance but because he was an elite wrestler. He reminded him that if he didn't invest in the training necessary to be the best, the camp training would come to nothing.

Wesley committed to stay in touch with Roquan and, on occasion, would call him and pray with him. He later discovered that Roquan's home environment was not very good at all. He lived in a drug-infested neighborhood, his dad was in prison, and his mom was addicted to crack cocaine. He was being raised by his aunt, who was struggling to raise him along with her own three children. Roquan really appreciated the fact that Wesley cared enough to take time to message him, encourage him, and even call him on occasion just for prayer. Wesley didn't know it, but he had a friend for life.

Roquan's situation fueled Wesley to continue to stand up as a leader on the home front, and his junior year was simply amazing. For the second year straight, he was a state champion in both the discus and wrestling. He was motivating athletes and other students to set goals and to work hard to achieve them, and he was at the top of his game not only athletically but also academically. He was well-known by sports enthusiasts from the entire area and by college recruiters from across the country. He was also well-known by sports reporters, and he even took a local reporter to his junior prom. It was a great story for the news channel, but it was huge for Wesley's reputation, creating even more publicity for him.

As a senior, Wesley was president of the Fellowship of Christian Athletes, and in addition to influencing students at his own school, he traveled to area schools to provide inspiration and encouragement there as well. He was once again a state champion in two different sports. His choice of colleges had been narrowed down to three. His decision was made when he was offered the opportunity to not only earn his degree but also be guaranteed a solid career after completing his degree program, make money while he attended school, and continue his wrestling career. Most appealing to him, however, was the opportunity to serve his country and to make his parents even more proud of him. Wesley had been accepted to the United States Naval Academy in Annapolis, Maryland, and would begin his journey to become a naval officer in July of the following year. This decision was made after much prayer, and it was one that sat well with his parents as well as with Pastor Johnson. He was training harder than ever, studying harder than ever, and serving God harder than ever. Wesley Heart was fully content with his life and the direction in which it was headed.

When he had free time, he would try to check up on all the ladies in his life. He talked to his mom every day, so she wasn't a part of the routine. His sister Tara was at the top of his list. She was now a college senior. He would normally call her about once a week just to chat. He was excited about her upcoming graduation and the fact that she would be at home for his graduation. He would also call his sister Patrice, who was an attorney in Spokane, Washington, as well as an Air Force veteran. He liked talking to her because she always gave it to him straight. She would let him know what it was going to take if he was going to be and remain exceptional. Sometimes, she was likely to use a few choice words in her communication with him, followed by an explanation of how she didn't mean to be offensive, but the world was not going to always be so caring and considerate.

"Besides," she would say, "sometimes it just feels better to say it like you mean it!"

Wesley always responded, "No, sissy, it feels better when you exercise self-control and hold your tongue."

"Just keep living, baby," she would say.

Their talks sometimes lasted an hour or more, and she would talk to him about women and how there's a time and place for friendships versus more serious relationships. She always told him that, for most people, middle school and high school are the time and place for friendships as very few people at that age are ready for a serious relationship. They don't even know who they are yet, so it really isn't too smart to add another confused soul to the mix. Nothing from nothing leaves nothing, which is why those relationships rarely go anywhere, and if they do, they usually don't end well at all. She would talk to him about being a man and about working and taking care of his responsibilities. "Cute don't pay no bills," she would say. "It takes a really desperate woman to let a man lay up and live off her, and it takes a sorry man to use a woman like that."

In her own way, Patrice gave Wesley the same wise advice he had received from his dad, except from a woman's perspective—a woman who was Southern and old-fashioned at heart. Wesley would listen, taking it all in, and about once every couple of weeks, he'd call to check on her. He would communicate with Amanda usually via text message, or via WhatsApp, depending on where she and Antonio were stationed. He would also message Sade every now and then on social media. He knew she wasn't following the instructions she'd been given, and when he would ask her about some of the weird stuff she was posting, she invariably attempted to pass it off as her just being silly. He often prayed for her. He didn't know how to help her otherwise, especially since she seemed no longer interested in wise counsel.

Lisa was the one person on his list who was hard to catch up with. Her elusiveness baffled him. She was no longer active on any of her social media accounts. When he would text her, she rarely responded; when he would call, she never answered the phone. He would often ask Tara how she was doing, and her response was usually a simple, "She's okay," or "She's fine, just keep praying for her."

The last time he had asked Tara about her, Lisa was heavy on his mind. Tara's response was the same, "She's doing okay, just keep praying for her."

"Tara, you always say that. What does that even mean? If I am supposed to pray for her, what exactly am I praying about?"

"Bro, you already know where this conversation is going. You know I can't talk to you about anybody's personal situation. You're a man with discernment, so just pray as you're led to pray by the Holy Spirit."

"Well, that's what concerns me, T. I keep feeling like Lisa's in trouble or something."

"If that's what comes to mind, then pray about that."

"Sis, quite honestly, if *that's* what keeps coming to my mind, I'm not only going to pray but I'm also going up to Greensboro to check on her myself!"

"Slow your roll, bro. I don't think she needs you to come to her rescue. I just think...well, actually I know that she won't be graduating in May."

"What? Did she fail a class or something? Is she in financial trouble?"

"Nothing she can't handle. It's just that her mom didn't come through for her as promised, so it's taking her an extra semester to graduate because she had to get a job. So that's probably why you're sensing trouble. It's no big deal, though, at least not anymore. I've been talking to her and encouraging her. She's good, but still keep praying for her and for her relationship with her mother, which you already know is not the best."

Tara had said far more than she wanted to, but she knew that if she didn't say something, sure enough, Wesley was going to figure out a way to be allowed to go to Greensboro to check on Lisa. She felt bad about telling him as much as she had. But at least she didn't share with him Lisa's true disdain for her mom, which was the worst part. She had some serious issues with her mother, and a lack of trust was at the root of it all. She had made some very distasteful statements regarding her mom. But Tara, knowing that it was all based on Lisa's temporary anger, would never share that info with Wesley.

What Tara didn't know was that Lisa had not been completely honest about what she was doing to make money. For nearly six months, Lisa had been selling drugs, but she couldn't bring herself to let even her best friend know that she had resorted to that. That way, if she ever got caught, it could never be proved that Tara was aware or involved in any way.

"Besides," said Tara, "she's coming home for spring break."

"And you really believe she's going to come this time? She's only been home a few times since she went away to college."

"Wesley!" Tara exclaimed, getting frustrated. "Everybody's homelife is not so perfect, ya know. Maybe she can't afford to come home more than that."

"Yeah, I know, T, and I can respect that. But come on, she practically grew up with us before she went to live with her mom. Why couldn't she come home and stay with us during her spring break?"

"Well, maybe that has something to do with the fact that there's a guy who lives at our house who is not a young boy anymore."

"Really, T! You make it sound like I'm going to attack her or something."

"Well, maybe *you're* not the issue, Wesley!" she said, letting her frustration get the best of her.

A few seconds of silence passed before anyone spoke. Tara knew that she had just breached her friend's confidentiality. As for Wesley, he couldn't believe what he'd just heard. Tara couldn't remember where she'd heard or read the statement before, but what popped up in her mind was that the next person to speak loses. She knew that her task now was to wait for Wesley to speak and then use what he said as ammunition for her response. Wesley had never heard anything so crazy, so he spoke.

"If you're saying Lisa is crushing on me, I'm seriously about to tell you just how crazy you are, because she doesn't return my texts, my calls, or even the letters I've written her." He laughed scornfully and said, "'Oh, I think he's hot, so let me just disregard all communication from him whatsoever. Oh, yeah, let me avoid him altogether when I actually do come home,'" he said, mocking Lisa. "You gotta be kidding me, T! If crushing on me is what she's doing, then she needs to take some lessons."

Tara chose her words carefully. "Bro, sometimes all you can see is yourself. Who said anything about Lisa crushing on you? How do you know I wasn't talking about Mom and Dad?"

"Tara, did you forget how well I know you? When you're telling half-truths, you start being indirect. So instead of saying that Mom and Dad were the ones who had an issue with Lisa staying with us during spring break, you say, 'How do you know I wasn't talking about Mom and Dad?'"

Shoot! she thought. *So much for that next-one-to-speak crap!*

"Bro, you're trippin'," she said. "Ain't nobody crushin' on you."

"Mmhmm, I hear you, sis. What else are you not telling me? That she was afraid to stay with us because she was afraid that she couldn't keep her hands off me? Or maybe she knew I was jailbait, so she just avoided me altogether?"

Oh my gosh, she thought. *This is too scary. This boy is a prophet in the making.*

"Bro, you're thinking more highly of yourself than you ought."

"Well, all I know is, if she *does* come home for spring break, I'm gonna find out for myself. I'm eighteen now, so we're gonna just see if anything has changed when I ask her out."

"Whatever, man," Tara muttered in frustration. "That's between y'all. Besides, I've heard that lie before. But, Wesley," she continued through gritted teeth, "if you say anything about this conversation, I mean anything at all, I will *never* forgive you!"

Tara knew that Wesley was very serious about asking Lisa out. She just hoped that, as always, he would be too busy to carry out his plan.

"No worries, sis," he said.

Chapter 19

Lisa actually did come home for spring break, and Wesley was hopeful that he would see her in church that Sunday. When she didn't show up, Wesley decided to call her.

"Hi, Lisa," he greeted. "It's Wes."

"Oh, hi, Wes! How are you?"

"I'm fine, thanks for asking."

"That's great! It's really good to hear from you. Is everything okay?"

"Yeah, I just thought I would see you at church today. Are *you* okay?"

"Oh, yeah, well, I overslept. Hey, wait, where is Tara? Did she put you up to calling me?"

"Actually, no, she didn't. I'm calling you because…well, I know that you normally come to church whenever you come home from school, and Tara told me that you were home. So when I didn't see you, I was just a little concerned. I've only seen you maybe twice in the past couple of years, ya know."

"Oh, look at you! So you're just becoming a little man now, huh?"

Little man? he thought.

"Checking in on me to make sure I'm okay? That is so sweet, Wes."

"So what happened to you this morning?" he pressed.

"Well, if you must know, I overslept. I was catching up with some old friends last night, and I stayed out kinda late. I tried to get Tara to come with me, but you know she is not going to hang out on

215

a Saturday night, especially if that choir of hers is going to be singing on Sunday."

"Oh, you know that's not going to happen," Wesley agreed. "Hey, speaking of the choir, you missed it today. That choir was singing like there's no tomorrow. And Pastor Johnson, as usual, was puttin' it down!"

"Oh, really? What did he preach about?"

"Well, he preached about you."

"Me? What?"

"Yeah, you. He noticed that there were a lot of people missing at church today, and he talked about those who stay out so late on Saturday that they don't make it to church on Sunday."

"You are not funny," she said, laughing along with him.

"That's the only thing I remember hearing him talking about."

"Yeah, right. I don't believe that for a minute, Wes. You are so dedicated you could probably recite the entire sermon word for word."

"Is my dedication a problem for you?"

"Hey, don't get your panties in a wad. Of course not, silly. But if you can dish it, you better be able to take it, you little punk."

"Oh, you're gonna pay for that one."

"Yeah, yeah. I'm really scared. Anyhow, as I was saying, I don't have a problem with your dedication. I love that about you, and in a way, I'm a little envious. But that's just who you are. You've been that way ever since you had that experience during revival that night years ago."

"Oh, you remember that?"

"Of course I remember that. It was an amazing experience, and no one could deny that you'd had an encounter with God that night. But if there was ever any question as to whether or not God was with you, it was proved the next night when you dropped that big guy who was trying to attack Pastor Johnson."

"Yeah, Amanda reminds us of that all the time," he agreed, laughing.

"Now, that had to be the power of God, because your little tail couldn't hurt a fly back then."

"Oh, really, is that what you think? That's funny, because I remember you telling me that you trusted me to protect you. So either you were lying then or..."

"Oh my gosh, Wes! You remember that? I was thinking about that just a few days ago! And no, I wasn't lying. I'm just kidding around with you. Like I said, if you can dish it, I hope you can take it."

Hhmm, so she was thinking about me the other day...note to self, he thought.

"Well, that was then. I'm a big boy now, ya know."

"Mmhmm, that's what I hear. I also heard that you're still the state wrestling champion."

"Yes, to God be all the glory. I've been the state champ for four years and the state discus champ for three."

"That's amazing, Wes! I'm so proud of you."

"Thank you, Lisa," he said, trying to change the tone of the conversation without being harsh. "I really wish...I...I really don't know how to say this."

"Say what? Just say it, Wes."

"Lisa, you seem to have gotten lost during this past school year. You didn't come home at all last summer. You didn't even come home during the Christmas break. I still don't know why, and in reality, it's none of my business, I guess. I mean, you're a grown woman now, but don't you at least *want* to see us? And maybe I shouldn't say 'us' because I can't speak for anyone but myself. But know that *I* really want to see *you*. And I can only hope that you want to see me too. But your actions lead me to believe otherwise. I understand that perhaps you can't always come home, and for different reasons. But you don't even return my calls or reply to my texts. And quite honestly, Lisa, that hurts. But like I said, I'm a big boy now, and I can deal with hurt feelings. I just don't deal well with not knowing how the people that I care about are doing, and as a matter of fact, I had already made up my mind that if you didn't come home for spring break, I was going to find you."

Lisa was at a loss for words. She could tell that he was not merely expressing a desire to see her face; she heard a yearning of sorts in his voice, and it made her a little nervous, especially the way he talked to her with the skill and confidence of a grown man.

She thought to herself, *Wow! Who is this man on the phone with me, and what happened to little Wesley?*

"I, uh...well, yes, I do want to see you. I want to see you all, Wes. I miss all of you guys. I mean, I talk to Tara pretty often, but I want to catch up with everyone. I just had some, uh...some personal issues this past year, and uh...I had to deal with it on my own. I'm sorry, but it's something I prefer not to talk about. But the good thing is that it's all behind me now," she lied.

Wesley noticed her discomfort in talking about her absence this past school year. In a way, he was sorry he'd mentioned it, but he felt as if he needed to confront her to see where her heart was before he popped his question on her.

"Lisa, I'm sorry. I didn't mean to put you on the spot like that, and I truly apologize if I made you uncomfortable. Just know that we...well, again, let me speak for myself. I love you, and although I might be acting a little selfish, I don't apologize for that. I want to see you. I want to know that you're okay. I want to see for myself that you're not putting on too much weight and that no one's abusing you. I want to see with my own eyes that you are not following some new, demonic philosophy that has you smoking weed and looking like a dude with your hair all locked up and tattoos and piercings all over your body, and I just..." He stopped his teasing before the truth spilled out. *I want to see you as the breathtaking woman of my dreams that you've always been.*

"Okay, Wes, I get it, I get it. Darn, demonic philosophy? I think you switched over to your father for a moment there. I was wondering if you'd put him on the phone or what."

"I know I sounded kind of fatherly there for a minute, but that's the protector in me. Now, you know I love the Lord, but I'll break a nose or two if I have to," he said, trying to keep it light.

"Oh, you're a nose breaker, huh?"

"I told you, I'm a big boy now, so if I have to play the role of nose breaker, that's cool if that's what's needed."

"Well, according to Tara, you're more like a heartbreaker."

"Listen, I don't know what she's talking about, because I don't fool with silly high school girls."

"Exactly! That's why they're heartbroken, because you won't give them the time of day. Then, on top of that, you had the nerve to ask the WXLT reporter to the prom. Now, if that wasn't being a heartbreaker…"

"You are so wrong, Lisa." He grinned. "I simply asked her on a whim. Listen, she was filling in for a sports reporter who was sick with the flu. She was covering one of my wrestling matches and interviewing me about my victory that night, which was huge for me because it earned me the chance to wrestle for the state championship. So being the fun-loving guy that I am, I asked her after the interview if I could be the reporter for a moment. She laughed and responded that if I didn't mind walking and talking, she would gladly answer any questions that I had. As we made our way to the car that she and the cameraman were in, I asked her where she was from, where she went to school, how long she'd been in her profession, and how it felt covering a sports beat since she normally covered community events. She answered each of my questions and told me that she was very impressed that I even knew her name, not to mention what type of reporter she was. She went on to answer each question thoroughly and said that she was used to sports coverage because that was what she covered when she worked for her college news team. We were just having fun when she asked me if I had any more questions for her. I was honestly just fooling around when I said, 'Yes, will you go to the prom with me?' She stopped dead in her tracks, turned and looked me in the eye, and with a huge grin on her face, said, 'I'd be honored, Mr. Heart. I would really like that.' I wasn't about to tell her never mind, especially after she seemed to be digging me the whole time, anyway. That would make me…"

"What?" Lisa prodded.

"That would make me really uncool."

"No, Wes, that would make you a heartbreaker," she teased, laughing loudly.

Wesley had to laugh, knowing that he had walked right into that one with his poor choice of words.

"Anyway, I'm not a heartbreaker."

"Well, the word on the street is that she was all over you at the prom and was trying to hook up with you a couple of days later, until she met the Equalizer, a.k.a. Amanda, who happened to be in town to put her in check."

"Yeah, thankfully Amanda got to her before Mom did. Anyhow, need I ask where you got your information from?"

"You already know."

Mmhmm, well, since Tara seems to be your source for information, did she also tell you that I want to be your man? he jokingly thought to himself.

"Well, Lisa, I have a question for you."

"Oooh, Wesley, baby, you can ask me anything you want as long as you're willing to walk and talk."

"I'm telling you, it wasn't like that!" Again, they laughed together.

"Hey, if you got it, you got it!" she said. *And trust me, you got it,* she thought.

"Oh, stop it, Lisa. So I told you that I really want to see you, and I'm hopeful that I can while you're in town. I want to know if you'll join me for dinner Wednesday night after Bible study, or if you want, I can pick you up early and you can just join me for the study."

"Aw, how sweet, Wes. Do you mean just you and me, or will Tara or your parents be there too?"

"No, it'll be just the two of us."

"Oh…well, okay, Wes. So is this, like, a date?"

"Well, it depends on how technical you want to be, but let's just say we're having dinner together, my treat, of course. You don't have to bring anything except maybe some conversation."

Who at his age wants conversation? Wow, this boy is really growing up on me, and now he wants to take me out? That's impressive…and kinda creepy too, she thought.

"You are so sweet," she said. "Wow, you really did miss me, huh?"

"Yes, very much, Lisa."

"Well, I would be more than happy to have dinner with you. I'm down for the evening, Bible study and all. What time should I expect you?"

"Five thirty."

"Okay, well, that works for me."

"Great. So do you like Italian?"

"It's my favorite!"

Yeah, I remember, he thought.

"Okay, well, I have a really nice place that I want to take you to. So pull out your red dress and high heels."

"Uh, please tell me that I didn't just hear lyrics from a Johnny Gill song," she interrupted, laughing heartily. Wesley joined her.

"Well, it wasn't intentional. It just kind of came out like that." *I certainly wouldn't mind seeing you in that, though,* he thought, being careful not to actually say it. "Uh, I didn't mean it literally, but you do need to know that it is a nice restaurant, in case you want to spice up your attire a little. I wouldn't want you to be uncomfortable or to feel as if you're underdressed."

"Okay, thank you for letting me know."

"You bet. Save your appetite, because you're going to need it."

"I'll do that. I can't wait!"

"Same here. I enjoyed talking with you today. I really wish I could have seen you instead, but I guess I can wait until Wednesday."

"I'm so sorry. I know I can be a slacker sometimes, skipping church, not coming home on break. I need to pull it together, don't I?"

"There's room at the cross for you, Lisa," he teased with a laugh.

"Oh, so now you want to quote gospel lines. You've gone from R&B to gospel. Sounds like *you're* the one who needs to pull it together."

"Don't try to make this about me. You were the one that said you needed to pull it together. I just agreed with you. All I'm saying is, there's room. 'Though millions have come, there's still room for one,' Lisa," Wesley said, laughing at his use of more of the lyrics to the song. He seized the moment while Lisa was laughing to switch songs. "I'm just letting you know, Lisa, that 'you don't have to stay in the shape that you're in, the Potter wants to put you back together again. I said the Potter waaaannts…'" He sang out the word *wants* just like Tramaine Hawkins's original version of the song.

"Stop it, silly," she demanded, laughing uproariously. "You're going to make me hurt myself over here."

"Okay, okay. Listen, I'll see you Wednesday at five thirty. Enjoy your day, Lisa."

"You too, Wes."

Chapter 20

As Lisa ended the call, a smiled spread over her face as she thought about all the dynamics of the conversation. This eighteen-year-old had just challenged her to be more spiritually, mentally, and physically accountable. He had expressed himself, leaving no room for guesswork about how he really felt, and by the time the conversation was over, he even had her laughing uncontrollably. *Wow, he's amazing,* she thought to herself, not for the first time.

Then she began to wonder what their conversation would be like on Wednesday night. She wondered how much his appearance had changed. She also wondered how he would treat her once he saw her, if he really wanted to see her the way he said he did. What were his true motives? *Will he be too forward with me? I certainly hope so,* she thought. As she burst into laughter, she said aloud, "I'm going to hell!"

Her laughter was interrupted when her mother responded, "I'mma *take* you to hell if you don't cut out all that noise!" Lisa thought about Tara's words of advice. Her assignment was to figure out a way to love her mother in spite of her actions. While she reserved the right to be angry with her mother, Tara had convinced her that what her mother needed more than anything was for somebody to show her unconditional love. Not knowing how else to respond, Lisa shouted back, "I love you, Mama!"

"Well, can you love me quietly, baby? Mama's got a headache," the hungover woman pleaded. Lisa's heart was suddenly heavy. For a brief second, she saw her mom as a victim. She was a victim of the anger and resentment that she carried in her heart over Lisa's father, who never knew that he had a daughter. He had entered the military just a few days after one encounter with Ms. Monroe. Embarrassed and afraid, her mom never sought him out to tell him, and she hated herself for it. She was a woman who had made some poor decisions at some of the most crucial points in her life, and those decisions had led her to the point of being a functional alcoholic.

Lisa wiped her tears and stood up. She walked over to the mirror, looked at herself, and said, "Unconditional love, baby. You can do this." She went into the kitchen and got a glass of water. Then she walked into the living room of the tiny apartment and knelt down in front of the couch, where her mother was sleeping. "Mama, I'm going to get you something to eat and something for your headache. Here, come on, sit up and drink some water."

"Oh, thank you, baby. Look in my purse and get some money out."

"I...I'm good, Mama. I got it. I'll be right back." This was a huge step for Lisa, who was determined that she was going to do her best to follow Tara's advice. Her actions that day marked the beginning of a new day in the relationship between Lisa and her mother.

The Wednesday-night Bible study didn't start until seven, but Wesley told her that he would be there at five thirty to pick her up because he wanted to make sure that he arrived before Pastor Johnson, just in case he needed anything. It was also his turn to open the building and prepare it for the study. Furthermore, he wanted to spend a little extra time with Lisa. When he arrived at her house, he was confident as he encountered Lisa's mother, who met him at the door and immediately started asking him questions about his intentions with her daughter. Lisa was impressed at his ability to remain calm and very respectful as her unrelenting, alcoholic mother, Betty Monroe, all but accused him of trying to lure her daughter into some type of inappropriate relationship. Lisa could have easily rescued Wesley, but she was so impressed with the eighteen-year-old's ability to remain collected and defend himself that she let the conversation go on for about five minutes before Wesley was able to convince Ms. Betty to just move on.

Once they got to the car, Wesley opened the door for Lisa, waited for her to get in, and closed it behind her before walking over to the driver's side of the 350Z. When she sat down, she realized that she hadn't thanked him. But before she could do so, Wesley had opened the driver's door of the two-seater, reached into the back behind the driver's seat, and pulled out a bouquet of flowers and, as he sat down in the car, handed them to Lisa and said, "I wanted to bring these to your door, but something told me that it might not be a good idea. I'm glad I decided to follow my gut, but I still want you to have them."

Lisa's heart was melting. *How could such a young man have such class?* she thought to herself. *How could he have more class than anyone I've ever gone out with before?*

"Wesley, that was so sweet. You opened the door for me, and now you're giving me flowers? I am so impressed."

"Well, you probably shouldn't be that impressed, because, uh, I have something that I need to tell you. I want to go back to our conversation Sunday and apologize to you again for the way I went off the deep end on you. I had no right to do that. It was selfish and tasteless, and I went overboard by prying and asking you questions that were none of my business. I was on cloud nine when you agreed to go out with me. But after a little while, the Lord burst my bubble by showing me just how wrong I was. I asked Him for forgiveness, and now I need to ask you for the same. I'm sorry, Lisa. Will you please forgive me?"

"Aw, Wes, you're melting my heart over here. You know, I had a similar experience that afternoon. I thought about everything you said, and I remembered the emotion in your voice and how you spoke up and voiced your feelings—not like a raging bull that was out of control, but like a real man expressing his feelings without trying to be hurtful and demeaning. That spoke volumes to me, because for the longest time, that is something I have struggled with, especially with certain people. But seeing how you expressed yourself really opened my eyes to some personal things that I've been dealing with, and long story short, because of you, I took a huge step in the right direction after we hung up. You might not believe me, but I was on cloud nine, too, because I could tell that you were genuinely concerned about me and that you wanted to see me. But then, like you, my bubble was burst when I thought about how I've treated you. One day, I'll be able to tell you the whole story, but for now, just know that I forgive you, and I apologize to you as well, and I hope you'll forgive me too."

"Of course. So what if we just start all over?" he suggested.

"I think that's a great idea."

"So do you want me to open and close your door for you again?"

"You mean that wasn't part of your apology?"

"No, that's a part of the standard package."

"Oh, so I get that treatment every time?"

"Every single time," he said emphatically. "Actually, the flowers are pretty standard too. While flowers are not for every outing, they are certainly standard on special occasions."

"I could really get used to this."

"Surely, you've had a guy open your door for you and give you flowers before, right?"

"Uh, surely not."

"Well, that's okay. You're in good hands tonight."

"I see that," she replied with a smile.

"So what about your favorite snack? I'm sure guys bring you that all the time."

"Wes, I haven't had much success with guys lately."

Great! he thought to himself.

"I don't even know if any guy knows what my favorite snacks are."

"Reese's Pieces and Coke, right?"

"Oh my gosh, Wes! You remembered?"

"Of course I remember. And I thought it would be a nice tide-me-over between now and dinnertime," he said, pulling the sugary combination out of the pocket of his door. The glass Coke bottle was encased in a bottle koozie.

"Wesley!" she exclaimed. "I...you're leaving me speechless. How thoughtful of you. Thank you, baby—baby brother, that is," she amended, catching herself. She decided to quickly shift the conversation, but before she could do so, Wesley beat her to the punch.

"So which is it? Baby or baby brother?" he asked, instantly serious. She decided to tease him as he put the car in first gear and began to drive very smoothly.

"What do you want it to be?" she asked.

"Before I answer that question, I should tell you that I've been waiting for this day, for this moment, for a very long time. I thought about your question the other day regarding whether or not this was like a real date. After thinking long and hard about it, I would really like to refer to this as our first official date. Now I understand that we may never have another one, and while my face might be broken, I'll find a way to get through it. But this moment is real for me, and I am going to seize the opportunity to take it all in. Most of all, I'm going to do my best to show *you* a great time. The point is, I know that's different from what I said on the phone regarding this night, and I just want to make sure that—"

"Wesley, are you kidding me?" she interrupted. "Have you forgotten that your sister and I are best friends? I've known about your feelings for me for a while now. But I never took that seriously because, first of all, you never approached me, and secondly..." Lisa hesitated because she knew that what she was about to say was not entirely true—at eighteen, Wesley was more of a man than most guys her age. He didn't hang out with just anyone, and he was his own person, not trying to be like everyone else just because it was the popular thing to do. Actually, she had watched him for years. Everyone loved him, and all the girls his age were crazy about him. She knew that he had a very close relationship with God. It was a relationship that she actually envied in her own way.

"Secondly what?" Wesley prompted.

"Secondly, you're just so young, baby." Lisa caught herself again but decided not to correct it this time.

"There's that word again," Wesley teased, smiling.

"Well, you never answered my question from the first time I called you baby," she responded with a smile of her own.

"I am totally okay with *baby*. I think *baby* would be really nice, and I could get used to *baby*." He noticed that his digital odometer read sixty miles per hour. He shifted to fourth gear and backed off the accelerator. "But seriously, Lisa, I don't want anything you don't want. Ya see," he said, trying to quickly lighten the mood by talking in his old-man voice, "there are certain thangs that are impliiied... when you start throwing around words like *baby*, and quite honestly, ya unda-stand, I don't think you can handle 'baby' right now."

"Oh, really?" She laughed. "You're the one that hit sixty in a thirty-five when I called you that, but you don't think *I* can handle *you*? Are you sure it's not the other way around?"

"Oh, don't get it twisted, missy," he rejoined, not even acknowledging that he just got busted. "I think you can handle just plain ole me. But I don't think you're ready for 'baby' me. Ya see, I'm a complicated man, Lisa, and to whomever I become 'baby,' she's gonna have to be ready for all this," he said, opening his hand and making air circles around his face and upper torso.

"You are too much!" she replied through a huge grin. "I'm scared of you."

"No need for that. But on a serious note, I would like to propose a toast."

"A toast? I think I need a bottle opener, and uh, you need a drink."

"Are you underestimating me, Lisa?" he asked, producing both items, one after the other, and passing both to her.

"Oh! I stand corrected. I should have known better than to doubt Wesley Heart," she teased as she opened both bottles and gave him his.

"Yes, you should," he agreed with a grin. "So as I was saying, here's to our first date. May we enjoy a nice dinner, pleasant conversation, and good times with each other tonight! Cheers."

"Cheers!" she rejoined as they clinked their Coke bottles against each other.

Lisa was fully attentive at Bible study. There were only about fifty people present, but Pastor Johnson taught as if speaking to a full house. To Lisa, it seemed this message was so clearly for her that there might as well have been no one else in the building. The topic was the God Who Understands.

Pastor Johnson began with the question, "Have you ever found yourself in a totally messed-up situation and you have no real rhyme or reason as to how you got there or what possessed you to stoop to that level?" As he taught, she thought about her current illegal occupation as a drug dealer. Although her predicament was truly temporary, she still couldn't believe that her life had come to this. Time after time, she reasoned to herself that at least she wasn't selling her body or transporting major drug shipments like others she knew; but those thoughts did nothing to make her feel better about what she was doing. It was her reality, and she knew there was no way to smooth it over or to minimize how painful it was to be in such a place, knowing that this went against everything she believed in. She had not told anyone about it, but for some reason, it seemed as if Pastor Johnson knew all about her. Of course he didn't, but God did, and tonight it was as if He wanted her to know that He cared and that He was going to work it out really soon.

Pastor Johnson ended the sermon by asking the congregation to trust God. "I know you got some messed-up situations you've gotten caught up in. Some of you are saying, 'I don't know how I'm going to get out of this.' Will you trust God with your situation? He understands, and He will deliver you. Is there anybody who needs prayer tonight? Somebody might be saying, 'Pastor, I don't just need prayer, I need a miracle.' Come on, let's believe God together for it."

Lisa got up and went to the altar, alone. As she made her way there, Pastor Johnson said, "It's so good to see you, Lisa," as if he were greeting her in the hallway after church. Then, sounding far more formal, he said, "Let's give God praise for Sister Lisa being back in town from college." While they applauded, he said, "You're all dressed up. Is that how they do it in Greensboro?"

Everyone laughed as Lisa smiled and replied, "No, sir, I'm just catching up with family after church tonight."

"Well, I'm glad you came to the altar, because I need to pray for you." Hearing this, Wesley made his way to the altar to assist in whatever way necessary. "Before I do, let me ask, Do you have any specific prayer requests?"

"Yes, sir. I would like to ask the church to pray for my mother and..." She got a little choked up as she continued, "And for our relationship. I also ask that we continue to pray for Sade Seabrooks. She, uh...she needs the prayers of the saints." Before Lisa broke down completely, she squeezed out past a large lump in her throat, "And please pray for me."

Pastor Johnson asked the church to extend their right hands toward her as a sign of agreement. Indeed, he prayed for Ms. Betty and Lisa's relationship, and for Sade. But as he prayed for Lisa, he shifted his focus to a prayer for God's miraculous protection. He prayed for her safety; he asked God to be a fence all around her and to shield her on every side. And before he knew it, he began to prophesy.

"God wants you to know that the enemy has strategically constructed a plan, a trap that was designed to destroy you. But God says, do not be afraid, for He has sent His angels ahead of you to protect you from harm. So in the same way that the enemy created the trap for you, in a much greater way, God has created a way of escape, and you, Lisa, will not be harmed. Let's give God praise for it right now," he encouraged.

Lisa had never felt so much relief. She knew that it was time for her to give it up. She had made all the money she needed to make in order to pay her tuition. She had also paid for her classes and room and board for the next school year, which meant that if she worked really hard, she could spend her summer retaking the classes she'd failed, and with a very full schedule for her final two semesters, she could finish strong and graduate the following May. So although it would take her five-plus years to complete her bachelor's degree, she would be finished and ready to move on to the next chapter of her life. What she didn't know was how she was going to be allowed to just walk away from Roquan, the drug dealer she worked under. He wasn't really the issue, but the kingpin, Mr. Lee, was very careful about dealers just walking away from the game, especially low-level dealers like Lisa. Worse yet, Mr. Lee had informed Roquan, even before Lisa was made aware, that she was being considered for an interview with the South Carolina Highway Patrol, and he did not like that scenario at all. Lisa knew that she needed nothing more right now than that prayer for God's protection in her life, and she felt as if the weight of the world had been lifted off her shoulders. She thanked Pastor Johnson as she left the altar to walk back to her seat.

Chapter 21

Wesley showed Lisa the time of her life that night. On the way to the restaurant, they talked about Pastor Johnson's prayer. Wesley shared with her that during his prayer time, as he prayed for her, he felt a need to pray for her safety and protection too. Nothing much came of that discussion, however, except for Lisa acknowledging that she'd started working at a local restaurant that wasn't in the safest of locations. Of course, she didn't reveal that she no longer worked there but was involved in something far more dangerous. Wesley wasn't buying it anyway, but he wasn't going to spend his time trying to pry out of her what she was not willing to talk about, for whatever reason. Besides, he knew that based on the prophetic word, God had it under control, whatever the real situation was, so there was no need for him to worry about it.

That Wednesday night was a beautiful time for both of them, and neither of them wanted it to end. He told her that he had been selected to join the US Naval Academy, where he would become a naval officer. He also related that after his schooling was complete, he had a five-year obligation to serve in the Navy. He wasn't sure whether he wanted to make a career of it, but he was sure that this was the right path for him. He told her that he wanted nothing but the absolute best for her. He wanted to be a part of her life, and although he hoped that this date would be the first of many over the years, he wanted her to be happy, which meant that if she met someone along the way, as long as that man made her happy, Wesley would be okay.

The night included talk about dreams, goals, and aspirations for rewarding careers and beautiful families someday, but it was not devoid of fireworks. When Wesley walked Lisa to her door, and even before she got out of his car, she just couldn't seem to keep her hands off him. Lisa found herself completely enamored by Wesley's presence, kindness, conversation, concern for her well-being, and everything else about him.

They spent another couple of days together that week, and she attended his county track meet, where he beat his personal best in the discus. They hung out together as much as possible, talking about the need to take it easy and be realistic about their expectations of a relationship at this stage in their lives. Wesley was focused on his upcoming commitments, and although he thoroughly enjoyed spending time with her, he knew that nothing serious could come of the relationship right now. His mind was set on two things: conditioning himself to become the best cadet in his class and one day, by the grace of God, becoming an Olympic hopeful.

Little did he know that, after his first year at the academy, his wrestling coach and athletic director would work through all the red tape for him to be granted special permission to compete and ultimately earn a spot on Team USA. This captured the attention of the superintendent of the entire academy, who, after meeting Wesley and seeing his status as one of the top cadets in his class, plus the fact that he had earned a spot on Team USA, had no problem signing off and making an exception for his military training to be delayed by one year to give the young man a chance to compete for his country in the upcoming Olympic Games!

These and a whole host of many other unexplainable events occurred that somehow seemed to just work out in his favor, and in the end, Wesley Heart was in London, England, competing against the most talented wrestlers in the world. How did this happen? How was he able to wrestle in the Olympics when, just two short years ago, he was a high school student? How was it possible that his entire immediate family, along with Pastor and Sister Johnson, was able to be there to witness him wrestle and win the silver medal for his country? How was he able to maintain his GPA and meet all the requirements necessary to continue his midshipman cadet status, even though he had been granted permission to delay his education and training for a year in order to compete? Wesley had only one answer to these questions: by the grace and favor of Almighty God.

When he returned to the academy, he was asked to be one of the speakers for a youth conference at a megachurch located ten minutes from the academy. The attendees were mesmerized as he encouraged them to pursue their goals and dreams with fierce intensity. He talked to them about the craftiness of the devil and about some of the tricks and tactics that he would use to throw them off course. As he continued his spirited message, many of the youth in attendance began coming to the altar, although no altar call had been given. The pastor and ministry leaders were caught off guard by this as they had never experienced anything like it before. For Wesley, however, it was a pretty common occurrence back home at Miracle Center. Recognizing the leadership's dilemma, he quickly asked the ushers, security, and altar workers to kindly stand down and allow the teens to come to the altar if they needed to. When he said that, it was as if the floodgates opened, and the youngsters started leaving their seats and making their way to the altar.

Wesley finished up his message as some began to cry at the altar. Then he told them that he wanted to pray for them before turning it over to the pastor for the invitation for all the listeners to become children of God. He led them in prayer as if he were a seasoned pastor, and as he closed his prayer for them, there was not a dry eye at the altar. Wesley had ushered in the presence of God in a way that amazed even him. Still, he had only one answer for how a fifteen-minute message could have such an effect on a group of young people: God's grace and favor.

It was that same grace and favor that opened the door for Wesley to eventually be offered a position as youth pastor at the same megachurch where he'd spoken, as well as at three different churches in the area, although he was not a minister. He was forced to decline each of them, given his time restrictions and his workload as a midshipman. He was also offered a position as a wrestling coach at two different schools, which he also had to decline. He stopped counting the number of declined offers to give private lessons to Olympic wrestling hopefuls from all over the DC, Maryland, and Virginia area. He did, however, make himself available to speak once per month at the church, as long as they were willing to extend the invitation to the public. Young people began coming from quite a distance to hear his encouraging and life-giving messages. In addition, Wesley developed a semiannual two-day training camp at one of the high schools to help gifted wrestlers excel to their potential.

His matriculation through his four years at the naval academy was supposed to be the type of process that started out very difficult and restrictive, with gradual improvement that led to eventual fun, privilege, and enjoyment. But he had learned how to make the most of every moment, and of course, he influenced the people around him to do the same. He formed tremendous bonds with his fellow midshipmen, professors, staff, and people from the community while he was there. He stood in utter amazement at all his accomplishments and, most of all, at the goodness of the Lord in his life up to this point. Before he knew it, he was nearing graduation and preparing to go to his first duty station as a surface warfare officer aboard an aircraft carrier set to sail from Pensacola, Florida.

His parents, Patrice, Tara, and Pastor and Sister Johnson were there for his graduation and commissioning week. He spent the week introducing his loved ones to his coach, his fellow midshipmen, and all the people who meant so much to him. He took them to a pre-arranged meeting with the megachurch pastor, which was scheduled to take place after the Wednesday-night service. However, during the service, the pastor called him up and thanked him first for his service to his country, and foremost to the Lord. They gave him a plaque expressing their appreciation for his service to the youth in that area. The man embraced Wesley and asked him if he had anything to say.

Wesley expressed his gratitude for the opportunity to serve. Then he asked those who were with him to stand. He introduced his parents, his sisters, and his pastor and pastor's wife. He told the congregation how grateful he was for them as they represented a portion of the village responsible for his success. He advised everyone in attendance, especially the young people, to take advantage of their village, the positive people in their lives who were willing and able to help them. Finally, he told them to stay focused on their dreams and goals, to work hard to achieve them, and to expect God to show up for them with the grace and favor needed to bring them to pass.

Upon graduation, Wesley was officially an ensign in the United States Navy, and he was just as proud that day as he was when he won the silver medal. He was ready to take command of his first assignment as an official commissioned officer in the Navy.

As for Lisa, she was working as a South Carolina state trooper. She knew that if she was ever going to have the caliber of man that Wesley represented, then she was going to have to be the caliber of woman that deserved such a man. She began, right then, taking detailed steps to develop herself into a self-confident woman, determined that she would have far more to offer a man than a pretty face and a nice body. Lisa Monroe was under construction by Almighty God!

She had managed to escape the danger of the life she had been living without any apparent repercussions, and for that she was so grateful. She had a difficult time, however, forgiving herself for it, especially without knowing the status of Fats, the guy she'd shot and left for dead. Still, she knew that she had to move on, and she was receiving counseling from the best in the business, which also happened to be her best friend, Tara Heart. Through counseling, she had decided to continue to hang in there with her mom and try to understand why she'd always been so angry and distant. Most importantly, she was working on her relationship with her God, one day at a time. She would attend church services and Bible study with Tara whenever her work schedule permitted, and she was learning more and more about how practical God is.

Pastor Johnson's teaching was quite different from what she had experienced growing up. She was raised by her grandparents in the type of church that espoused that every blessing seemed to require a major move of God. Pastor Johnson focused more on teaching people how to walk with God day by day so that whenever there was a need, large or small, their faith in Him was strong enough to believe

Him for the best outcomes without Him having to move heaven and earth merely to meet the needs of His people.

Indeed, Lisa was growing in her faith, and she often prayed regarding what to do about Wesley. They had managed to stay in touch for a couple of months after their first date years prior, but once he entered what's known as Plebe Summer, a seven-week training period for freshmen entering the naval academy, their communication dwindled down to nothing, as he was focused on being the head of his class, and she was focused on getting her mind clear before entering the police academy. When his rigorous training was over, he was indeed the number one cadet midshipman in the freshman class, in part because he cut off virtually all communication with everyone to focus on achieving that distinction. Although he did inform everyone of his intentions, the lack of communication did not help whatever hopes of a relationship had existed, and it was certainly not easy to resume.

To add insult to injury, it wasn't long before Lisa began *her* twelve-week training at the South Carolina Police Academy. Back then, she was so in awe of Wesley's accomplishments she decided to take a similar approach to him just to see if the concept of focus was as strong as he made it seem. She informed Tara that she would only call her when she needed her, and she informed her mother that she would only call her once a week on Sunday evenings. She was not as physically fit as Wesley—one would be hard-pressed to find *anyone* who was. During the course of her training, however, she experienced significant improvement in her physical fitness. The same was true of her ability to use a handgun. At first, she had a great deal of trouble because she was trying to flush Fats out of her mind. He seemed to pop up every time she squeezed the trigger. However, because her shooting skills were so bad, and partly because she was so physically attractive, the instructors gave her a lot of attention on the shooting range, and she ended up graduating as the highest-qualifying shooter in her class. After finishing the first twelve weeks at the academy, she was required to complete twelve weeks of law enforcement training in the county she would be assigned to.

Upon her graduation, her mother and grandparents were there. Tara and Mr. and Mrs. Heart were also present. She was so grateful to see the love and support from the Heart family and to see that her grandfather, who was now in a wheelchair, had made the sacrifice to come. She was overcome with emotion as they approached to congratulate her. Mr. Heart had given her a brief speech that helped her pull it together. She promised that she was going to start coming to church once she got on a regular schedule. She also told them that she was going to make her way to visit them some time. They presented her with a gift for her college graduation and a gift for her academy graduation. Pastor and Sister Johnson also sent a gift by them. She was once again overcome with tears when Tara gave her a gift and also handed her one from Wesley.

She wanted so badly to talk to him and to at least thank him for being so thoughtful. He had always been thoughtful toward her, and she had always seemed so unappreciative. This was something she wanted to correct immediately. She was so proud and happy that day. She was also grateful that God had seen her through everything. When she arrived back at her mother's apartment that evening, she decided to try to contact Wesley. To her disappointment, his voicemail picked up on the first ring. She determined that she could say it best if she wrote him a letter anyway, which was exactly what she did. But each time she attempted to mail it, she lost her courage. She felt that perhaps what she'd written was too emotional or that perhaps she'd gone too far in what she was asking, even though she simply expressed a desire for them to start communicating more. Before she knew it, four days had passed and she had not mailed the letter. Then she received a letter in her mother's mailbox with no return address, but the postmark was from Greensboro.

Congratufreakinlations, you're a police officer now! Woohoo! I'm sure you can tell how happy I am for you. Yeah, whatever. Your new title does not scare me at all. I'm gon' tell you this one time: stay away from my boy. He's doing his thing at the naval academy, and in the near future, he's going to be compet-

ing in the Olympics. The last thing he needs is to be distracted by people like you, who don't even have the common decency to holla at him every now and then. Now, he's getting his career off to a good start, and he don't need people like you in his life. I'm tellin' you, Lisa…no calls, no texts, no telling him how you want to be his girl now and all that BS. If you had some sense, you coulda been his girl long before now, but it's too late! This is your one and only warning. Leave him alone or else!

    Photocopied on the bottom of the letter was a picture of her at her police academy graduation with Mr. and Mrs. Heart and Tara. Lisa was at a loss for what to do. She knew that she couldn't report it on account of her past, and she couldn't pursue it personally since it was from so far away. It troubled her that members of the Heart family were in that picture, and consequently, she couldn't even talk to Tara about it.

    Lisa knew there was only one person who could have sent the letter—Roquan, the drug dealer she had worked for. She was almost 100 percent certain that it was him. The reference to "my boy" confirmed it even more, as he had made mention that he was going to let her walk away from the game only because of Wesley. Somehow they knew each other; Roquan even said that Wesley would call him and pray with him on occasion.

    She was angry and uncertain about what to do. She thought about sending her letter to Wesley anyway, just to prove to herself that she wasn't afraid. But she *was* afraid. She feared for the safety of Tara and her parents, and she was not about to involve them in someone's games. She also knew that Roquan was likely to hurt someone; he had a bad reputation from his days as a low-level dealer. Now that he was in the majors, he seemed to be a bit more cautious, but that wasn't enough to flush out of her mind the fact that this was the same guy that had put a gun to her head not so very long ago. Upon weighing her options, she decided that she was not going to crumble to pieces now. She was an officer of the law for the state of South

Carolina, so she would slowly and methodically play the game with Roquan. So for now, no communication with Wesley.

As time went on, upon conducting some self-evaluation, Lisa decided to work on personal growth and becoming the best state trooper she could be. The more she looked at her life, the path she had taken, and the fact that she was not that far removed from her past, the more she wondered whether having a relationship with *any* man at this point in her life, including Wesley, was in her best interests. She also pondered whether a relationship with her would be in Wesley's best interests as he was in the process of making a life for himself as a naval officer.

Before she knew it, another couple of years had gone by without any further threatening letters or pictures, but she still had a host of questions about initiating contact with Wesley or not. Would he look at her with contempt and think that she only wanted him now because he was no longer a mere college student but a successful military officer? Would he wonder where she'd been while he was going through his most challenging and most joyous times, or why she'd stopped responding to his letters, texts, e-mails, or phone calls, infrequent as they were? Would it be an issue for his parents or for one of his siblings for them to date each other, given how they'd sort of grown up together? She concluded that it must not be God's will for them to be together at this point in life. She finally decided that she wasn't quite ready for a relationship, and she was not going to contact him until she had peace about it. Instead, if he was still interested, then perhaps he would let her know.

Little did she know that Wesley had come to much the same conclusion. After all, he was the one who had put himself out there time and again, usually without so much as an acknowledgment. In his mind, if they ever had a relationship, it would not be at his initiation.

If Lisa had sent even one of the many letters she had drafted and discarded, things might have been very different for the two of them. She had put the ball in his court, and he had put it in hers and, moreover, decided to move on with his life. In fact, Wesley eventually met someone else.

Chapter 22

Wesley had once again begun training hard. In fact, he began a camp for gifted wrestlers at a gym in Pensacola, and the response was overwhelming. This motivated Wesley to consider Olympic competition again, as his conversations with Tara had revealed that he was never fully okay with not winning the gold. In addition, his prayer revealed that there was an even greater calling on his life—a calling to be a minister of the gospel of Jesus Christ. He spent significant time communicating about this calling with Pastor Johnson, whose heart was overjoyed, since he recalled what the Lord had shown him years ago regarding Wesley becoming his successor one day. Although he didn't yet feel the liberty to share that revelation with Wesley, he saw the hand of God at work as Wesley shared with him his desire to come home once he was out of the military and use his gifts and talents to help him in the work of ministry.

Wesley was earning and saving his money in preparation for building a life for himself and the family he'd always dreamed of having. By now, he knew that a lengthy career in the military was not for him, although he was proud of his exemplary military service and looked forward to finishing out the remainder of his five-year contract. Nevertheless, he wanted to return home to Columbia so that he could be there for his parents, who were not getting any younger, for his pastor and church family, whom he missed dearly, and for his community, the community that had loved and supported him during his developmental years. However, he didn't want to return home alone. He was tired of being alone and had decided that if it wasn't meant for him and Lisa to be together, he still deserved to be happy, and some young lady was very deserving of all the love he had to give.

Petty officer first class Lareka Huey was a Navy hospital corpsman. She, too, was stationed at the naval air station in Pensacola, studying to be a nurse and planning to go to officer's candidate school to become an officer. To Wesley, Lareka was not Lisa, but she was pretty, smart, sharp-witted, and intriguing. She seemed to walk right into his life at precisely the right time—or perhaps it was the wrong time. It was a time when he needed somebody to talk to, someone who understood him and his relationship with God, someone with whom he could share his joys, sorrows, and if things worked out, eventually, his life.

However, dating Lareka raised a couple of problems. The first was that she was an E-6, a noncommissioned officer, while Wesley was a lieutenant junior grade. As a result, they were not allowed to date each other according to military policy. If their relationship was discovered, they could be court-martialed by the military for fraternization, which could cripple a military career for both of them. They knew what they were doing was wrong, yet both became willing participants in the desensitization that accompanies attempts to justify unjustifiable behavior.

Over the course of a few months, Wes and Lareka became really good friends. They would travel miles away just to spend time together without being seen by anyone who might know them. Lareka was coming to the end of her enlistment contract, when she could either re-enlist or simply walk away. She had always wanted to re-enlist and become a career military woman. As a matter of fact, she was close to finishing nursing school, and she was planning to attend OCS the following summer. However, she told Wesley that she was willing to make the sacrifice of pursuing nursing as a civilian so they wouldn't have to hide their relationship any longer.

Lareka's willingness to give up her dream in order for them to be together spoke volumes to Wesley. She was quickly capturing his heart. But given the man that he was, he was not willing to allow her to give up her dreams for him. Yet he was falling for her and didn't have a clue as to how to bring resolution to their problem. He finally prayed and asked God to give him wisdom, and Pastor Johnson immediately came to mind. When he finally made the call, it was as if Pastor Johnson had been expecting the phone to ring.

"My son," he greeted Wesley with love and pride in his voice. "I am so happy to hear from you. Let's talk. Tell me what's on your mind." Not surprised at all by Pastor Johnson's to-the-point greeting, he spilled his guts, telling him about almost everything from his feelings about Lisa to his newfound "friend," Lareka, from St. Louis. Pastor Johnson didn't contribute much besides an appropriate "Mmhmm" or "I see" until Wesley was finished talking and asked him what his thoughts were.

"Well, son, so much of what you just said speaks for itself. It sounds like you've given up on Lisa, which is a bit of a surprise, given how you held out hope for so long. She has really stepped it up, by the way. She has always been a beautiful girl inside and out. I have to admit, though, son, I never saw in her what you saw until now—not that I was supposed to see it. That was for you to see, not me. I only saw fragments, bits and pieces of what she had the potential to become…you know, the total package that she is today. I see it now, but you saw it when y'all were only teenagers.

"At any rate, I can't say that I blame you, though. If she's not interested in you, there's no need to continue to waste your time. You deserve someone who is going to give back to you the love you have to give. So now, you're trying to forge this relationship with Ms. Lareka, and you're trying to determine if she's the one for you, right?"

"Yes, Pastor, that is correct."

"Well, like I said, what you just shared with me speaks for itself. And what you didn't share speaks volumes too, son."

"Uh, I'm not sure I'm following you, Pastor."

"Well, you said that Ms. Lareka is a petty officer first class. Now I don't know everything about the ranking structure in the Navy, so correct me if I'm wrong, but I believe that's an E-6, which in the Army is a staff sergeant." Wesley immediately knew where his pastor was headed, but he knew better than to interrupt, because there was always wisdom to be found in his rambling reasoning. "And you," Pastor Johnson continued, "being the fine young man that you are, have been promoted to lieutenant junior grade, which I think is the same as a first lieutenant in the Army—that's an O-2 pay grade. Now, again, I don't recall all the Navy ranks, because you know I was just an ole infantry foot soldier in the Army back in the day. But I do recall that Es and Os don't mix. So my first question is, How did you, a commissioned officer, even come close to having a relationship with her, an enlisted troop?

"And please don't say it just happened. You two have gone out of your way to deliberately bring this relationship to where it is today, wherever that is. Now, even outside of any spiritual advice, what does military law dictate in regards to that? Both of you bear responsibility for disregarding the obvious and jeopardizing both of your careers. You claim that you are not willing to let her sacrifice her dream of a military career to be with you long-term, but that is exactly what you're doing, son, because if you guys get caught, that could very well put an end to the dream. And by the same token, Ms. Lareka says that she is willing to give up her dream career for you. Well, that's what's about to happen if you guys don't open your eyes.

"Son, you two may have a lot in common, and you may understand each other, but neither one of you is thinking clearly. Something is clouding y'alls judgment, especially yours, son, because you are sharper than this. And you are an officer in the United States Navy—a proud one! So my question is, What is it, Wesley?"

"Uhh…I'm not sure, Pastor."

"Well, based on what I'm gathering from the Holy Spirit, something is very wrong here, and I believe it's either one of two things or both. Wesley, are you having sex with that woman?"

Wesley was caught off guard, though not by the question, since they had always had the type of relationship where they could talk about anything, no matter what. He was taken aback, however, at how accusatory his pastor suddenly seemed. Lareka went from being referred to as "Ms. Lareka" to "that woman." It was almost comical to Wesley, until he thought about the fact that he needed to respond, truthfully.

"No, Pastor, I'm not," he said softly.

"But…?" the older man asked, waiting for Wesley's response.

"No *but*, Pastor."

"Well, it sure sounded like there was some uncertainty in your response."

"No, I'm very certain we have not had sex, but I just know that at the rate we are going, it might not be long before we end up there."

"End up there?" Pastor Johnson exclaimed. "Come on, son, you know good and well that you don't just end up there. Lust, just as with any other sin, is first conceived in your mind before it is acted upon and becomes sin. So you don't just end up there. It's a process, you know that."

"Yes, I do, which is why I needed to call you. As it stands, I'm still Wes, the virgin. Honestly, Pastor, I don't even know how I'm still a virgin. In college, I found myself in some crazy situations. I'll spare you the details, but all I can say is but for the grace of God. But still, I'm having all these feelings and emotions surrounding Ms. Lareka," he said with emphasis in a sly attempt to bring dignity back to her name, "that make it hard to tell what's real and what's not."

"It really isn't that difficult, son. You've known from the beginning that this relationship is off-limits. You just admitted that where the relationship is heading is taking you down the wrong path, so why would you continue? You are not just an officer, you are an Olympic medalist, son. Have you considered the damage that being found out would do to all those young men who are aspiring to be like you?

"And what about the kingdom of God, Wesley? You have been called to a higher place of service, to serve as a minister of the gospel of our Lord! You cannot afford to be haphazard, because the enemy is not haphazard. He has obviously launched a strategic attack against you, which means that you have to be even more purposeful and strategic against him! Let's take a look at the enemy's plot against you. Take a look at how being found out would discredit the sermons that you've preached to all those back in Maryland and to those you mentor and encourage now. Think about how your testimony would instantly become a lie in the minds of those who are not mature enough to know the difference between the man and the mistake. Think about the counseling, advice, love, appreciation, and respect that you have earned in the lives of so many people. Take a *good* look at it. I mean, you need to really take a moment and take it all in, because you're risking it all, son. And once it's gone, it's gone! You can go back to the Olympics and win the gold twelve times. You can preach and teach and get the whole world saved. But what people are going to remember is that you were an officer screwing around with some enlisted woman. Can you see the attack, son? Do you see how the devil is playing for keeps?"

Wesley was stunned. He hadn't realized just how clouded his judgment had become. Indeed, he had not fully counted the costs of his foolishness, and what Pastor Johnson had just said was causing him to want to kick himself for being so shallow and haphazard. How did he become so unaware, so desensitized to the perils of such a risky relationship? How could he know with such certainty that he was heading straight toward a sexual relationship with Lareka and still be so passive? He wasn't sure what to say. The wisdom of God had just slapped him hard in the face, and he was so grateful for it. But now he was scrambling for words.

"Um. Thank you. I, um...I really appreciate you pointing out so many things that I should have been able to see. I really don't know what to say. My vision is not just clouded—the truth is, I've been flying blind, man. I've been dancing with destruction, and I was just about to get dipped. But I still don't understand *how*, Pastor. You said that my judgment is clouded because of one of two things. We know it's not sex, so what is the other thing?"

"The other thing is what I presumed your issue to be in the first place—Lisa. You're not thinking clearly because you haven't fully resolved your feelings about Lisa. I'm certain that someone like Tara could explain to you the science behind it, but basically, in your resolve to settle down, you are looking for characteristics in a person that remind you of Lisa. I've never seen Ms. Lareka, but I'm willing to bet that she looks a lot like Lisa. I'll bet she's absolutely gorgeous, just as charming and witty, and she probably understands you too, huh?"

Again, Wesley was speechless. He had never denied that Lareka was a physical work of art. Nor had he ever denied her charm and wit. And yes, he loved the way that she listened to him and how she seemed to get him. But not once did he ever make a connection between Lareka and Lisa.

"Are you there, son?" Pastor Johnson asked.

"Yes, uh, I...yes, sir, I'm still here," he muttered. "I just never made the connection. Lareka is, uh...you're right, Pastor, she's Lisa all over again. I guess I've got some work to do. If I'm honest with myself, I have to acknowledge that I'm a little lost right now. Lisa obviously doesn't want me, but somehow she's still haunting me after all this time. I thought I'd found someone who had the potential to really make me happy, but I can't pursue that relationship because there's too much at stake. I understand that I need to end it, right now. But I also need to bring closure to the woman who is still occupying space in my mind, and I honestly don't know how to do that, Pastor. Do you think I need to talk to somebody?"

"Yes, you really do, son."

"I guess it needs to be somebody from home, but besides Tara, who do you recommend? I can't talk to anybody here, because I might end up letting it slip during one of my sessions...you know, about my relationship with Lareka, and we both know I can't afford to do that," he said sadly. He was intrigued to discover that Lisa was still his issue, since he had resolved to just live life without her. He didn't allow himself to dream about being with her anymore. He had forced her out of his mind—his conscious mind, that is. But somehow, she was obviously still hanging out in his subconscious mind, and he needed to get that resolved once and for all. He continued his discourse. "I'll be home for ten days from Thanksgiving through the end of November, and I can set up something then if you know anybody."

"Wesley, first of all, relax, son. You're going to be just fine. You've spent so much time taking care of everyone else, ministering, counseling, serving at all times of the day and night. But it's okay for *you* to get help sometimes."

"I...I just feel so strange right now, Pastor. Inasmuch as I could possibly comprehend, I had made up my mind that I was done with Lisa. I just can't believe she still has a hold on me. I went through months of processing her out of my mind. I finally asked myself why. How did I become so crazy about Lisa Monroe? We never had a dating relationship. We never had sex or anything close to it. I loved her as a kid, but to her, it was puppy love, and she had no problem telling me that. If she had been just a couple of years younger, though, I'm telling you, we would probably have about eight kids by now. There would have been no college for either one of us, no military, none of that! We wouldn't have had time for that, because our time would have been spent working and making babies, and when we weren't making babies, we would have been perfecting our craft at making babies, if you know what I mean."

"Wesley!" Pastor Johnson exclaimed, but he was laughing hard.

"Sorry, Pastor, I think I just slipped over into lust for a minute, but I'm telling you, my man...listen to what I'm saying to you, man of God. There would have been no relief in sight for her...none!" Wesley and Pastor Johnson laughed again.

Pastor Johnson finally said, "Okay, I think I get the point."

Wesley continued, "But honestly, I wasn't just physically attracted to her. I loved everything about her. I loved talking to her, and I loved listening to her. It was as if she were just made especially for me. Whenever I was in her presence, I was instantly better! I had more confidence, I could think more clearly, and I think I was even a better athlete when she was around. I'll tell you a story. One day, during my senior year of high school, Lisa was home from college on spring break. I had wanted so badly to see her, and Tara told me that she would be at church Sunday. Well, she didn't come to church that Sunday, so I called her that afternoon and asked her out. We planned a date for that Wednesday after Bible study.

"We went to an Italian restaurant and had a great time. The food was delicious, the conversation was awesome, there was plenty of laughter, and it just was a beautiful night. We shared a very passionate kiss in the car before I walked her to her door. Once we got to the door, she kissed me again. Now, I'll admit, I was shocked and kind of scared. I was shocked because I wasn't initiating *any* of this and because she wasn't just some high school student. She was a senior in college who had always claimed that I was more like a little brother to her. So to have her come on to me like that was shocking. Don't get me wrong, I loved every minute of it, except for the fear that her mother, Ms. Betty, was going to open the door and catch us smooching on her apartment porch. I had already had one run-in with her earlier that evening when I picked Lisa up. I'd held my own pretty good and was able to get her to calm down and to back up off me. But now, here we were, standing on her porch, engaged in a lip-lock, and in that moment, I was in such a state of euphoria that Ms. Betty was liable to get body slammed had she come out on that porch, talking junk to me again."

"Wesley!" Pastor Johnson was laughing again. "Surely, you wouldn't scoop the young lady's *mama*, would you?"

"Pastor, are you hearing me?" he asked, laughing and sounding just like his dad. "At that time, this was a dream come true—Lisa Monroe had just engaged me in a moment of passion for the second time, and I was not ready to be disengaged. I'm telling you, I would have slammed Ms. Betty so hard she would have thought I was the Rock!" Wesley replied, laughing uproariously.

"You're killin' me, Wesley!" Pastor Johnson laughed. But Wesley continued.

"Then I would have stood over her and said, 'Who do you think you are, interrupting my magical moment with your daughter?' Then, while her mom was lying there, trying to come to terms with her WWF debut, I would have reached for Lisa's hand and said, 'I'm sorry, baby, can we please pick up where we left off?'" Again, the two men shared hearty laughter. Pastor Johnson was very glad to hear that reminiscing about Lisa had caused Wesley to seriously perk up. As he wondered how long it had been since the young man had laughed like this, the light came on for him.

Wesley continued, "Anyhow, thankfully there were no interruptions, but as you can imagine, I was on cloud nine. We finally ended our kiss, and we looked at each other for a moment before I broke the silence by thanking her for an awesome night. I told her that I would call her the following afternoon. She closed her eyes, took a deep breath, and nodded. Then she took out her key, opened the door, and went inside. I was heading back to my car when I heard my name being called again. I thought it was her mom, Ms. Betty, about to give me a hard time about Lisa again, but it wasn't. It was Lisa. She came running out to me in the parking lot, so I met her halfway, thinking that perhaps she had forgotten to tell me something. To my surprise, she grabbed my jacket and pulled my head down for another kiss right there, in the parking lot. I was in shock. She told me that we really needed to talk and that she would call me the next day. We talked each day for the rest of the week, and she came to see me at the county track meet that Saturday. That was when I broke my personal record twice in the discus back-to-back in the same set, one throw behind the other. Do you remember that, Pastor?"

"Yes, I remember it like it was yesterday, because you almost took the field judge's head off with that first throw. I guess he was used to your norm, but you shocked us all that day. You broke the state record, and on your next throw, you broke it again. The crowd was clapping and cheering for you. When they announced it over the intercom, the announcer explained that it wouldn't count as a state record until you actually did it in the state meet. Then he said, 'Let's encourage Wesley Heart by giving him a round of applause,' and the crowd went crazy. I guess you've always had that crowd-pleaser anointing, huh? I also remember that, after your event, when everyone was congratulating you, Lisa gave you a big hug there in the stands. I thought it was a little over the top at that time, but I figured that she was just happy for you—until she grabbed your hand and the two of you walked up the stadium stairs together, holding hands. It makes more sense now that I know what had transpired a few days before."

"Wow! You *do* remember. We met at the Chicken Coop restaurant after the track meet. We agreed that a relationship would still be awkward at that point in both our lives. Both Mom and Dad were working that Saturday and were unable to attend the track meet. When I got home, I barely had time to call them to share the news about my new record before Lisa called me. We talked almost all night until Mom came home and made me get off the phone about two in the morning. We talked about our dreams and goals, and she told me that she was very tempted to change her mind about us, but she knew that it was best for both of us to just wait and see what the future held. Looking back, I believe that God was intervening on our behalf, because I would have been all in.

"At any rate, the point I was trying to make is that there was nothing too serious there to bind us together. Was there passion? Yes, there was plenty of that. But there was no commitment or anything that transpired between us that would lead me to having some type of attachment to her back then, and certainly not now. As a matter of fact, I'm really not too fond of her anymore, Pastor."

"Uh, you'd better explain that comment, Wesley."

"Well, it's simple. I have graduated college at Navy, been commissioned as an officer, I've been promoted since then, though I was on my way to being demoted by fooling around with Lareka. I've even competed in the Olympics...the Olympics, Pastor! I even won the silver medal! But I haven't heard from Lisa in the way of greeting, encouragement, congratulations, or much of anything else with the exception of an occasional 'Tell Wesley hi,' communicated through Tara. On the other hand, I've written letters, to which I received little response. I've sent cards, I sent a gift for college graduation, another one for police academy graduation, and the list goes on and on. Don't get me wrong, I never send a gift looking for one in return. The point is that I have demonstrated effort, interest, and a celebration of her life and accomplishments. I've shown love and genuine concern, and yet it has not been reciprocated. Now, where all the passion went, I don't know. But she has since sent a clear message to me that she is simply not interested, and I...I'm just...I'm okay with that."

"But how do you know there's not a good reason, son? Furthermore, are you sure you're okay with that, Wesley? Because you don't sound too sure to me."

"Well, I don't know what her reasoning is, but I can't imagine anything being so bad that she can't reach out to me *sometimes*. I'll admit, it still hurts a little, because I just knew that she was the one. I've been crazy about this girl since I was about thirteen years old, Pastor. I thought that her being rooted so deeply in my heart just *had* to be God's doing, but I guess I just misjudged that one. In some ways, I wish that I hadn't spent so much time being hung up on her, but I understand that it'll all work together for my good somehow. It's just one of those things that you learn to live with and move on. I'm just...I'm okay with it, ya know? But anyhow, let me tell you who's not okay with it—Sade Seabrooks."

"Oh, so you still stay in contact with her? That's great, Wesley."

"Yes, sir. We made a vow to each other after her dad's death to remain friends and stay in touch with each other."

"I remember you telling me that sometime ago. I'm glad to see that you guys are honoring your word to each other."

"For sure, but I have had to keep my distance from Sade."

"What do you mean? Does she have an issue with *you* or with *Lisa*?"

"She's none too fond of Lisa. I've even been forced to go into ministry mode with her about Lisa, but it's all my fault. Had I known that she was still hopeful that there would one day be something between us, I wouldn't have said anything about Lisa just out of sheer respect. I thought she was over me."

"I never knew there was anything between you and Sade."

"Trust me, it was completely one-sided. I never had any romantic feelings for her. I actually used to wonder whether she was bisexual, and that was a turnoff to me. In college, she dated this guy named Jarvis, who worked at Lisa's school, UNCG, which is just a few minutes away from North Carolina A&T. But the whole time she was dating him and posting things about their relationship, she was messaging me, letting me know that she was 'still down for whatever,' to use her words.

"I don't know what to think about Sade. She's just, uh...weird. For example, she is a very attractive woman, or at least she used to be. Right now, though, I don't know what she's got going on with her hair and her attire. Then, when I message her, she makes the weirdest comments at times. All I can do is pray for her because I really don't know how else to be her friend at the moment. At any rate, she does not like Lisa. She wouldn't be hostile toward her or anything like that, but she has made it known that she does not appreciate how Lisa has treated me."

"But why, Wesley?" Pastor Johnson asked. "Sade is a grown woman now, and surely, she understands that people have a right to make their own decisions about whom they're interested in. There has to be more to the story."

"I feel the same way, and I have expressed that to her. I think that's what helped her to kind of calm down about it. I believe Sade has some much-bigger issues, though. Don't get me wrong; she's functional, but she's unstable. I think she stopped her therapy too soon. Like I said, I see her every now and then on social media, and she seems to be bouncing from one job to another. I know her relationship with God is obviously suffering too. She doesn't have a good sense of self-worth, and she never got over her dad—not his death, but the way he treated her. It's very weird, Pastor. It appears that she only has romantic concerns when it comes to me. In her mind, it's like I came into her life when she needed me most and rescued her from her dad. She talks about how she had thought about killing him herself, but because of me, that didn't happen. And she still mentions how brave I was to stand up for her and her mom. So in the back of her mind, she wants to give me something in return—herself.

"Thankfully, the Holy Spirit gave me enough sense not to tell her that I don't want what she has to offer. Instead, I just told her I was unable to accept anything in return. So we're still friends. But in her own twisted reasoning, since she can't have me, then the person that I choose better treat me right. At least this is my assessment of her. Who knows, I could be totally wrong about everything I just said. She's just hard to figure out, Pastor. As a matter of fact, despite all that, we really don't talk much at all. I don't even know what she does for a living anymore, or even where she lives right now. But at the end of the day, if you think I need counseling, you should have a conversation with Sade.

"But as for me, I've been training myself to be okay with Lisa's antics for quite some time. When I came home for Thanksgiving during my sophomore year of college, I tried for days to contact her. When I learned that she was going to have to go to school for an extra year or so in order to finish, I wanted to go see her and spend the day with her. I wanted to encourage her, and honestly, I wanted to see if there was something still there between us.

"I even took a thousand in cash out of my savings just to help her out with tuition. I was still in college, but I was making a little bit of money, especially with the speaking engagements. I never charged anyone, but people insisted on giving me a check every time I spoke. Being the tightwad that I am, I was only spending about a hundred dollars a month. Truth be told, I would have given Lisa every dime of my savings if she had needed it. But she never so much as answered my calls—no text message, no e-mail, nothing.

"One day, after a couple of failed attempts to contact her, not knowing that I had just called her, Tara called her, and she answered right away. So needless to say, it's been quite some time since we've actually talked. To be brutally honest, to hear you say that I'm somehow still holding on to her is baffling to me, but I know that you are my pastor for a reason, and you are not quick to speak on things that you are not sure of. I know you too well, Pastor. I know that you've been praying for me, and you were probably waiting for my call, weren't you?"

"Well, let's just say that had you not called me, I was going to call you before the evening was done," the man offered with a chuckle. "You were under attack by the enemy, and the Lord usually won't let me go too long without at least some knowledge of what's going on with the people that I shepherd, especially those who have a strong connection in Him."

"Man of God, you're the best. I'm going to let you go, but do you have a therapist in mind that you recommend for me to sit down and talk to about all this?"

"Wesley, you probably don't want to know who I have in mind."

"If you're referring to Tara, I'd rather not. Normally, Tara would be my go-to therapist, but I just don't feel like she's the right person this time, given her relationship to Lisa."

"I have no doubt that Tara can remain objective, Wesley, but I'm not talking about Tara, son. The person you need to talk to is Lisa."

Chapter 23

She was dressed in a US mail carrier's uniform. She noticed the name Randall Street as she walked briskly toward gate 1. The appearance of her body was the epitome of frailty and malnourishment, and it was hard to look at. However, it was even more difficult to observe the look of fear and terror on her face, yet there seemed to be a flicker of determination in her eyes. In her hand she held one letter as she made her way toward the gate. The letter was inside an envelope that seemed to be golden in appearance. It was obviously several pages thick, as the envelope was full and had an extra stamp on it just in case it exceeded the maximum weight for a single stamp. She glanced at the address on the envelope:

> US Naval Academy
> Wesley Heart
> PO Box 42944
> Annapolis, MD 21412

When she saw his name, her pace slowed while her breathing increased. After a few more steps, she stopped. Her breathing was frantic. She considered her doubts as to whether she should continue. She also considered the voices in her head that told her she didn't deserve him, that she didn't have what it took to love him the way he deserved to be loved, and that if he knew the whole story, there was no way he would accept her.

She looked at the letter again and said aloud, "If he can't accept all of me, then maybe he's just not the one for me." She looked at her mail carrier's uniform and wondered why she was wearing it. "Don't you get it?" she asked herself. "Lisa, you were made for this," she said. "You have what it takes. Now let's go." Suddenly, Lisa bolted through the gate in a full sprint. Her destination for the single letter that she carried was the mailroom. She determined that if she could just get the letter in the mail, then it would be out of her hands and in the hands of God.

She ran as fast as she could. However, her sprint ended abruptly when she heard out of nowhere, "Stop right where you are! Drop the envelope and put your hands in the air where I can see them!" When she turned to see who had given her such a command, she found herself more confused than ever and unable to make any sense of what she saw—because she saw herself! And she was wearing her police uniform.

"Lisa?" she asked. "What am I...I mean, what are you...listen, I don't have time for this. I have to go mail this letter, and if anyone knows that, it's you."

"I can't let you mail that letter. It contains the whole truth about your past. I know you're about to say that everybody has a past, and that's true. But if Wesley finds out that you were a drug dealer, how do you think that is going to help your cause, missy? When are you going to stop being so simple-minded? Surely, you haven't thought this through. I mean, you're actually going to tell him that you shot someone and left him for dead? Girl, you must be on crack. That's why you look the way you do, because you're doing stupid stuff. You're trying to be all sanctified and holy, confessing your sins and all that. Well, let me tell you something: you better hope you're really saved, because if you don't hand over that envelope, I'm gonna bust a cap right in your—"

"Lisa!" her mail-carrier self exclaimed. "What is wrong with you? You know how God has turned my life around. And you know what it's taken for me to get to where I am. Why are you fighting me on this? You know God's voice, and you heard His instructions. You also know me and that I'm not the same person I used to be. I'm walking with power now—the Holy Spirit is right here with me. So are you really going to try me now?"

"I sure am."

"Girl, quit trippin'. I fear God, not you."

"Lisa, if you take one more step…"

"Then what?" she screamed. "Are you going to shoot me? So I guess you're gonna *cap* the Holy Spirit too, huh?"

"I got a fifteen-round clip and one in the chamber."

"Lisa, I'm going to mail this letter."

"Give me the letter, Lisa!"

Mail-Carrier Lisa suddenly attempted to step around Police Officer Lisa, and Officer Lisa immediately pulled the trigger.

Pop!

Lisa jumped so hard that she nearly fell off the bed. She was dazed and disoriented, yet she was relieved to know that this was just a crazy dream, although it had seemed so real. Her body obviously thought it was real too. She was sweating, her breathing was heavy, and her heart was racing. She flopped backward on the bed as she muttered to herself, "Oh, gosh! I've got to get off this graveyard shift. I've had some crazy dreams, but me against me is just too much to handle."

As she pondered the meaning of her dream, she spoke aloud. "I will be sure to get Wesley's contact info today, and I am going to call him before this week is out and see if he's willing to hear me out. I'm certainly not going to take any chances with the mail, e-mail, text, or any type of message-delivery platform after that dream." She chuckled.

She noted that the clock read 9:48 a.m. and realized that she had time to relax and rest for a while before her Thanksgiving reunion with the Heart family. However, she wondered how in the world she was supposed to relax after a dream like that. She decided to try to think happy thoughts. At first, it was difficult as she thought about the letter she had received from Roquan after her graduation from the police academy. She had prepared herself to play his game, but she hadn't heard any more from him since the original letter, so she concluded that his temporary obsession with Wesley and the Olympics had passed.

Eventually, she was relaxed enough to begin thinking about how her Thanksgiving was going to be. Mr. and Mrs. Heart had always been so kind and welcoming toward her from day 1. They took her in and treated her like one of their own whenever she was in their home. Amanda, who was always the life of the party, was married and had two sons now; she couldn't wait to see her again and meet her family. She saw Tara regularly, and if she had to name one thing she was grateful for, it would be the friendship, understanding, and love that Tara had always demonstrated toward her. She had never met their much older sister Patrice, who had moved out and joined the Air Force even before the other siblings were teens. Mr. and Mrs. Heart had given birth to Patrice while they were still in high school, but they had tried to rear her in the most wholesome way possible, even though their relationship with each other hadn't always been wholesome.

Tara couldn't contain her excitement about seeing Patrice again. She had shared her excitement with Lisa along with all the reasons she was so excited. What she didn't share was the news that Wesley would also be present, since he had asked her and Pastor Johnson not to say anything to anyone about him coming home. Although Lisa was unaware that Wesley would be there today, she imagined seeing his face and wondered how military life was treating him.

Once again, Lisa was drifting in and out of sleep. She was reminiscing with much regret about the first time Wes had shown interest in her. She thought about all the twists and turns that her life had taken due to bad decisions and choices. Her mind was in overdrive.

Things could have been so different, so much better for me, she thought. *I'm sure he's dating somebody now, though. He's probably head over heels in love with some military chick, but then again, I don't know that for sure. Why do you always expect the worst, Lisa? All you can do is try. You've got to try. Come on, girl, where is your faith? Wait, what am I talking about? Try what? I must have dozed off to sleep.*

Lisa's eyes popped open. Her eyes snapped toward the clock, which read 9:56 a.m. She repositioned herself to a more comfortable position and was instantly back in the mode of semisleep that comes along with working third shift. With her eyes open, she stared at the wall.

"I need a fresh start, Lord," she said aloud. "I have made some major mistakes, and I'm facing the music every day of my life. I'm tired of living like this, not knowing if or when a part of my past might decide to just show up on any given day. I know that we can't just pretend that my past no longer exists, but are You willing to at least help me get to a better place? I really don't know what that means, but when Pastor Johnson was teaching the other day, he said that Your Spirit prays for us about things that we can't even understand. Tara tells me all the time that You *are* willing to help me, but I have to receive the help. So here I am, God. I need help, please."

Lisa wasn't sure whether her prayer was being spoken or was just in her head, or whether she was awake or asleep. But Lisa was at peace. She knew that she was truly connecting with God. Her eyes were wet with tears, and she continued her prayer while simultaneously trying to get some rest. *Gotta get my prayer life back. I must shake off my past. What happened happened, and...I can't change that. Gotta move on with my life.* Lisa opened her eyes and closed them again. She was trying to guide her self-talk, but she was drifting off to sleep again.

You need to show yourself some love. All you do is work and pretend to build a relationship with your mom. When are you going to get real with yourself? You go to the gym because that's less time you'll have to spend dealing with your mom. You go to your mom's house supposedly to make sure she's okay, but you use that as an excuse to not have to be alone with your thoughts for too long. You have to be true to yourself, Lisa. When you are true to yourself, you can be true to everyone else.

She recalled Tara's recent advice to listen to her conscience, since that is where the voice of God can be heard. The thoughts, prayers, or whatever it was were now flowing freely as Lisa stopped resisting the urge to make it make sense in her conscious mind.

And speaking of your mom, you really need to talk to someone about your feelings toward her. Again, if you are true to yourself, you have to acknowledge that you blame her for everything that's wrong in your life. But you're a grown woman, Lisa. When are you going to start taking responsibility for your own life? I'll say it again, it starts with being true to yourself. Only then can you be true to everyone else, including God. Get your mind off Wesley. There are two people that you need to focus on at this point in your life, Jesus Christ and Lisa Monroe. You asked for help? Rest assured that help is on the way!

"Ugh!" she muttered as she jumped again and wondered who said that. She had clearly heard someone say, "Help is on the way!" But what was that dream about, and furthermore, who said that? She checked the clock again; it was 11:15 a.m. She decided she couldn't lie there any longer, listening to her thoughts. She was going to take action. It dawned on her that she had fallen asleep while praying. The last thing she remembered was asking God for help, and now, as she woke up, she clearly heard the words "Help is on the way!"

"I think God just spoke to me," she said excitedly. "Or maybe it was an angel." With a huge grin on her face, she got up and put on some coffee. The coffee was stale because she didn't drink it often, but she figured it would help her get going. She got in the shower, and her thoughts began whirling again.

I really have some work to do. My life is a mess, and I have to make some changes. She finished her shower and dried off, donning her thick bathrobe. She went into the kitchen and poured a cup of the coffee. When she came back into her bedroom, she grabbed a coaster and set the cup on her nightstand. Wanting to feel her best, she chose a favorite outfit, then went back into the bathroom, determined that she was going to put her best foot forward with her hair and makeup. She took her time to make sure everything was as perfect as possible without having someone else do it for her. Then she dressed in her favorite True Religion jeans, which fit her perfectly, added a cream-colored camisole and a burnt-orange blazer, and completed the outfit with beautiful tan boots.

Thinking the coffee was cool enough to drink, she took a sip and nearly spit it out because it was so stale. After brushing her teeth again to get the taste out of her mouth, she refreshed her lip liner and lipstick, then gave herself a final once-over in front of her full-length mirror, twisting and turning to look at herself from head to toe.

"Even I have to admit I'm stunning today!" she announced with a laugh. Grabbing her purse and sunglasses off the counter, she strutted out of her apartment, purposely twitching her hips in a moment of humor. She cranked her Honda and let it run for a minute, since she didn't drive it every day now that she had a police cruiser. After letting the engine warm, she pulled away from the curb, deciding to stop and grab a coffee from the convenience store to help her wake up. She would take her time driving to the Heart residence, which was about twenty minutes away. She didn't turn on any music, preferring to see where her mind would carry her during the drive.

All she could think about was Wesley as she sipped the sweet black coffee as she drove. At the forefront of her mind was whether or not Wesley would be even the slightest bit interested in her. The more she thought about him, the more she couldn't believe how blind and even rude she'd been to him. Wesley would have been perfect for her. He had written her more than a few letters while he was away at school, and with the exception of the first one, she had failed to respond to any of them or to at least text or e-mail to say that she had received the letter. Each one of them bore a sincere expression of his desire for her to be well, to passionately pursue her dreams, and to refuse to compromise her true self for anything or anybody. He always expressed his feelings for her, and he always ended his letters with a phrase that said something like, "Perhaps the day will come when the two of us can forge a real relationship. Maybe not. But let's both commit to personal growth. With that, we can't go wrong. You have my commitment."

But between the stress of passing her final year of classes and the fact that she had become a drug dealer to pay for them, she just didn't have the time or the courage to respond to him. Upon graduating, she received an offer for an interview with the South Carolina Highway Patrol, a job that she had applied for during a career fair nearly two years prior. Given her former illegal occupation, she was fearful that if she got the job, someone would come along and make it known that she had been a drug dealer, or perhaps she would have to arrest someone from her past and somehow one of these scenarios would cause her to lose her job.

After several years on the job without that happening, she still wasn't at peace. Although she genuinely liked her work and worked very hard to be her best every day, she was always looking over her shoulder and wondering whether each day was going to be her last as a state trooper. Her relationship with her mother had improved, but it was still somewhat strained. She worked, she worked out, and she tried her best to follow Tara's advice—to love her mother unconditionally. She recognized that her life was stressful, so at least she tried to destress through working out, and whenever she wasn't working overtime, she would pamper herself with occasional massage and spa treatments. In her current state, there was no room for anything else or anyone else, and in her mind, there was certainly no room for a man like Wesley. Pondering all this made Lisa sad. She realized that she needed to make some changes.

"Lord, I won't be surprised if Wesley doesn't even answer when I call him," she said aloud. "I won't even be surprised if he never speaks to me again. Well, I know he's not that type of person, so I know he'll speak to me. But he is fully justified in not having anything to do with me, given the way I treated him. I had so much going on, and I didn't want Wes or his family to ever find out what I was doing, nor did I want them to be in any danger. So I avoided them like the plague, except my friend Tara, who just refused to leave my side. But You know I did it to protect them. I danced to the music, and now that it's time to pay the piper, I'm so afraid. I so deeply regret how I've treated Wes and his family. I ask You to forgive me. I'm going to ask his family to forgive me today, and I'm going to ask him to do the same whenever I get to talk to him.

"Honestly, I don't deserve a man like Wesley. While I can't use that as an excuse to justify why I never responded to him, I just felt like he has always been on another level from where I am. I've felt that way about his entire family. I just never felt good enough to truly belong. I know that is so wrong, because they *always* accepted me for who I am. Where I needed polishing, Mrs. Heart buffed me right out and treated me with so much love and affirmation, as if I were her own daughter.

"The truth is, the problem is me. The other day, I was thinking about the time several years ago when Wesley took me out to dinner. It felt so good to be treated like a real woman. He treated me like I was a queen, like I was his queen. I had never been treated like that before, nor have I since. He was not looking for anything in return. He simply wanted my company and conversation. He just wanted to be good to me, Lord, and the truth is, since we're dealing in truth here, I had no clue how to handle that. So instead of growing and learning from it, I ran from it. I ran from him, and it was certainly not because of him—it was me.

"It's still me. I've been dealing with my demons for a very long time, and now it's time to do something about it. I owe him a sincere apology. I promise I'll get his contact info before I leave, and I'll call him this weekend. Perhaps I can even explain a little bit about what I was going through during that time in my life. It's no excuse, but it might add some perspective to the utter lack of response to his attempts to express his care for me. Because he's close to You, I hope he'll at least understand, if nothing else. I ask You to help me to learn whatever lessons I can learn from all this and show me how to gather up the pieces of my scattered life. I know this is only one step in the right direction, but I promise You that I'm going to do better. I just need Your help."

Lisa was feeling the effects of her lack of sleep as well as the coffee. She was also truly feeling the conviction of the Holy Spirit as she immediately began heeding His advice to be true to herself. As she exited Interstate 26 and came to the stop sign at the end of the ramp, she removed her sunglasses and grabbed a small package of tissue from the visor. She checked that there were no cars behind her, then took a few seconds to dry her eyes, take a few deep breaths, and remind herself that her senses were heightened from the coffee that she had been consuming during the drive. Before she pulled away from the stop sign, she looked in the mirror to check her makeup again. When she looked into her eyes in the mirror, the words came up in her mind: *Help is on the way!* She smiled and breathed a sigh of relief as she pulled a Breath Savers mint out of her purse and popped it into her mouth, put her sunglasses back on, and continued making her way to the Heart home.

She was being eaten alive with nostalgia as she looked around and noticed the familiarity of the place where she'd spent so much time growing up. *Calm down, Lisa. This is your family. Enjoy your time with your family. Stop thinking about the past. Just commit to doing better. Be true to yourself, baby, be true to yourself.*

"Relax, girl," she told herself as she stepped out of the car and headed up the driveway. As she walked up the steps and onto the front porch, the door opened.

"Wow!" popped out of her mouth before she could stop it. It was Wesley, looking like he had just finished a photo shoot for Calvin Klein. Lisa, who had stopped dead in her tracks, was speechless. Worse yet, her glossy lips were hanging open, and she felt paralyzed with apprehension since she had no clue how he would respond to seeing her. A million thoughts danced in her head. *I shouldn't have come. I didn't know he was going to be here. He probably hates me. God, help me. I don't know what to do. Oh my goodness, here he comes. God, he looks so good. Lord, I'm really lusting right now, and that look in his eye is not helping at all. He certainly doesn't look like he's upset with me. Okay, fix your face, girl. You need to say something. Oh my gosh, is he going to...*

Wesley slowly walked up to within inches of where she was and, without saying a word, stood still right in front of her as they stared at each other. He thought about his conversation with Pastor Johnson and knew that what he needed most during his time on leave was to spend some time talking to Lisa. He needed to know why or how she was still somehow lingering in his subconscious mind, even though he had given up on her a long time ago. Standing face-to-face with her, however, perhaps helped him to begin answering some of his questions. Lisa Monroe had an effect on Wesley that was not easy to explain. He was very glad to see her. He was even happier that she not only looked breathtakingly beautiful to him but also healthy and well, as if she had been taking good care of herself.

Still, they had not exchanged a word with each other, but Wesley needed to see her eyes. He reached out to remove her sunglasses from her face and placed them on the ledge of the porch. When he looked into her eyes, he saw pain and regret. He also saw hope and expectation. He saw the face of a woman who had been bruised and scarred and yet unwilling to allow her battles to get the best of her. She was drop-dead gorgeous on the outside, but on the inside she was more like a tangled web. In that moment, he saw her for who she really was, and it was not a pretty sight to see—at least that would have been the average person's assessment. But to Wesley, it was the sight of the most beautiful girl in the world. It was the sight of the woman who needed him to be the man who needed her. It was the sight of God's perfect provision and His perfect timing made manifest right before his eyes, and he was overcome with emotion.

Wesley opened his mouth to say something, but nothing came out. He extended his hands, placed them just above her waist, and leaned his tall frame down to kiss her. It was definitely not what he had planned, but it was just right for the moment. It was what he wanted. *She* was what he wanted, and whether he could actually have her or not wasn't going to stop what was about to happen in that moment. To his amazement, although she hadn't moved from her spot on the porch, she stood on her tiptoes and placed her hands on his face to kiss him. They were moving toward each other when their magical moment was suddenly shattered by an overzealous member of the Heart family.

"Hey, Lisa!"

Chapter 24

Wesley wasn't sure whether or not his mom had just saved the day, but he was very sure that she had just ruined the moment. Embarrassed, both Wesley and Lisa attempted to gather themselves.

"Uh, Ms. Elizabeth, hey!" Lisa exclaimed, a little too brightly. "It's really been a long time, too long! How are you doing?" she babbled on.

"I'm fine, baby, and from the looks of you, you're doing well too," Mrs. Heart replied.

"I am, thank you. I don't get to see you all at church because I have to attend during the week, given my schedule. I know you all are there on Sunday mornings. It's been a while, but I'm back."

"So I heard! Tara told me, and I think that is wonderful news. All of us, like sheep, have gone astray, but, honey...His mercy endures forever! Come on and give Mama a hug. Come on in. Everyone's going to be so glad to see you!"

"Yes, I was just expressing to Lisa how glad I was to see her too, Mom."

"Yeah, I noticed that. I don't know what you two got goin' on, but we'll talk about that later, son."

"Aw, there's nothing to talk about, Mama."

"Oh, yes, there is, Lieutenant *Junior Grade*! Now, there's a time and a place for everything."

"You're right, Mama, and sometimes, the time is right here, right now, in this moment," he said, locking eyes with Lisa once again and stepping close to her again. He was kidding around, but he caught both Lisa and his mother off guard with his boldness.

"Wesley!" Lisa admonished with a huge grin on her face. Looking up at him, she slapped him on the arm, which, by the way, was leaner than ever. "Cut it out before your mom knocks both of us off this porch." She turned toward Mrs. Heart and said, "I'm sorry, Ms. Elizabeth. Our behavior was inappropriate, and I didn't mean any disrespect."

Mrs. Heart was actually elated to see what she had always known in her heart to be inevitable between the two of them. Now she wished she hadn't come outside at all, so that they could have had their moment of reacquaintance or whatever they were about to have. But she was Mama, and it was only right for her to have something to say about it. Despite her intuition about the two of them one day hitting it off, Mrs. Heart was completely blindsided by what she had seen. *Have the two of them been in a long-distance relationship? Surely, they weren't just spontaneously drawn to each other like that, were they? But the Lord truly does work in mysterious ways,* she thought to herself.

"Don't be ridiculous, Lisa," Mrs. Heart said. "I don't feel disrespected. I'm just wondering where all this is coming from. I mean, when did you two become an item?"

"Actually, Mom, we're not an item," responded Wesley. "We were, uh, trying to become an item when we were so rudely interrupted, so if you'll excuse us," Wesley again joked as he stepped toward Lisa again. This time, both Lisa and Mrs. Heart slapped him on opposite arms.

"Boy, get yo butt in this house!" his mother commanded as she pointed toward the door. She was on the verge of releasing an explosive grin, so she widened her eyes, gritted her teeth, and pursed her lips in an effort to convince both Wesley and herself that she was serious.

"Wesley, I don't believe you," remonstrated Lisa, though it was clear she was teasing. "Ditto to what your mom just said. In the house, right now. Let's go!" But Wesley saw straight through the antics of both women.

"Okay, okay, I'm going in. I'll be there right after I tickle this look off Mama's face." As he finished his sentence, he grabbed his mother and tickled away. Mrs. Heart was laughing so hard that everyone came outside to see what was going on. Although it was late November, the temperature was seventy-one degrees in Columbia that day. Everyone came out to find Wesley and his mom engaged in a dance of tickles, laughter, and swats as both Mrs. Heart and Lisa tried to whack him hard enough to make him leave his mom alone. Indeed, it was a sight to see as everyone joined in the swat fest.

Wesley, completely unaffected by their blows, decided to let it go and let them think they'd convinced him to do so. When the laughter settled, everyone took turns greeting Lisa, whom they hadn't seen in years, and the Thanksgiving reunion was on. Lisa was having the time of her life as she greeted everyone. When she saw Amanda, the two of them embraced and held each other as they cried. Then they looked at each other, embraced again, and cried some more. It was a very sobering moment.

"Come on over here, Antonio," Amanda called. "Lisa, this is my husband, Antonio Trent."

Lisa looked up and saw what appeared to be Goliath himself coming toward her. Antonio was six foot eight and weighed 320 pounds. "It's nice to meet you, Antonio," she greeted warmly.

"The pleasure is all mine," he replied, hugging both Amanda and Lisa, who were still embracing each other. "So this is Lisa, huh? It is so nice to finally meet you in person."

"Lisa, Antonio and I have you to thank, in large part, for a closer walk with the Lord," Amanda continued.

"Me?" asked Lisa, her surprise evident in her voice.

"I'll explain later, but we thank God for you. During some of your most difficult times, when you thought you were all by yourself, you were not alone, girl. We were stationed in Germany at that time, and God would put you on my heart to the point that I couldn't sleep at night. I would wake Antonio and tell him what was in my heart concerning you. He would wake up with me and say, 'Come on, baby. Let's pray for her right now.' I know he was glad when you came on through, so he could get some sleep again!" Amanda teased.

"Amen," Antonio agreed with a laugh.

"We both were just thankful that you did come through what-ever it was," Amanda continued. "We knew that Tara knew what was going on, but she wasn't at liberty to share, so it was truly a situation where we had to rely on the Holy Spirit to guide us. It's a very different type of prayer when you don't know any details, but it's more pure because you have no room for judgment and all that. So I just want to say thank you for whatever you've been through. I still don't know all the details, but I know that it was too heavy a burden for you to carry alone. Whatever it was, just know that it was not in vain, because while we were praying you through, God was binding Antonio and me together and drawing us closer and closer to Him. But we'll talk more about it later, because I have a word to share with you regarding someone from your past."

Through their tears, they thanked each other. Lisa was amazed to discover that God had been there for her even when she felt like no one was there and no one would understand. She was almost an emotional basket case at the thought of it all, but there was a humorous side to the story that kept her from going over the edge. Her mind briefly drifted back in time to the Amanda that she'd grown up with, who had never been this serious about the things of God, or about anything. In fact, Amanda was the one who would give them all a hard time about being so serious about church, especially Wesley. She would mock him, she would imitate Pastor Johnson and his wife, and she would also mimic people dancing before the Lord or giving a testimony. As her mind drifted back to the present, she was able to dry her tears for the moment.

"I love you, Amanda, and I'm so grateful that you both took the time to pray for me. If you only knew what I've been through," she said, shaking her head and starting to cry once again.

"Well, I hate to interrupt the church service while y'all are giving your testimonies and all that," Patrice teased, lightening the mood a bit. "I don't know this young lady, but why are y'all messing up her makeup like that? She didn't come over here for that. I'm Patrice, and I have heard so much about you," Patrice said in greeting, turning toward Lisa. "It's so nice to finally meet you! Give me a hug, tears and all!"

Lisa was nearly overwhelmed by all the love. She hugged this nice lady, who squeezed her tightly. Patrice released her grip but left one arm around Lisa as she said, "You lift up your head and dry your tears, baby. We all have been through something, things we can share and things that we can't tell anybody about. You're still dealing with some of that right now, I can tell. But mark my words and listen to me real good now! If you don't even remember my name, remember this: help is on the way!" With those words, Lisa lost it again. Patrice sensed that they'd connected right then in that moment, though she had no idea why.

"Now, you take that word and be encouraged," she continued as she pulled Lisa into her bosom again and let her cry. "Now I'm the one messing up her makeup!"

Lisa worked really hard to pull herself back together quickly. Although her recovery wasn't as quick as she had hoped, she was able to keep from falling apart completely.

"It's okay, sweet pea," Patrice comforted. "Even the golden child over there has had his share of problems. He just doesn't tell anybody about his stuff except Pastor Johnson. That's what's wrong with him—he needs somebody to talk to sometimes."

"Wait, hold up, sis," said Wesley. "First of all, you were introducing yourself to Lisa and encouraging her. So how did *I* become the topic of your conversation? Secondly, what's up with that 'golden child' stuff?"

"That's right, Patrice, leave your brother alone," demanded Mrs. Heart.

"It's the truth, Ma. He listens to people's problems all day, every day. He has to counsel them, coach them, chastise them, help keep them out of trouble, then he has to preach to them and try to give them spiritual insight and guidance. He works all the time and has no outlets—none! At least he used to wrestle, but even then he was punishing people so bad that nobody wanted to spar with him."

Everyone laughed, including Wesley. He was standing there with his arms folded. He had a smile on his face as he took it all in. He was thoroughly enjoying this time with his family. This was what they did; it was just their way of loving one another and embracing family. Patrice hadn't been around for most of their growing-up years. She would show up for graduations and major events, like Amanda's wedding and the birth of her children, and Tara and Wesley's high school and college graduations. She had also footed the bill for the entire family to attend the Olympics in London to see Wesley compete for the gold. So she was very familiar with the family dynamics, and she was abreast of what was going on in everyone's lives. By far, she was the most outspoken one in the family, and in many ways, she was like a second mother to all her younger siblings and didn't have a problem challenging any of them.

"Patrice, I'm going to spar with you if you don't hush," Mrs. Heart warned. "Wesley is a grown man who's focusing on his career. He'll pursue all that when the time is right."

"You're right, he *is* a grown man, Ma, so why are you talking up for him? He can speak for himself if he has a problem with what I'm saying," she challenged, looking at Wesley.

"Oooooooh," everyone said together.

"Sis, be warned. If you can dish it, you better be able to take it."

"Ooooooh!" they all said again.

"Bring it, li'l bro! All I'm saying is…look, you all were there! You saw him break that man's shoulder in the Olympics! That doesn't happen with grown men. In high school, yeah, it's possible, but I'm telling you, this man needs somebody to talk to. God said it is not good for man to be alone. You need somebody to talk to, bro, a shoulder to cry on, ya feel me? And I ain't talkin' about no Pastor Johnson. You need a woman, bro!"

Soft sighs and whistles came from everyone at that point, because each one of them, including Wesley, knew she was right. Patrice still had one arm wrapped around Lisa's shoulder, but even Lisa had pulled it together and was thoroughly enjoying this.

Wesley spoke up. "Okay, okay. I'm about to get real ghetto right here. Uhh, where yo man at, Patrice?"

"Whoooaa!" the entire group chanted loudly.

"Oh, don't sleep on me, bro! He might be on his way over here right now!"

Everyone responded with cheers.

"We can talk about what 'might be' all day," Wesley responded.

"Mmhmm, and speaking of 'might be,'" Patrice shot back, "your woman might be, uum, let's see…nonexistent!"

"Oooooh!" they all said.

"Give it up, bruh!" Antonio voiced from the back.

But there was absolutely no way that Wesley was going to give it up. It was just family fun, but he was not a quitter. Oddly enough, he was at a loss for words. Although only three seconds had passed since Patrice's last blow, it seemed like an eternity. His arms were folded, and he was still smiling and nodding as if he had a comeback.

"Or she might be…" He paused saucily, looking at Patrice.

"Well?" she taunted.

Suddenly, the light came on. He turned his gaze from Patrice to Lisa and spoke up very firmly.

"She might be standing right in front of me, needing to be held in my arms instead of yours."

There was complete silence.

"Patrice is right," Wesley continued. "I need a woman in my life. As of a few weeks ago, I was in a relationship. But during a conversation with Pastor Johnson," he said with emphasis, pausing and glancing quickly back at Patrice, "I realized that the relationship was…let's just say, headed in the wrong direction." He looked back at Lisa and continued, "Ever since I was a kid, Lisa, I've been crazy about you."

"Yep, shoal have," Mr. Heart said from the background.

"Yeah, we all thought it was puppy love because you were older than me, but I knew that it wasn't. I finally concluded that you just were not interested in me, so I let it go and moved on. I dated people over the years, but there was nothing serious until my most recent relationship. But in talking with Pastor Johnson, who, while not a therapist, is certainly anointed to be my pastor, I realized that the person I was dating subconsciously reminded me of you. After my conversation with him, I began praying and doing some soul-searching. I was shocked to discover that *everyone* I tried to have a relationship with reminded me of you."

"Nothing has transpired between us that would cause me to have such a deep-rooted affinity to you, but somehow, you've really got a hold on me. I don't know if you're in a committed relationship or not. Something tells me that you're not," he said, smiling slyly in reference to their meeting on the porch, "but we need to talk. Now, it was not my intention to have this conversation out here in front of everybody, but since they *all up in my business*"—he said it loud-ly—"let the record show I came here to see my family, and I'm going to enjoy my family while I'm here, but I also came because I have some unfinished business with you. You're in my heart, and I owe it to myself to find out why, and to find out what's in your heart. So if you're willing, we can talk later, since we have such a great cloud of witnesses right now."

Though everyone broke out in laughter, no one moved. There was no way they were going to just walk away from this show unless Lisa just refused to talk in front of everyone. Once again, tears were coursing down her cheeks, but Lisa stepped out of Patrice's embrace and extended her hands toward Wesley.

"Wesley, what I have to say actually should be said in front of everyone. I owe you an apology. You have been so good to me, but I've treated you so badly. I'm sure you remember when you were a senior in high school and you asked me out on a date. The way you treated me that evening made me feel as if I were the queen of the world!"

"That's my boy," Mr. Heart said softly.

"I mean, you were a high school student, but to this day, I have never, ever had anyone treat me with such dignity and class."

"Mmhmm," Mr. Heart mumbled again.

"You brought me flowers, you opened and shut the doors for me, you even told me how to dress because you had done research to find out that my favorite food was Italian, and you had selected the best Italian restaurant in the city just for me. At the end of the night, you didn't want anything from me except to know that I'd had a good time. You're one of a kind, Wesley Heart. Your entire family is one of a kind."

Lisa was determined to finish, despite her tears. She paused for a moment and continued.

"So after that night, I did some soul-searching myself. I concluded that you deserved someone just as special as you are, and with everything that I had going on in my life, I felt I was not that person. My grades began to decline during my junior year, and I lost my scholarships because I was doing so much traveling back and forth from school to home to keep a check on Mama. To make matters worse, I was supposed to receive a letter informing me of my financial aid probation, but I recently discovered that, along with a few other students, I was set up by an employee who worked in the financial aid office. I got caught up in some crazy stuff, y'all. This employee deliberately discarded our probation letters so that by the time we found out we were in trouble, we were already on academic suspension, which meant that if we were going to graduate, we had to come up with the money out of pocket.

"As it turned out, this financial aid employee was working for a drug dealer who was trying to get desperate students to work for him. Except the plan wasn't that obvious. It was a very elaborate scheme designed to trap people before we even knew what happened. Some of the students ended up transporting drugs across state lines, others even went so far as to exchange sexual favors, and some of these kids wound up doing all kinds of things just to get the money to pay tuition. Thankfully, I didn't get caught up in that. But trust me, I did my dirt."

"Lisa?" Tara spoke up.

"I'm okay, Tara, I need to do this."

Tara nodded.

"I started out working as a waitress in a restaurant," she continued. "What I didn't know is that the restaurant was owned by the kingpin. Before I knew it, I was the campus drug dealer, selling weed and pills to students on two different campuses. Imagine that, me, a drug dealer. But I can't deny it. Now granted, I was probably the most naive drug dealer ever, but I knew that if I got caught, I was going down. And I didn't want any of you to have any connection to me whatsoever if that happened. But Tara never gave up on me. I have a lot to be thankful for, but most of all, I'm thankful for my friend Tara for her unconditional love toward me.

"Wesley, I didn't know you were going to be here today. I came here to apologize to this beautiful family and to ask for everyone's forgiveness for becoming so distant. But seeing you here and hearing what you just said lets me know that God is more real than I could ever imagine. I'm so sorry for the way I treated you, ignoring your texts, letters, and cards. So many times I wanted to reach out to you, but I just couldn't do it, knowing that you were possibly headed to the Olympics. That was an opportunity of a lifetime, and I simply refused to do anything to jeopardize that.

"But, Wesley, I kept every letter and card you ever sent me. I have newspaper articles about many of your college accomplishments. I even contacted the naval academy for a copy of the program from your college graduation and your commissioning ceremony. I have articles documenting your Olympic journey and victory, and I recorded the two wrestling matches that actually aired on television. You would think I was some type of stalker or something." She tried to joke, trying to lighten the moment a bit. "What I'm trying to say is, Wesley, you're in my heart too. You always have been ever since we were kids and you were down there at that altar, being filled with the Holy Spirit. Had you been a couple of years older, we wouldn't be having this conversation. But since I'm not a child molester, things took a different turn, and here we are. But, Wesley, I can't allow you not to know the truth about me, nor can I expect you to still feel the same way about me, knowing what you know now," she said, tearing up again.

"Well, why not, Lisa?" Wesley asked, pulling her close to him and causing her to gasp. He wiped her tears with gentle fingers. Still, she pushed away from him a bit. "Lisa," he continued, "didn't you hear what Patrice said? Every one of us has skeletons."

"But there's more!" she cried.

"I don't care! All of us have *more* to tell if we keep digging. But no one is asking you for that."

"But you should know what else happened..."

"Lisa, please. I already know what I need to know."

"Wesley, I shot someone!"

Everyone gasped.

"Uh-oh," Mr. Heart murmured softly in dismay.

"It was my last drug deal, the last freaking one!" she exclaimed, dropping her head for a moment to try to pull it together long enough to finish. "I had made up my mind to get out, because everything had gone too far. School was out, and I had actually walked for graduation. But I had one more class to take. I had made the money I needed for school, but I had gone from selling on campus to selling on the streets, so I knew I had to make a change, and my big break had finally come. I had already told the dealer I worked for that I had been hired to work with the South Carolina Highway Patrol and I wanted out. Believe it or not, he was cool with that.

"He said, 'Your Finest!' That was the name he'd given me. 'I need to advise you that I was already aware of your new job. I have a couple of friends there who had already told me about you. I just need you to know that either you will seal your lips or I will seal them for you...permanently.' He pulled out his .45 and put it to my head as his phone began to ring. 'If I hear so much as the slightest hint about any aspect of this operation, I promise you, the end of your police career will be the least of your concerns. Do you understand me? You're not to talk to anyone about any detail of your life, not your financial problems, any school personnel that you know, any details about the restaurant manager or employees, nothing! You feel me, Your Finest? Now you can go all hero cop on me, but 'round here, heroes die quick!' I quickly agreed as he answered his phone. When he finished, he holstered his gun and started talking again.

"'Hey, Nature Boy's got a flat tire and a trunk full of dope. I gotta go take care of that. So what I need you to do is just deliver this to the park for me, and as long as I never hear from you again, we're done. Now, I'm tellin' you, I'm stickin' my neck out for you. I'mma smoove things over with Mr. Lee, and I'm doing this for one reason—it's because of my boy Slam, from your hometown. I understand the two of you pretty tight, or at least he want it to be that way. I'm sure he don't know what you involved in, and I came close to tellin' him a couple of times myself. But I just didn't feel it was right at that time. I guess I know why now, since you got a chance to get outta here and do something with yo life. So I'mma take the hit on this one, but it ain't for you, it's for him. That brotha ain't neva done nothin' but help me. He ain't neva judged me. Matter of fact, he the one that takes the time to pray with me. My own blood don't even do that. This brotha is the truth, and I don't know, maybe you just ain't attracted to him, and that's cool. But you can't deny that he that real deal, though. Anyhow, make this drop to Fats at Union Park—big light-skinned dude with a green hoodie. Now, gimme a buck, which is what he owes, and get out!'

"Everything was in slow motion. I pulled a hundred-dollar bill out of my pocket and gave it to him and left. I couldn't believe I'd just had a gun to my head. It was as if the devil was saying, 'You're not just going to walk away. This is going to cost you.' But I remembered the prayer for protection and the word that the Lord spoke over me through Pastor Johnson. So I went to meet this guy Fats in an abandoned park in Greensboro. It was supposed to be a quick exchange—you know, the drugs for the money and I'm out. But for some reason, the guy tried to take the bag of weed from me, and I know I should have just let him have it, it was my last deal. But in that moment, though I can't explain it, all I could see was my mom and that handgun pressed into my temple earlier. I had so much anger and malice toward Mom in that moment because I blamed her that I was in the situation in the first place. That anger was literally controlling me.

"So with this guy trying to pry the weed out of my hand, I took my foot off the brake pedal, and when I did, he fell over into the car. He tried to pull away, but he was a big guy and couldn't keep up with my car, which was rolling. I wasn't going to let go of the bag, and he wasn't either. So I reached down beside my driver's seat and pulled out a .38 I had started carrying when I started selling in the streets, and I shot him. Again, all I could see was my mother's face. It was as if she'd had the gun to my head. I was so angry that, somehow, I shot him again. This time, he let go of the bag and fell backward to the ground, and I…I left him there as I sped away. There was no way I was going to bring you into that. But I need you to know that, Wesley. You need to know what happened." She stood there gazing sadly into his eyes. She had stopped crying, but she seemed to have run out of words.

"Are you done?" Wesley asked calmly.

"Well, I…yeah."

"If that's what you needed to tell me, I'm glad that you finally found the courage to do that. And I appreciate your concern for me and my family. It says a lot that you intentionally shielded us in an effort to—"

"Wesley!" she shouted, interrupting his ecclesiastical rambling. "I just told you that I shot someone and left him for dead! Did you even hear me?"

"Yes, I heard you, Lisa. Did the guy die?"

"No!"

"So are there pending charges against you or something?"

"No!"

"No, Wesley." Tara spoke up. "There are no pending charges, and he didn't die. As a matter of fact, he's clean now, and he's a therapist, just like me. We met each other last month at a conference. He shared his testimony, and of course, although I couldn't say anything, I knew that he must be the very person Lisa shot."

"Boy, God has a way, doesn't He?" Mr. Heart said softly.

"But, Wesley," Lisa began again, obviously stunned. "I don't get it. Aren't you…I mean, don't you want to know…uh, I guess what I'm trying to say is that, surely, you have *some* thoughts about everything I just told you…don't you? Surely, you have *something* to say?"

"Yes, I do, Lisa," he said calmly. "I admit, I'm a little taken aback by the fact that you worked for Roquan. I knew that once he got injured, he dropped out of college and turned to the streets. But I had no idea that you knew him, and of course, I didn't know that you worked for him. But if you're waiting for me to pass judgment, I have no stones to cast." He added, "So you got into trouble and God got you out. That's what He does, Lisa."

"Have mercy!" Mr. Heart said a little too loudly in the background.

"You were young, desperate, and like most of us when faced with such situations, you made a decision that wasn't seasoned with wisdom. But don't you know that we serve a loving God who is a great deliverer? He knows how to take even the shameful things in our lives and use them to our advantage. Look at you! You went from one side of the law to the other, and you're still carrying a gun. Except now you have been granted the authority to carry it and to use it if need be. Besides, you were set up, Lisa. You were preyed upon by these guys at a vulnerable time in your life.

"So my thoughts are that all things are working together for your good. Stop condemning yourself. God has delivered you. The only one who still has you bound is you. Can you imagine how God must feel knowing that He sent His only Son for you? He gave what He treasured more than anything else so that *you* could be delivered and set free from everything that held you captive. But instead of walking in that freedom, instead of living a life of gratitude and celebrating the freedom that He so graciously gave you, you continue to remind Him of why you shouldn't be free. Please, do Him and yourself a favor and stop it, Lisa. Let it go. Walk in your freedom and rejoice. Hearing that awesome testimony you just shared, we're certainly rejoicing for you."

"Mmhmm," Mr. Heart said in the background.

"Yes, we are, Lisa," said Mrs. Heart. "Nobody here is holding anything over your head, baby."

Again, Lisa's tears seemed to have come out of nowhere. She had never looked at God's grace in this way before.

"I guess I should be happy, huh?" she squeaked out.

"Yes, you really should, Lisa," Wesley said. "When God looks at you, He sees who you are. What you did in the past has been washed away through the blood of Jesus. Your sins have been cast as far away as the east is from the west, so He sees you as the masterpiece He created. I'm standing here face-to-face with His masterpiece," he said as he lifted her chin so that he could look into her eyes. He wiped her tears and continued, "You're a woman who is broken, a woman who, like all of us, has scars and bruises. But you're still standing. You're also a woman who has literally cried away all her makeup." He smiled after teasing her, wiping more of her tears as everyone snickered. "But you're still absolutely beautiful to me. So please stop trying to convince me of all the reasons I shouldn't love you and just embrace the moment. This moment, Lisa. Not your past, not worrying about tomorrow…embrace this moment right here, right now. I think you'll find that it can be very special if you just learn to be present in this moment. Do you think you can do that?"

Lisa nodded, and Wesley leaned down and kissed her right there in front of the whole family.

"Yes! You go, Wesley!" The whole family was celebrating, and Lisa was embarrassed, but she really didn't care. Wes released his gentle kiss, and as she wiped her own eyes, she had an epiphany. It was because of her own misguided thoughts that she had been kept away from this angel standing in front of her, but now that she had been enlightened, she wasn't going to allow herself to miss this moment. She placed her hands behind his neck, pulled him down to her height, and kissed him for real.

"Hey, heeey!" the siblings all cheered.

"Well, well, now." Mrs. Heart beamed.

Patrice chimed in, "Girl, you better work," as she high-fived both of her sisters.

"That's all right, son," Mr. Heart encouraged.

"Those two were made for each other," Antonio pronounced firmly.

Suddenly, Amanda and Antonio's son called out from inside the house, "Grandmaaa, I think the turkey is burning!"

Epilogue

Wesley and Lisa spent time together every single day of his leave. They had agreed to take things slowly since they had a ton of catching up to do and since Wesley had a few more years left in the military.

Lisa was growing by leaps and bounds in her faith and in her walk with God. She spent her time attending worship services at least once a week and more often as her schedule allowed. She was heavily involved with the women's ministry at Miracle Center Church. She worked out at the gym and at home, and she studied the Word of God, learning how to meditate in it and apply it to her life.

She stood in awe of how God had completely turned her mother's life around as well. Ms. Betty had met an old man outside the grocery store, a man that the locals used to call Street Preach. He shared the gospel of Jesus Christ with her that day, and she accepted God's glorious invitation! She joined Alcoholics Anonymous and had been clean for months. All this was mind-boggling to Lisa, especially knowing what miserable lives both she and her mother had led not even a year ago.

Lisa and Wesley talked every day until he headed out to sea. She became more than that "someone to talk to" that Patrice had joked about. Even by phone and FaceTime, she brought out the best in him. She challenged him to go back to being his absolute best again in everything that he set out to do. That had always been his MO, but he seemed to have abandoned the mindset during the time he was with Lareka. Of course, he challenged her too. The mere notion that he had chosen her to be his lady out of all the available women challenged her significantly. What challenged her even more was how he seemed to look beyond her flaws and rough edges, and even what he initially perceived to be her avoidance of him over the years. The fact that he was even willing to listen to her reasons, to accept her as she was, past and all, and to love her even in her current state was more than enough to challenge Lisa to her core. She was determined to become the best woman she could be, whether she and Wesley made it or not.

Lisa was slated to be the only one who was going to be surprised when, only a year later, on Thanksgiving Day, Wesley planned another surprise visit to his parents' house to make official what God had set in motion last Thanksgiving—or, in his mind, back when they were teens. Although it wasn't as romantic as he'd always imagined, he planned to propose to her at his parents' home. He wanted everyone to be there who was there last year, with the addition of Lisa's mother and grandparents, whose blessing he had received about a month ago. Pastor and Mrs. Johnson had also been invited, along with Sister Patterson, who had always been a mentor of sorts and one of his greatest supporters from church.

He had told Lisa that he would be home for *Christmas* and that she might as well be prepared to spend every single day with him. He e-mailed her a detailed list of what they were going to do each day and asked her to let him know if she wanted to add to or subtract anything from the list. Although he was serious about the list of outings and activities during his Christmas leave, Lisa was completely unaware that he would be home for three days during Thanksgiving as well, which was when he was planning to ask her to marry him. His dad was going to pick up Lisa's family and keep them hidden once Lisa arrived. Wesley had asked her to FaceTime him once she arrived at his parents' house and got settled. She was unaware that this would be his cue to show up out of nowhere and propose to her.

The big day finally arrived, and surprisingly enough, everyone was on time for the noon arrival—everyone, that is, except Lisa. She was still working third shift, but she was off Thursday through Sunday and didn't have to return to work until Sunday at midnight. Tara had called her the night before, and they had agreed to go Black Friday shopping the next day, but they hadn't talked since then.

"It's not like Lisa to be late without calling," Tara fretted, whipping out her cell phone. "No answer. All right." She demanded everyone's attention loudly. "Nobody spilled the beans, did they?" Everyone denied any bean-spilling.

"Lady Johnson, did you tell Lisa that Wesley was coming home for Thanksgiving? I know you can't keep a secret."

"No, I did not!" the pastor's wife announced indignantly. "I kept my mouth shut…this time." They all laughed.

"Okay, let me call her again right quick," Tara muttered. She sighed when there was no answer. "Lord, we've got to get her off that third shift."

"We can handle oversleeping," Amanda said. "I just pray she's all right."

This prompted Pastor Johnson to speak up. "Well, if y'all don't mind, I just feel that now is a good time for us to call on the Lord, if that's all right, Brother Rory?"

"Of course, Pastor," he agreed. "Come on, everybody, let's pray together."

As everyone was gathering, Tara stepped out and went downstairs, where Wesley had just finished adorning himself in his dress blues. Tara told him what was going on.

"Listen, T," he said, "I've had this gut feeling all morning. I thought it was just butterflies about asking Lisa to marry me, but something is not right, sis. I…I'm gonna ride with you, okay? In fact, we'll take my car. It's out back. Come on, hurry, T!"

Upstairs, Pastor Johnson was already praying with everyone else. "Father, You are worthy to receive glory and honor. We praise Your holy name right now in this moment. We are not the type of people who sit around expecting the worst. Instead, we expect that whatever is going on with Lisa, You've already prepared her for it. So we pause to say thank You in advance. Father, if by some measure this situation requires a miracle, we're thankful that You've already written out the details of that miracle and You have prepared those involved to move along with You. Thank You for the safety and protection. Thank You for the release of Your mighty power and Your ministering angels right now. Thank You that even You Yourself have gone before us, making the crooked paths straight. We thank You and praise You for all things, and we declare that all is well. In the mighty name of Jesus Christ we pray. Amen."

As they finished praying and praising God, Tara came back in to say, "Okay, everyone, Wesley is going to drop me off at Lisa's apartment. She just got off work this morning, so she probably overslept. I'm sure that's all it is, so Wesley will stay out of sight, and I can help her get ready. Now, remember, Mr. and Mrs. Monroe and Ms. Betty, you all will have to hide in the living room once we get back, just long enough for Lisa to greet everyone. Then Wesley will come from downstairs and surprise her. When you hear him say that he has something to say to everyone, that's when y'all will come on out of hiding—that should get Lisa's attention. By the time Lisa turns back around to hear Wes's announcement, he'll be down on one knee. Amanda, can you take the lead on all that?"

"I gotcha, sis."

"Okay, now, y'all know Lisa, so even with me helping her, it's going to take her a good hour to get ready, so please, go ahead and eat so that you all can be relaxed and excited for the big moment. We'll be back before you know it."

"Try calling her again, T," Wesley said as they sped up I-26.

"No answer. The phone still rings through to voicemail."

"Okay. I'm gonna believe God that she's all right. I don't know how, but I gotta get my woman off this night shift. Long-term, it's not good for a person's body, anyway, but times like this make it hard on everyone involved. I have a few ideas once I'm home for good."

"'My woman.' You felt that one down in your soul, didn't you, bro?" Tara asked, trying to lighten him up a bit. He smiled as they began rehearsing their plan for once they arrived at Lisa's.

Wesley parked a few doors down from Lisa's apartment, and they both noticed a very nice blacked-out '65 Chevy Impala.

"Wow!" Wesley exclaimed. "Whose car is that?"

"I don't know. I've never seen it, but that is super nice!"

"Yeah, well, I guess you can go on in and wake her up," he continued, "but, Tara, listen to me. When you open the door, yell out her name until you hear her respond. Please don't just walk into her bedroom. She has guns, ya know."

"Come on, bro, she's my best friend, remember? Don't you think I've done this a time or two? I'll give you a thumbs-up once she responds." Tara pulled out her key to Lisa's apartment and walked up to the door. She put the key in the lock and was about to turn it when the next-door neighbor's door opened.

"Are y'all here to check on Officer Lisa?" a frail-bodied lady asked timidly.

"We are. Is she okay?" asked Tara, immediately concerned.

"Uh, I think so. It's just that I heard her yelling and shouting at someone about an hour ago. I think she was on the phone."

Tara thought, *Who would she be arguing with? Her mom is at our house.*

"I called the police about three minutes ago," the lady whispered. "I think I hear the sirens now, so maybe you should wait until they get here."

Okay, first of all, why is this lady whispering all of a sudden? Secondly, why did she wait until three minutes ago to call the police if she thought there was an issue an hour ago? And third, I don't hear any sirens. This woman's imagination is in overdrive, Tara thought. Nevertheless, she decided to join the lady in the festival of secrets as she whispered back, "Yeah, maybe I should wait for the police. But do you know whose pretty black car that is parked out there?"

"No, but that's what concerns me. The car pulled up, but no one ever got out." *Okay, enough talking,* Tara thought. She turned the key as she whispered, "I need to go in and check on my friend. The police will be here in just a moment, anyway, so I'll be okay. Be sweet and stay right here, okay?"

The lady spoke up a little louder, begging her to wait, but Tara ignored her as she gave the door a push.

"Lisa!" she called out. "It's Tara. Are you okay?" She heard a faint reply from the bedroom.

"Come in. I'm back here."

Turning to give Wesley a thumbs-up, she entered the apartment and closed the door as Wesley pulled out of the parking space to head back to the house. Tara made her way down the hall toward Lisa's bedroom.

"Girl, if you don't get up outta that bed. We've been waiting on you, boo. I tried several times to call you but—"

When she entered the bedroom, she stopped dead in her tracks. Lisa sat on the edge of the bed half-dressed, mascara running down her face, and she appeared to either be nervous or afraid—or maybe both. Tara was shocked to see one knife beside Lisa on the bed and another Marine Ka-bar on her nightstand.

"Lisa, baby, what on earth is going on?"

"It's Roquan," Lisa replied, fresh tears falling. "He's threatening me again, Tara. He told me that my career and maybe even my life would be over if I set one foot outside my door this weekend. I…I don't know what he's talking about. He kept saying, 'Don't act like you don't know that my boy is coming home to propose to you today.' I told him Wesley was still at sea, but he doesn't believe me. He keeps talking about how Wesley is at home and he's going to propose to me. He told me that Mama and Grandma and Grandpa are all at your house, waiting on me to arrive for the proposal. Then he called them, Tara. He called my family!"

"Lisa, calm down," Tara began.

"No! He has my family's phone numbers, and he called them using another phone. I actually heard their voicemail pick up. I know Mama won't answer if she doesn't know the number, but her voicemail picked up on the first ring, and she never turns off her phone. And my grandparents are always at home, but their voicemail eventually picked up too. So I figured I'd call them myself, and I'm getting voicemail too. Something is going on, Tara. If you know anything, you got to tell me. Roquan is crazy!"

Tara would never forgive herself if she ruined Wesley's surprise, but she was totally at a loss for words—and not to mention totally afraid. "Lisa, you've got to calm down."

"No, Tara! He's not playing. He says I can't show up at your house today, and…and he says that Wesley will probably come over but I am not to let him in. He told me to tell him that I can't marry him and that I'm just not ready for a relationship right now. He's threatening me, and he knows I can't go to the police about it. 'One more round,' he said. 'My boy's got one more shot at the gold, and after that, I don't care what y'all do.' He's crazy, Tara! And he's making me think I'm crazy. So I've been in here, praying, crying, and trying to figure out the best move to make. Every time I get up the nerve to call you, he calls back with more threats. It's been years since I heard from him, but he's obviously lost it. He says he's watching my every move, and I think that's his car out there! I know God is looking out for me, because had I brought my weapons inside this morning, I know I would have tried him by now, because I refuse to be a prisoner in my own home!"

"Okay, Lisa, wait. If that is Roquan's car, wouldn't he have called you back when I came in? I even stood there and talked to your new neighbor next door before I unlocked your door. So if he was really—"

"What?" Lisa interrupted. "Tara, I don't have a next-door neighbor."

"Lisa, I talked to her, a sweet elderly white woman, in the apartment right beside you. She was talking to me, then she suddenly started whispering and was trying to get me to wait on the police. She said she heard you on the phone yelling and said she had called the police—"

"Oh gosh, Tara!" Lisa gasped.

"What, Lisa?"

"She must be a police informant! But right now, she's our only hope. Quick, go get the hammer under the kitchen sink! Hurry, Tara!"

Lisa's phone rang. She answered.

"Oh, so you gon' just call somebody over here to see if I'm really watching you?" Roquan roared. "Well, I am! You think I'm playin' witchu? Okay, so check this out, I'm about to show you how serious I am!" The phone went silent.

Outside, as Wesley neared the apartment complex exit, the front of his 350Z was nearly taken off by three unmarked black SUVs entering the complex with flashing blue lights. There were no sirens, just lights. Immediately, he felt the pit return in his stomach, and he knew it was not because he had just avoided a wreck. Wesley put the sports car into first gear, whipped it around in a trail of white smoke, and followed the SUVs. As he turned into the entrance to Lisa's building, he also noticed three or four Richland County police coming up behind him.

The SUVs had two people in each vehicle. The lead vehicle pulled directly behind the Impala and even bumped into the back of it. Officers exited the vehicles rapidly, most of them dressed in camouflage clothes, boots, and helmets, with rifles and shotguns aimed at the Impala, shouting, "FBI, get out of the car now!" Wesley unwisely parked his car where he had parked before as he watched additional officers assume backup posts.

Roquan, however, was not in the car. Suddenly, the agents heard a 9mm handgun discharge and the sound of shattering glass coming from behind the building. Roquan had shot out Lisa's patio door to get into her apartment. The agents moved quickly and methodically to take their posts, one at the corner of the building and another at the patio entrance, to ensure there would be no outside interference. The lead agent entered Lisa's apartment and cleared the open kitchen and den area, while a team of three entered and carefully moved down the hallway. They could hear Roquan shuffling around in Lisa's bedroom, making threats under his breath. The team leader quickly threw a flash grenade through the doorway as they braced themselves for the loud, bright blast. The men immediately breached the room to do a sweep of the bedroom, bathroom, and closet. They found Roquan lying on the floor beside the bed, temporarily blind, deaf, and very disoriented. They retrieved his handgun, which was about eight feet away near Lisa's dresser. They quickly cuffed him, but Lisa and Tara were not visible.

Announcing themselves, two agents opened the closet door, thinking the women must surely be inside. But the only thing they saw in the closet was a huge hole in the wall that led into the apartment next door. Using the hammer to break through the wall, Lisa and Tara had escaped to safety and, along with the informant, were now outside with the Richland County police officers on the scene.

The FBI agents brought Roquan back to the front of the building as two ambulances pulled up and stopped right behind Wesley's car. He had been wise enough not to get out of his vehicle, even when he saw the police escorting his sister, his woman, and some elderly woman to safety. However, now that the situation had settled down, he decided to step out of his car and try to find out what in the world was going on. Two of the SUVs whipped around and pulled in right behind the ambulances. The agents sat Roquan on the ground in the empty parking spot right beside Wesley, and an EMT came over to check his vitals. *Roquan?* Wesley thought, staring intently at the man.

"Sir, I need you to go back inside," one of the agents instructed.

"I'm sorry, sir, I don't live here, and you guys have my car blocked in."

"He's okay, Agent Spencer," offered a female agent whose jacket and cap identified her as FBI. "I actually need to interview this gentleman."

Me? Wesley thought in shock.

"Hello, Mr. Heart," the agent greeted. Wesley looked over in surprise when the voice sounded vaguely familiar. He examined the woman's face closely, trying his best to identify this person who obviously knew him—but with her eyes hidden behind her dark sunglasses, he was stymied.

"I'm sorry, do I know you?" Wesley asked, thoroughly confused.

"Right this way, please," the woman requested, ignoring his question and escorting him to the passenger side of her SUV.

When they both were inside, she removed her hat and sunglasses and asked, "How are you, friend?"

Wesley was astounded. "Sade? When did you...uh, I mean, I thought you were..."

"What? You thought I was what, Wesley?" She smiled. "A failure? An addict? A statistic? A victim of circumstance?"

"No, I didn't mean...I meant...Sade, I was just trying to say..."

"Well, you were right. I was all that, Wesley. Look, I know I've been MIA for quite some time. But I've been on a mission, a rather-long journey, in fact," she said, pulling out a towel and wiping her face. "Now, granted, I had a season in my life of just making stupid decisions while still hoping for good results. And I often thought about some of the things you used to tell me when you thought I wasn't listening. But I *was* listening. I was listening to you, Mama, and believe it or not, I even had a voice of reason inside my head." She smirked. "I thought about all that I was putting my mother through, and she had already been through enough. I thought about your commitment to be my friend even when you thought I'd lost my mind. Boy, you don't give up, do you? Most of all, I couldn't shake that set of instructions your pastor gave me, especially once I hit rock bottom. So I started following that advice little by little.

"At the same time, I started dating a guy named Jarvis, who worked in financial aid at UNCG. I noticed pretty quickly that his lifestyle seemed to be much larger than his income. On a whim, I decided to start doing some investigating and discovered that I was extremely good at it! Over time, I continued to date him only to find out more about who he really was and what he was involved in. By the time I graduated—which I know you didn't think I'd ever do—I had almost figured out his whole scam single-handedly, and I took it to the FBI.

"But I was yearning for more! It was like something inside of me was pushing me to pursue this passion. Out of nowhere, the thought came to mind to apply to the FBI. After they conducted a deep background investigation, I entered the training academy. While there, I soaked up the training like a sponge. They say that I have a rare instinct for solving problems and cases, an ability that few people have. I'd already told them about Jarvis, and after they checked out my story, they put me on the case. The FBI arrested him a couple of weeks ago, and he is singing like a mockingbird.

"At the top of his list is your boy Roquan over there, who knows his time is running out. As it turns out, he's not just fond of you—he's involved in an elaborate gambling ring where he placed a huge bet on you so that if you were to win the gold next summer, he'd win close to a half-million dollars. Even if you win the silver again, he'd still make out pretty good.

"Also, I'm sorry to tell you this, Wesley, but your ex-girlfriend, Lareka, worked for Roquan. He was using her to get information about you—your training, your plans to compete, your health, everything. Then when you broke up with her, you basically put an end to her assignment. But Roquan figured there could only be one reason you'd do that—Lisa. So he decided to take matters into his own hands.

"His original goal was to convince you that Lisa was no good for you, but he couldn't find anything to use to do that. I slowed him down tremendously when I started taking down his boys one by one. He had pretty much decided to leave you alone until Jarvis got arrested. He knew then that he was probably next, which meant you competing and winning in the Olympics was his last hope of putting away a nice chunk of money, since gambling money is guaranteed regardless of the status of his freedom. So when he heard you were coming home again, he put together this plan to stop you from proposing to Lisa.

"I've been working undercover for years. I've been a financial aid employee, a janitor, a student services coordinator, a recruiter, a drug dealer, a drug user—I've even been a man a time or two," she said with a chuckle. "That's why so many of my responses to you have been so weird over the years. Still, you never gave up on me. So I made a vow to God that if He allowed me to stay on this case, I would do everything within my power to give you the chance to fully enjoy your life with the woman of your dreams, without her looking over her shoulder each day. Trust me, I have dirt on people from the statehouse to the jailhouse in both Carolinas. So as far as Lisa is concerned, she's good. She can truly relax now. I have the evidence needed to completely clear her with the South Carolina Law Enforcement Division. She'll be back to work in no time."

"Sade, you're amazing, and I...I'm so proud of you," he responded warmly. "You have an amazing testimony of God's goodness in your life. I'm so sorry for everything I've put you through, and I don't know how I could ever repay you."

"You didn't put me through anything, and you don't have to repay me for doing my job. It's just the nature of the beast. I love what I do. Besides, I'm going back to being a regular agent after a short vacation in Puerto Vallarta."

"Nice! I truly hope you enjoy yourself. Is there anything I can do for you, Sade? I just wish I knew how to thank you."

"Well, you could join me on my vacation," she joked.

"Some things just never change, huh?" he replied, smiling. "My vacation of a lifetime is in the back of that ambulance, and in just a minute, I am going to get her out of there and ask her to marry me."

"Trust me," she said. "I didn't go through all this for you to be with somebody other than Lisa. Just make sure I get a wedding invitation, and we'll call it even."

"That's it?

"That's it.

"Pinky swear?"

"Pinky swear."